IMPERFECTION AND IMPARTIALITY

Also by Marcel Wissenburg and published by UCL Press

Green liberalism: the free and the green society

For Masja and Martin

Imperfection and impartiality

A liberal theory of social justice

Marcel Wissenburg

University of Nijmegen, the Netherlands

Routledge
Taylor & Francis Group

LONDON AND NEW YORK

Published in the UK in 1999 by UCL Press

Reprinted 2003
By Routledge,
11 New Fetter Lane, London, EC4P 4EE

Transferred to Digital Printing 2003

The name of University College London (UCL) is a registered trade mark used by UCL Press with the consent of the owner.

ISBNs: 1-85728-850-5 HB
         1-85728-851-3 PB

British Cataloguing-in-Publication Data
A catalogue record for this book is available from the British Library.

Typeset in Bembo
by Graphicraft Limited, Hong Kong

Contents

CONTENTS

Acknowledgements

Long ago, this book began life as a PhD thesis. It was then called *Justice from a distance* (Wissenburg 1994). Over the years, both contents and title changed repeatedly, in the last two years of its recomposition (1996–8) mostly in reaction to another book I was writing at the time, *Green liberalism* (Wissenburg 1998). Particularly in Chapters 7 and 8, I discuss themes that I have also discussed in the latter book; despite minor differences in the wording, the substance of both chapters is, I believe, now consistent with the ideas expressed in *Green liberalism*.

Everyone who was involved in the making of *Green liberalism* was also indirectly involved in the creation of *Imperfection and impartiality* – in particular my sponsor for the last three and a half years, the Foundation for Law and Government (REOB), which is part of the Netherlands Organization for Scientific Research (NWO), and the members of the Department of Political Science, now part of the School of Public Affairs, at the University of Nijmegen. In addition, I owe thanks for their ideas, guidance, help, suggestions, advice, support or absence of obstruction to a few dozen people who read parts of this manuscript itself. I hope I have not forgotten anyone if I mention Mark Bovens, Ad van Deemen, Andrew Dobson, Rob Gilsing, Bob Goodin, Steven Hartkamp, Bob Lieshout, Grahame Lock, Cor van Montfort, Paul Nieuwenburg, Ewout Ossewold, Carmelita Parisius, Larry Temkin, Marin Terpstra, Albert Weale and countless participants in numerous conferences and workshops. One conference in particular has exerted a lasting influence on this book: the one on Human Rights fifty years after the creation of the United Nations in Sintra, Portugal, funded by the Friedrich Naumann Stiftung of the German Freie Demokratische Partei in 1994. Although they may not have realized it, João Bettencourt da Câmara, Luis Bustamente, Raul Campusano, Goh Cheng Teik, Ehud Ben Ezer, Sabira Faquirá, Elsa Kelly, Ewa Matuszewska, Mahmut Ongoren, Kunga Tsering, Juan Urioste and others there completely restored my faith in the human capacity for impartiality. I am especially indebted to Brian Barry for his very careful and friendly comments on the one-but-final version of this book, and to Caroline Wintersgill and

ACKNOWLEDGEMENTS

Claire Hart of UCL Press for their time, help, energy, thoughtfulness, ceaseless patience and delightful e-mails – and in the case of Caroline, also for persisting that this book be published by UCL Press.

Of course, despite the efforts of all these people I did not always yield to their better judgement. Hence the usual disclaimer applies: I and I alone am responsible for any misinterpretation, misrepresentation, misunderstanding and mistake in this text.

Perhaps no one is irreplaceable, but in writing this book two members of our species were more irreplaceable than anyone else – and not just for their intellectual contributions. Without Masja Nas and Martin van Hees, this book would never have been what it is, we would not have been who we are or where we are now, and life would have been far less interesting, at times not even interesting at all. The four years in which we were colleagues, friends and nearly neighbours (we are still friends, but unfortunately the rest has changed) were, not coincidentally, among the best of my life. In this best of all possible worlds, I have been remarkably fortunate to meet people like them.

Finally, I could not have completed this book without opportunities to reflect and relax. I thank everyone at Café Mahieu for tolerating a guest who at times neither talks nor hears, only stares and writes, and I am extremely grateful, especially after these last emotionally exhausting weeks, for dancing and talking shop, but most of all for just talking, with Hester Moerbeek. Friends should be more important than books; I regret that I so often forget that.

Marcel Wissenburg
Nijmegen, June 1998

Part I

1

Introduction

Book, chapter and verse

One reason why we live in states and societies is that there is no escape. We are born into them, we do not choose them or create them. Rather, they design us and our desires, needs, habits and customs; our own contribution as individuals to their make-up is usually negligible. We are in chains from the very first moment of our existence – even though by nature we may be free.[1] Only collective action can change state and society. We also live in chains because it is the only alternative to a state of universal warfare, as Thomas Hobbes believed, or to a state of universal fear and insecurity, as less pessimistic contract theorists argued. We are not angels and we do not as a rule expect our fellow humans to be angels; we need them in chains to protect ourselves, and we chain ourselves to chain them. Yet the bare existence of a state is not enough to warrant its preservation. In places like Afghanistan, Sudan, Somalia, Rwanda, parts of the former USSR and former Yugoslavia, state institutions totally disintegrated even when the state seemed omnipresent.

Our individual chances of having a life worth living depend on the existence of protective and, as such, necessarily oppressive institutions, but institutions also depend on us. To exist and function, the institutions that make up states and societies require our active support; to give this support we need good reasons, and one among many good reasons is thought to be justice. To paraphrase Augustine, it is justice that makes the difference between the state and a band of robbers; it is justice that legitimizes institutions. And justice happens to be the subject of this book. It is not my intention to claim, let alone prove, that justice is all that counts. A society needs many other virtues to provide a haven for our wandering souls and even then it is not necessarily a safe and comfortable place to be. Justice is a necessary, not a sufficient condition for a life worth living, yet even in the very limited sense in which I shall interpret justice it makes a fundamental difference.

3

INTRODUCTION

This book deals with *distributive social justice*, more specifically with the recent version of the eternal debate in political, social and legal philosophy about the two questions central to this problem: how should we distribute the benefits and burdens, the joys and bores, of society, and why should we accept these distribution rules? Both are traditional questions in political philosophy, but, assuming that political philosophy is not, they are also very practical. A society cannot function without some support from its members, or at the very least without the absence of resistance on their side. The perception of distributive injustice in the societies of which we are members and citizens frequently leads to such resistance. Tax evasion, for instance, need not always be inspired by pure egoism. Sometimes, as in the United Kingdom during the Poll Tax times or in the Italy of the *Mani Pulite* (clean hands) campaign, a refusal to pay is legitimized as a form of resistance against a government that misuses its legitimate share of the social product, that unfairly redistributes it, or that burdens taxpayers in an unfair way. On occasion, the legitimacy of taxing itself is denied by objectors who feel that the money is theirs and no one else's to spend. Tax evasion is still a relatively innocent example; there is not a day when the papers do not report violent struggles in societies near and far over the proper distribution of power, freedom, opportunity, welfare, or plain food.

Before anything else is said, the reader should have some idea of what is meant by a distribution problem. Imagine eight persons trying to divide one pie of which they all want a quarter. There are four types of solution to this problem. One is to take the parameters of the problem as given and ask who should get what, and why. This is the pure distributive approach. The other three types of solution are what I call (following Goodin 1984) supply-side solutions: one could simply exclude at least four persons, one could change the preferences of at least four persons, or one could bake a second pie. Supply-side solutions are not necessarily illegitimate or immoral – quite the contrary – but they do not solve the distribution question. They only displace the problem. A supply-side strategy creates other distributive questions: who and how many should be excluded, and why? Whose preferences should be changed, in which direction, and why? Why should all eight get a quarter of a pie – do they equally deserve it, need it or have a title to it? The pure distribution problem, then, is that of distributing benefits or burdens without changing the parameters: one pie and eight people claiming a quarter of it. Within these limits, the theorist of distributive justice tries to find morally acceptable rules for the division of the social pie.

This book is, furthermore, concerned mainly with the quest for an *impartial* theory of distributive justice. The idea of justice is intrinsically related to that of impartiality: it has to do with giving and receiving what is in some way objectively due, not with what parties subjectively prefer. Moreover, a standard for justice, a criterion for what is objectively due, cannot – as I shall argue in more detail later – be justified with an appeal to a higher, substantive moral truth. There is no ultimate source for moral justification, and if there were it would, in our world of moral pluralism, be irrelevant. The best we can do is try to

4

formulate impartial standards, standards that are compatible with every reasonable moral code, every reasonable view of the good life. This means that we do not just want distribution rules to be *applied* impartially – what Brian Barry (Barry 1995: 11) called first order impartiality. We also want second order impartiality: we want the rules themselves to be impartial, that is, whether some situation should be seen as beneficial or undesirable should be determined impartially, the way in which it is to be treated should be determined impartially, and the rules for these two judgements should be chosen under conditions of impartiality. As a matter of fact, Barry observed that we often care less about first than about second order impartiality. We want to be partial to our friends in need, yet we do want to justify this behaviour with an appeal to a shared, if possible impartial, higher standard.

It probably has not escaped anyone's attention that we live in a morally divided world. We do not agree on what is good or the Good, few of us even have more than an inkling of our own private view of the Good, and those who do or think they do usually find that others cannot be rationally persuaded to share their views, unless one considers the sword an intelligent argument. In absence of a universal consensus on the good, and in an attempt to avoid the opposite position of universal cynicism and self-interest, moral and political theorists beginning with John Rawls (Rawls 1971) have discussed a third approach that might offer a way out: the idea of a reflective equilibrium. Basically, this means that one tries to imagine circumstances under which we could assess moral issues impartially, and at the same time convince our imperfect selves with their self-interest and theories of the good that these circumstances reflect reasonable, universally acceptable conditions for moral judgements. It is this attempt to strike a balance between impartiality and imperfection that gives this book its shape: in Part II, I develop a new version of the impartial judgement machinery, in Part III I apply it to the question of distributive social justice – and in the next two sections, I shall try to summarize both parts without giving away to much of the argument. I would not want readers to feel that they bought a book but only needed the first 20 pages.

Finally, the debate to which I just referred focuses on the idea and content of a *liberal* theory of social justice, which the theorists involved identify implicitly, and some outsiders like Ewald (Ewald 1986: 550–52) explicitly, with distributive justice. The notion of impartiality regarding the individual's conception of a good life is central to this liberal understanding of justice. It has found its classical expression in John Bordley Rawls's *A Theory of Justice* (1971), the book that set the agenda for the ensuing debate and for my own small contribution to it. The issues I discuss are familiar: how should goods and freedoms be distributed over a society, and why should we accept the distribution rules? For very simple and quite frustrating logistical reasons (time, space and money), I have not been able to deal separately with the issue that immediately follows the formulation and defence of principles of justice: what should people do, or refrain from doing, to protect and support (their principles of) justice? Nevertheless I try to rise to the occasion where the occasion arises, in particular when discussing communitarian justice (justice within the community) in Chapters 3 and 10.

Although this is a book about political theory, written by a political theorist, it is not relevant only to the initiated, the theorists of social justice. It may be as interesting as the whole debate on justice itself is to political philosophers on the one hand, and to economists, jurists, political scientists, sociologists and social psychologists on the other. Some, particularly continental, philosophers, sometimes complain about a lack of philosophical rigour in the debate. I think this is a misunderstanding, but even if it were not, such a deficiency should be seen as an invitation to join in rather than as an excuse for expressing disapproval. I hope to come some way towards opening the debate to these less interested philosophers by exposing the philosophical foundations of the debate where this is expedient, and by linking its political themes to traditional and new philosophical questions. Empirical social scientists often voice a diametrically opposed complaint: the debate would be too theoretical, too abstract, and unrealistic. I can do little about this – just two things. In the first place, I can and do claim that the debate, like any other debate, empirical or not, should be judged on its own terms, terms that I hope to elucidate. The justice debate in political theory should not be understood first and foremost as a contribution to progress in empirical sciences. It is a debate about the just society, interpreting the world from its own point of view. Secondly, although I cannot elude the trait that gives political theory a bad name to some (i.e., its being theoretical), by invoking more of the far from transparent conditions of the so-called real world, I at least want to raise its relevance for the reflection on the moral foundations of modern states and societies, whether they be liberal democratic or not. Which, by the way, makes this book worthwhile for anyone who is interested in the wellbeing of his or her society.

Impartiality

A central assumption of mainstream (a.k.a. liberal) social justice theory is that rules or principles of justice can be accepted as morally valid only if they are both impartial and chosen under conditions of impartiality. This means that liberal theorists of justice are interested in two distinct questions: (1) how is an impartial choice of principles of justice possible? and (2) what should these principles be?

I shall answer these questions in the same order, the first in Part II and the second in Part III, for three reasons. First, it seems to be the logical thing to do: one cannot justify principles without first knowing what justification requires. Secondly, the role of an impartial justification procedure is not necessarily limited only to that of justifying principles of distributive social justice. Even though this book and liberal theorists in general are focused on that particular issue, a reflective equilibrium between impartiality and imperfection may serve to support other moral principles as well: principles of non-distributive justice (e.g. criminal and commercial justice), principles of non-social justice (e.g. in the family or community, between societies, species or generations) and moral principles other than those of justice (e.g. self-government, benevolence, friendship). Being a separate issue, the theory of impartiality deserves separate treatment.

A last reason to split this book in parts is aesthetical: in texts, I prefer the straight line to the crooked. The more popular alternatives to a foundations first, implications later strategy are Rawls's (first the basics of the theory, then abstract implications, then an extended theory, more implications, more refinements, and so on) and Barry's (a bit of theory, some implications, the next bit of theory in response to gaps in the first bit, new implications, and so on). Although they make the heavy element, the moral theory part, more digestible, they increase the risk that parts of a text are taken out of their context and understood as representative of a complete theory of justice. Many readers of Rawls, for instance, are unaware of the difference between his general and special conception of justice, of the amendments made to his two principles, or of the ins and outs of his four-stage sequence of original positions for the application of these principles. Selective reading may also create the impression that a theorist considers the theory to be complete and finished, indubitable, uncriticizable and impossible to improve on – as if it ever can be. I hope that my choice to follow a straight line instead makes it easier to distinguish between necessary assumptions and axioms on the one hand and valid implications on the other. This is not to say that the straight line does not have its own disadvantages. One quite unfortunate result is that Part II of this book may seem to offer little justice theory and Part III little about the impartial foundations of justice theory (although the latter part could, in principle, be read without prior knowledge of Part II). This Introduction is written to serve the potentially bewildered as a guide, a mental map of the book's main topics and theses.

Above, I briefly discussed the current debate on the premises and content of an impartial liberal theory of distributive social justice. Chapter 2 will deal in more detail with this debate, with the themes upon which it centres, with the specific definition of social justice that participants in it use, and, to top it all off, with a few words on the vocabulary of justice theorists. On the one hand, this chapter helps to distinguish justice from other virtues, distributive justice from other basic forms of justice, social justice from other virtues of society, and the liberal approach to social justice from two alternative traditions, the Christian and socialist schools. On the other hand, it describes the liberal approach as one aimed at defining a neutral or impartial distributive social structure, one that tries to offer maximum opportunity for the development and realization of individual plans of life and theories of the good, while at the same time promoting typically liberal and allegedly 'self-evident' social ideals.

The remainder of Part II discusses justification procedures and in particular the possibility of defining and defending an Archimedean point (in John Rawls's terminology, or archpoint in mine), that is, a universally valid procedure for designing and defending equally universal principles of justice. For reasons explained below (Chapter 5), I shall opt for the contract theory model as being most consistent with the idea of impartiality. In the contract model I use, principles of justice are justified by the consent of disinterested individuals who are well informed in general, but who need not be too well informed about their own lives.

To those acquainted with John Rawls's theory, this may sound familiar. Despite superficial similarities, however, there are important differences both in the shape of this archpoint and in the assumptions behind it. The archpoint must be seen as a reaction to the shortcomings that (mostly) others detected in comparable constructions, shortcomings that will be discussed in Chapter 3. There are more similarities between my archpoint-based contract and Brian Barry's alternative 'Scanlonian' contract theory (which I shall introduce in a moment). I designed the archpoint, in particular, to meet the two most important lines of critique brought in against Rawls's, Barry's and other modern liberal theories of justice.

On the one hand, liberal theorists of justice, in particular Rawls, have been accused of not being impartial (universalistic) enough. Their theories would be based on all sorts of 'too substantial' assumptions about what matters to and about an individual: what is right more than what is good, what is efficient more than what is beautiful, negative liberty more than positive liberty, liberty more than equality, political freedom more than economic wellbeing, one's own fate more than that of others, the individual more than his or her environment, and so on. In short, they would presume without argument the universality of values that are typical of modern Western societies only, particularly of the still smaller group of genuine liberals living within those societies.

On the other hand, liberals have been criticized by communitarian theorists for being far too universalistic (impartial). In the first place, liberals would build their theories on an inadequate representation of the individual. In Rawls's theory of justice, for example, principles of justice are chosen by individuals behind a so-called veil of ignorance, which prevents them from knowing any particular fact about their individual lives. The result must be something like a Dance of the Vampires in a state of enlightenment: they cannot look at themselves in mirrors, hear their hearts thumping or feel their blood pumping, they have no sense of the time or place of their existence, no feelings of love and hate, and above all no knowledge of anything that distinguishes them from others. By separating the self from its social context and moral convictions for the purpose of creating an impartial individual, liberals following Rawls's example would disregard the social construction of the self, as well as the strong identification of the self with its convictions. One cannot, it is said, strip oneself of one's heritage (even if we could be conscious of all our judgements and prejudices) – not without losing everything that defines the individual. Consequently, liberal theories would not be able to convince 'real' individuals, as these will not (want to) recognize themselves in such morally neutered creatures. More basically, the demand that individuals be impartial will result in moral impotence. No goals or aims of individuals and no ideals of society can ever be justified, nor any moral community sustained, if the highest moral principle, impartiality, demands that all other principles be considered culturally specific, and hence coincidental and unjustifiable. For the sake of completeness, I should point out that this last objection is also supported to some degree by several liberals (e.g. William Galston and Joseph Raz), who understand it as a lack of room for perfectionism.

The answer I propose to these charges (in so far as they may be justified) is, first, to admit that there are indeed limits to the evaluative potential of justice as impartiality, but that this need not conflict with a communitarian view of justice. Basically, impartial principles of justice put limits to the validity of communitarian views on morality. Justice as impartiality is minimal justice. If we value impartiality (and I argue that we do, or at least ought to), then we must accept that there *are* certain things people should do or should not do, regardless of their personal convictions and regardless of whatever consensus on morality may exist in their communities. On the other hand, anything goes *within* these limits. Beyond the emphasis it puts on respect for basic human values and human dignity, the notion of impartiality has little evaluative potential. It thus leaves room for any kind of consensus, compromise, discourse and conflict about principles that are typical for their specific time, place and culture.

In Chapter 4, I shall propose a more impartial alternative to the existing accounts of moral relevancy and the human good which, as said above, have been criticized for containing too many contingent factors and thus for being too typical of liberals living in liberal societies to be called really impartial. The key notion in this alternative is that a liberal theory of justice should be impartial towards certain basic reasons for behaviour rather than towards any list of social goods or moral ends. The latter are destined to be socially or culturally specific and there is, moreover, no reason why they should not be open to rational critique. These basic reasons, so-called full reasons, bear a certain resemblance to virtues or categorical imperatives. They do not prescribe the goals or ends of human action, and are therefore independent from the contingent factors distinguishing particular societies. Instead, they merely indicate *how* one would want to act and what the *quality* of one's actions should be, regardless of circumstances. I call a person's set of full reasons, for want of a better and less theological term, a plan for a full life.

The range of people who are familiar with Rawls's now more than 25-years-old theory, terminology and concepts is still far larger than that of those familiar with the theory of justice Brian Barry developed in his *Treatise on Social Justice* (Part I: 1989, Part II: 1995).[2] Both because of the immense popularity of Rawls and because Barry's theory can be seen as a reaction to Rawls, I have chosen Rawls as my point of reference in this book. Wherever opportune, however, I have included comments on Barry's theory for those who are acquainted with it – much like functional sex in an otherwise dull movie. I believe that Barry's answer to the question of impartiality in justice theory is far superior to Rawls's. I am bound to, of course, because there is a far greater resemblance between my archpoint and the contract theory Barry developed on the basis of Thomas Scanlon's

(Scanlon 1982) alternative to Rawls's original position, than there is between the archpoint and the original position. Yet there are still substantial differences that make my theory distinct from, though not necessarily better than, Barry's.

In the first place, my aim is to reach a higher level of impartiality than Barry's second order impartiality. The theory presented here is meant to be 'reasonable' or 'acceptable' or 'non-rejectable', from all reasonable points of view, and not just, as it is in Barry's treatises, acceptable from the points of views of the current set of actually existing persons with their necessarily limited set of reasonable conceptions of the good (cf. e.g. Barry 1995: 11, 69). It has been argued that Barry's references to *particular* societies could be mere slips of the pen and that the flaw in Barry's conception of impartiality lies instead in the co-operative motivation Barry attributes to his contracting parties (Horton 1996). Horton is certainly right on the latter point, but Barry's pen simply slips too often.

Speaking as a theorist, I believe Barry misrepresents impartiality by making it a kind of common denominator of a limited number of particular moralities. Yet from a practical point of view, his theory may well be far more viable than mine. This is a second difference between Barry's theory and mine: his prime intention is to make impartiality viable, whereas mine is to take it seriously and see where it gets us. The result of the latter approach is twofold: it gives us impartial principles of justice for every society regardless of its composition in terms of moralities (perhaps less substantive principles than Barry's, but substantive enough to have radical implications for real life), and it offers room for both communitarian and Barry-like conceptions of justice in concrete societies.

Thirdly, my theory differs from Barry's in offering a clear and distinct concept, full reasons, to fill a gap left by Barry. Barry made a distinction between goods that are essential to the fulfilment of a person's plan of life and those that are not, attaching special weight to the former (cf. Barry 1995: 84), but he never explained on what basis the distinction was to be made, whereas I have tried to do exactly that. Consequently, I explicitly allow critique on the contents of plans of life, whereas in Barry's theory plans of life sometimes seem to be immune to critique.

Since the question of impartiality and the answer to it are of a quite abstract nature (impartiality is a general moral concept, not specifically political), and since I cannot, like the social scientist, take refuge in tables and graphs to lighten up the text, I shall try to offer the reader relief in another form: wherever possible, I shall stop the train of thought for a moment and let two fictional characters discuss the real-world political implications of theoretical impartiality. Any similarity between these characters and existing persons is purely coincidental.

Imperfection

Part III opens with a brief summary of all the conditions for an impartial judgement described in the preceding chapters – plus, for those who prefer fiction to dry theorizing, no fewer than two dramatic scenes depicting impartial people contracting for justice. The inclusion of Chapter 6 in that part theoretically allows the reader who wants to do so to skip the tedious impartiality talk in Part II or to save it for later, and move on to questions of justice immediately. The doctor does not recommend this, though. If the conditions posed on impartial judgement are first read as assumptions, the rest of Part III may easily be seen as nothing more than an exercise in informal logic, the relevance of which escapes the attention. The result of reading Part III separately may be that the reader is ultimately forced to start reading again, this time in Part II.

With this brief summary, the time has finally come to apply the machinery to the question of social justice, that is, in more appropriate but less digestible words, to the description of a metric or meter of social justice consistent with the view of impartiality developed in Part II. Basically, this means that I want to discuss principles of justice, who should get what and why in a just society. Yet the term 'metric' is somewhat broader than principles: a meter of social justice is a system of rules, measures and variables, certified as just for a society, which together determine what should be distributed, by whom, to whom, in which proportions and on what grounds. What most distinguishes the metric presented here from others is its definition of the subject of justice, society, and its radical distinction between two sorts of distributable goods, basic needs and further wants.

Current theories of distributive justice usually start from a simple model of society: one state, one shared language and history, one equally healthy and sane population, no intermediate levels of government, and no international trade, contact, or responsibilities. The only complicating factors are those within a population: differences in age, sex, colour, religion. Once a distribution scheme has been designed for this relatively simple society, further complicating factors are added, preferably one at a time: children, embryos, disabled citizens, Nazis, Nietzscheans and other intolerant fundamentalists, future generations, animals, the Third World, and so forth. This is a very satisfactory method for designing consistent principles fitting an imaginary world, but that is not the world we live in. If, following Rawls, the theory of justice should give us criteria for evaluating the basic structure of society and the institutions distributing our fundamental rights and freedoms and determining the basis of our expectations concerning our future, then we should at least give up the idea that each person's basic structure is made up of only one political authority, the centralized nation-state, and that all citizens of the same state necessarily share the same basic structure (cf. Miller 1998). The necessary changes in this hypothesis being made, social justice can be brought back to its true proportion, that of a tentative generalization of the individuals's 'basic structures'.

A second issue widely discussed in justice theory is that of the equalisandum. According to its formal definition, (distributive) justice requires that equals be treated equally and unequals in proportion to their inequality. Allocating shares in proportion to the relevant differences between individuals, however, requires an impartial yardstick by which to measure the value of 'shares', the so-called equalisandum. (I shall express shares in terms of formal rights, using a logical conception of rights first imported into political philosophy by Hillel Steiner (1994).) If the basic criterion of impartiality is to be respect for full reasons and for the plan of a full life defined by them, measures like utility, desert, pure equality, or primary social goods will not qualify. Respect for full reasons, I argue, can only be expressed adequately if basic needs, that is, rights to the opportunities and external resources needed to practise one's full reasons, are equally distributed – an equalisandum which I call equality of options. However, there is more to be distributed than conditional rights to basic needs and inalienable rights to the individual's internal resources needed for a full life. This remaining category of further wants cannot be measured in terms of options, as they are at most accessory to a full life. Their relevancy to the full life lies in their being the object of social conflict and possibly the cause of the disruption of society, which by itself is inimical to a full life. Accordingly, and using 'envy' as a pars pro toto label for all the sources of conflict, I shall claim that envy-containment is the best defensible impartial equalisandum for further wants. Such a formal criterion obviously leaves room enough for the culturally, historically and socially specific conventions that communitarians so zealously defend.

These two proposals – for a more subtle understanding of the subject of justice and for an almost perfectly individualized notion of the equalisandum – will make it clear that I do not consider social justice to be an easy mathematical exercise of distributing one and only one type of good, say, apple pie or utility, over a clearly delineated and defined group of equals. The real world is not that simple, people are not that simple, and their appreciation of goods and rights is not that simple. A theory of justice that takes the plans of life of individuals seriously, a liberal and impartial theory of justice, must take account of these facts – and learn to deal with them, or more precisely, learn to deal with the fact that justice cannot be meted out with mathematical precision.

To make matters worse, Part III is one extended argument in favour of diversity and differentation. Principles of justice have subjects and objects: the *x*s to whom *y*s are attributed, and the *y*s that are distributed among the *x*s. Chapter 7 is devoted to the identification of subjects or, as I prefer to call them, *recipients* of justice in general and social justice in particular. Since justice is about treating equals equally and unequals in proportion to their inequality, we need to know what makes recipients equal or unequal. Assume the existence of a welfare state, that is, assume the legitimacy of a government taking money and goods from some citizens and redistributing them to others. Is there a relevant difference between the homeless beggar who gambled away his money and the bag lady whose husband first drove her insane and then kicked her out of her house – whose claim to social benefits is more valid? Why exactly is the difference between the two relevant or irrelevant? Is it irrelevant because they are both human, relevant because they are not both responsible for their circumstances, irrelevant because they are beyond salvation, relevant because one had courage and the other was too weak? And what if we add a third recipient – a starving man in a faraway place, a great ape in a small cage, your unborn daughter?

The argument I shall make is that the morally relevant differences between recipients require us to differentiate between *degrees* of recipiency. It follows that we cannot hope for one clear demarcation line between valid and non-valid claims of recipients; there will be many. Life, consciousness and agency make a relevant difference between humans and rocks, enough to dismiss rocks as recipients, but not between citizens and foreigners, nor necessarily between humans and animals. Responsibility can make a difference, but only in a limited sense: if we take impartiality seriously, we should also be prepared to take individuals seriously whose ideas of the good presume a less or more cautious attitude towards risk than ours. Membership of society also makes a difference, yet since 'society' is not a clear-cut concept, the difference between members and non-members changes into a difference in degrees. The good news is that one clear distinction can still be drawn: that between real and possible persons. Against the taste of our times, I shall claim that members of future generations cannot be recipients of social justice – although we may have other moral obligations towards them.

Distribution creates a relation between people and things: objects, goods, acts, experiences, duties, benefits and so forth. Chapter 8 discusses these objects and asks which kinds of things there are and which of these can and cannot be the object of distributive justice. Since 'things' is an ugly word and one that does not describe the quality of the relation, I shall replace it by a more complicated term and even more complicated concept, that of formal rights. Every 'thing' and every state of affairs can be described in terms of permissible and forbidden acts, attributed to (distributed over) individuals. Not only does this allow us to economize on words, it also allows us to see where irrelevant conflicts over scarce resources originate (too general and uncalibrated rules of property, possession, use and freedom of action) and to avoid these.

In practical terms, the most fundamental question in matters of distributive justice is whether there are any rights at all that a society can (re)distribute – in particular, whether property and income can be redistributed. After all, it is all nice and amusing to discuss principles of justice, but if individuals have absolute property rights, natural rights to the fruits of their labour or absolute freedom from interference in their affairs unless they violate the freedoms of others, there would seem to be little sense in talking about social (re)distributive schemes: justice could only refer to the voluntary acts of individuals. Then again, rejecting the priority of individual rights literally opens up the road to serfdom: if my possessions are not mine but society's, the acts by which I got them may also be society's to rule, and if my acts are not mine, then neither is my body, my mind, my self.

In the end, I conclude that libertarians like Robert Nozick and Hillel Steiner, both taking a natural rights position, are wrong in two respects. A natural rights perspective is quite unhelpful and in fact redundant; what matters is whether people, preferably impartial contracting parties, have good reasons to recognize specific rights and any overall distribution of rights. Moreover, the fact that rights must have a social basis does not imply that we will all become slaves of society. There are good, impartial reasons to recognize some rights as absolute and untouchable – though not all.

In the course of this discussion, I make a distinction between four different categories of rights. First, there are things that simply cannot be the object of rights: square circles, the ghost realm and other impossibilities. Next, there can be absolute rights to the things that make a self a self: parts of body and mind. Finally, there are two particularly interesting categories of conditional rights: based upon their relevancy to a person's plan for a full life, we can distinguish between rights to goods, acts and so forth that may fulfil basic needs and those that may satisfy further wants. A claim to x as an individual's basic need, as a necessary condition for a full life, can trump any other individual's claim to x on the basis of his or her 'mere' desires.

One more, possibly odd, conclusion is drawn in this chapter: in so far as social justice is concerned, it does not matter how the distribution of rights in a society is actually organized, in the form of a perfect and complete free market, a planned economy, or anything in between. What matters is that there is some kind of institution to safeguard a fair distribution in some way.

At this point, we know 'who' gets 'what', and we know that justice requires equal treatment or proportional equality. But since rights do not mean the same to individuals, we still need one more instrument: a measure of equality, the equalisandum (Chapter 9). Since I have already discussed this element of the book at the beginning of this section, I shall not waste more words on it than necessary. Interpreting a distinction made by Brian Barry between goods that are crucial and those that are not crucial to the realization of a plan of life, I argue in favour of two equalisanda: equality of options and envy-containment. The first prescribes an equal distribution of rights to basic needs, that is – in full – an equal distribution of those rights that individuals require in order to live a life in accordance with their full reasons: their private criteria for the quality of their lives and actions regardless of the contingent circumstances in which they live. The second equalisandum, envy-containment, determines that all further distributable rights be distributed in whatever way minimizes conflict in society, thus maximizing the chances of leading a full life.

There is an element of utopianism in the expectations of readers and writers of theories of justice, even though justice is necessarily a remedial virtue for an imperfect world: ultimately, we all want to know what a just society would look like. In so far as the result of developing a theory of justice is knowledge, not opinion, we know who is entitled to just treatment, we know to what recipients are entitled, we know how to measure it and we know why we should accept these conclusions, but it all remains abstract. A description of the just society could give us something to compare the real existing world with, something to help us choose and support policy aims, perhaps even some sense of strategy.

In the final chapter of this book, I shall describe my impression of this imperfect utopia – a necessarily imperfect impression. The greater part of that chapter is devoted to distilling a series of principles of justice out of the preceding analyses. These principles are flexible in one respect, rigid in another. They describe and prescribe the most fundamental human rights, and in that sense they are rigid, but their formulation leaves room for a multitude of possible shapes of society from libertarian near-anarchy to communitarian near-totalitarianism. Any of these possible societies should be considered capable of meeting the demands of an impartial, liberal theory of justice. Although many liberals may welcome this conclusion as an unexpected blessing, there was no way in which it could have been avoided. The real existing world is simply too complex. It contains a diversity of distributors, not just one state per nation, society and co-operative venture; it consists of subjects in varying degrees of recipiency rather than basically homogeneous individual humans who only interact (all in equal amounts) among themselves within a closed society; it is a place where several categories of rights are distributed, categories that cannot be reduced to one simple measure; and even though a degree of generalization is possible, the most fundamental needs of recipients dictated by their most fundamental criteria for a good life remain invariably private. This should not be taken to mean that the measure of justice presented in this book is inapplicable to the real world. It is difficult but far from impossible; I have tried to describe its application to several real(istic) issues elsewhere (e.g. Wissenburg 1998: 161 ff.). There are so many real worlds to which it can be applied that an analysis of even one question of distributive justice in even one community would (and did) take a whole book – and it would still tell us nothing about an ideally just society. All we can say about 'the' shape of 'the' just society is that there is no such thing; only side-constraints within which liberty and plurality may flourish. The rest is silence.

To cut a long story short and summarize it as provocatively, even politically, as possible, this book defends the following series of theses: if we take justice seriously, we must take impartiality seriously; if we take impartiality seriously, we must accept that it can only serve to justify protection of our most basic needs, that it cannot support any principle for the just distribution of the rest of society's benefits and burdens, and that it cannot justify one particular form of state or society – not even a night-watchman state. How exactly we distribute benefits and burdens and how we shape society depends on time, place and culture, on substantive, perhaps even communitarian, views of justice. There is no impartial criterion available, no appeal to impartiality possible. All that an impartial theory of justice can defend is a minimum demand: that the state or its equivalent be at least a dozing night-watchman. As a consequence, each appeal to the impartially justifiable status of particular policies becomes circumspect. In a truly short short summary: taking impartiality seriously only gets us so far – but it does get us somewhere.

Part II
The Archimedean point

There is no agreement on the divisions of justice.

Samuel Pufendorf (1991: 31)

2

Justice in society

Social justice and other virtues

The natural thing to do, confronted with a vague or ambiguous concept like social justice, is to ask what it means – or more precisely, to ask if there are any conventions on its meaning. Aristotle opened the fifth book of his *Nicomachean Ethics* with the dullest of propositions, announcing his programme for a conceptual analysis: 'With regard to justice and injustice we must consider (1) what kind of actions they are concerned with, (2) what sort of mean justice is, and (3) between what extremes the just act is intermediate' (Aristotle 1959: 1129ª1). These are some of the questions on which I shall touch here, albeit in relation to the *liberal* idea of social justice only. What I have to offer in this section is a probably very dull list of the terms used by liberal theorists of social justice and of the concepts they represent.

Let me start with the clearest distinction, the one between *moral* justice, the normative or evaluative concept, and *legal* justice, which is more or less synonymous with positive law. Ideally, legal justice would be fully compatible with moral justice. In practice, laws are of course designed and applied with reference to moral justice as well as other criteria, which means that discrepancies between the two can and do arise. As from now, I shall use the term justice to refer to moral justice exclusively. The concept of (moral) justice is often used in connection with ideas like the *good*, the *right*, and *morality*. The connotations of these three terms differ from language to language and from author to author, yet there seems to be a certain consensus on their hierarchy: what is good is a broader concept than, and embraces, what is moral. The domain of justice is in turn more limited than that of morality. The fourth term, right (as in 'the right thing to do'), is more promiscuous: it can refer to 'straight' or correct behaviour, correct reasoning, honesty and legality. In justice theory, it is used as an equivalent of rationality, justice or, most often, morality (cf. Frankena 1962; for a dissenting view, see Brandt 1979: 306–7). However, this does not tell us anything about priorities. In John Rawls's theory, for instance, justice has priority over the right and the right over the good (see e.g. Rawls 1971: 30–32, 395–7).

Next on our list is a distinction between justice and different conceptions of *rationality*. Some authors treat the two as directly related. Richard Brandt, for instance, sees principles of justice as part of the social moral code that would be chosen by perfectly rational people (Brandt 1979: 308), people who have gone through cognitive psychotherapy, a process in which their desires are confronted with all relevant available information and in which they are 'de-conditioned' if their desires turn out to be indefensible (cf. Brandt 1979: 113 ff.). Here, rationality comes down to acting in accordance with established facts. Note, however, that Brandt is not completely succesful in reducing justice to rationality: whereas justice is based on desires or principles we *should* (positively) have and cherish, (Brandtian) rationality is and can only be concerned (negatively) with determining which desires we should *not* have. A second interpretation of rationality is offered by the rational choice theorist, David Gauthier, in his *Morals by Agreement* (1986). He completely neglects the theme Brandt concentrated on: the origins and merits of individual preferences. 'What is good is good ultimately because it is preferred, and it is good from the standpoint of those and only those who prefer it' (Gauthier 1986: 59). Having excluded the possibility of moral judgements about values, preferences and autonomy, he then seeks to show that justice and morality, understood as impartial constraints on rationality, and rationality understood as the pursuit of one's greatest interest or benefit (Gauthier 1986: 7), are fully compatible: impartial actors involved in the bargaining process called 'society' are by (his) definition necessarily rational actors.

Despite the existence of such dissenting opinions, I want to point out that there *is* some intuitive difference between justice and rationality. Whether rationality be understood as the maximization of benefit, as consistency with known facts, as the capacity to think logically, or in any of the other ways we may encounter later on – it will always be associated with *necessity, given certain aims* (such as maximum personal benefit). In contrast to this, justice, morality and ethics are concerned with justifying the choice *for* those same aims.

Rationality, morality, the good and justice are distinct criteria by which one can judge societies, individuals, actions and states of affairs. There are scores of others: 'love and mercy, of course, go beyond justice' (Passmore 1979: 27), or 'the virtue of a state is its security' (Spinoza 1951: 290). Feminist philosophers influenced by Carol Gilligan have argued for an ethics of care to supplement or even overrule the 'cold jealous virtue', as David Hume described justice (see e.g. Baier 1987: 42). I shall not take a position on this issue. It is not my intention to claim that justice must be the first virtue of a society, merely that it must be *a* virtue of society. Whether it can or should at times be overruled by other virtues is an interesting and important question, but not one I can treat here.

Within the broad concept of justice we can make further distinctions to isolate the more restricted concept of social justice. One possibility is to look at the *location* of justice, but unfortunately this will not help us much. Following Aristotle, some theorists of social justice understand justice primarily as a virtue of the individual, a *disposition* of the acting subject (Aristotle 1959: 1129ª7). Others see justice as a trait of *social interaction* between individuals rather than as a feature of intentions (e.g. Nozick 1974: 151). And still others, notably John Rawls and his disciples, consider justice to be first of all a property of the *structure* of social interaction: 'the primary subject of justice is the basic structure of society' (Rawls 1971: 7).

Herbert Kitschelt has suggested a second distinction between (at least) two types of theories of justice: those immediately based on and justified by 'substantial or formal norms, values, or principles' like utilitarianism, and those based on and justified through procedures, regardless of the outcome of those procedures, like John Rawls's and Jürgen Habermas's theories (Kitschelt 1980: 392–3). Unfortunately, modern justice theories of both types exist. Moreover, the distinction itself is useless. First of all, both approaches end up referring to *some* substantive source of justification (cf. Rawls 1995: 179). Secondly, whether or not some theorist's principles of justice are *in fact* justified with a direct reference to some substantial norm, or whether such norms are to be 'found' in a roundabout way by some procedure, is irrelevant here. What counts is whether either course is *theoretically* possible, and often both are.

Apparently, then, if we try to characterize the recent debate on liberal social justice as one, united but distinct, approach to justice, we have at this moment little more than an annoyingly vague notion of a common subject: the idea of justice in (the basic structure of) society, rather than justice among strangers, international justice, justice in the family or God's justice. There is nothing typically liberal about social justice being concerned with justice in society; the subject is not a monopoly of liberals. It is just one of the slogans and topics that popped up in European political debates in the first part of the nineteenth century, along with other social-isms like social science, social feeling, social responsibility, and social politics.[3] Until the 1900s it was mainly a political slogan of the leftists of those days, the radical liberals and the first socialists, a slogan symbolizing the existence of an alternative to *laissez-faire* capitalism and its reduction of justice to legal justice.

There are, however, two aspects in which the liberal approach to social justice can be distinguished from others. One is its focus on a series of typically (modern) liberal values, the foremost being impartiality; I shall discuss this aspect later. The other is that it understands social justice as, for the most important part, a problem of distributive justice, rather than as one of general justice or one of both general and distributive justice. The latter two approaches are characteristic of what may be called the Thomistic and the Marxist paradigm of social justice. Let me first explain these terms and then introduce the three paradigms.

In the fifth book of his *Ethica Nicomachea*, Aristotle distinguished seven categories of justice, beginning with *justice 'in general'*. A just person in this general sense is one who furthers, maintains, and protects the good of the *polis* (ideally expressed in its laws) in the interest of the *polis* – in other words: the common good. The six other categories of justice are called 'special' kinds of justice: distributive justice, commercial justice, corrective justice, political justice, household justice, and finally equity. We can disregard most of these terms here. Commercial and corrective (or retributive) justice are the two sides of what Aristotle calls remedial justice and Thomas Aquinas commutative justice. They relate to the voluntary and involuntary exchanges between individuals – say, commerce and crime. Equity rectifies injustices that would be caused by the strict application of formal rules of (legal) justice without regard for special circumstances – say, if a judge were to fine a biker for ignoring a stop signal, thereby actually saving lives. Household and political justice are domains for the exercise of justice rather than genuine forms of justice: they concern the proper duties and rewards of officials and those of independent members of the household.

The more important terms are distributive and general justice. *Distributive justice* concerns the distribution of whatever can be lawfully distributed among the members of a *polis*, following the rule of proportional equality or (Powers 1996) proportionality: each person's share should be proportional to his or her worth as established by (local) law. In modern justice theory, references to positive law as the ultimate standard of a person's worth have virtually disappeared in favour of moral standards.[4] *General justice* is an invention of Thomas Aquinas's, who copied and systematized Aristotle's categories of justice. In his view, general justice is the mirror image of distributive justice. Whereas the latter determines what a *polis* owes its members, the former determines what the members owe the *polis* (cf. Aquinas 1975: 88–91, 2–2q61; Shields 1941: 11). One of John F. Kennedy's most famous statements immediately springs to mind.

The idea that social justice is first and foremost a matter of distributive justice goes back at least to Henry Sidgwick, whose work had a deep and lasting influence on Anglo-Saxon analytical philosophy, the breeding ground for the liberal theory of social justice. In his *Methods of Ethics*, Sidgwick wrote: 'We may observe that the notion of justice always involves allotment of something considered as advantageous or disadvantageous' (Sidgwick 1962: 268). Yet, as I said before, other approches do exist. They all follow Justinian's definition of justice ('the precepts of law') as: *honeste vivere, non alienum lædere, suum cuique tribuere* – to live honourably, not to injure another, to render each his due.[5] They all define social justice specifically as *suum cuique*, to each his due. But they do not all interpret 'due' as distribution.

What I call the Thomistic paradigm developed for the greater part out of the critique Pope Leo XIII voiced against capitalism and socialism in his 1891 encyclical *Rerum Novarum*. His own views on social justice left a deep mark on the official Church doctrine, as in Pius XI's 1931 encyclical *Quadragesimo Anno* and others (cf. Davies and Walsh 1991: xii ff.; Hickel 1984: xxiii), on dissenters within the Church (e.g. Maritain 1947; Shields 1941), and on non-Catholics inspired by either Thomism or the idea of personal salvation central to Leo's views (cf. Hickel 1984: xxiii; see also Dooyeweerd 1957).

Leo XIII stressed the responsibility of citizens for the wellbeing (the good) of their society and fellow-citizens, a thought we can immediately identify as being consistent with the Thomistic theory of general justice. Leo's approach to the social question was that it should be answered not only by the state but also, and even primarily, by the citizens. Social justice could not be enforced by the state, at least not without endangering private property (which is a natural right of every human being), and it should certainly not be enforced by means of a revolution. The lack of social justice and the danger this posed to societies whatever their momentary form originated in a lack of personal social virtues: greed and cold-heartedness on the side of the capitalists (Leo XIII 1991: 43, 58), anti-harmonious socialist aggression on the side of the workers (Leo XIII 1991: 16, 58).[6] The task of the state was to protect both property and workers (the last by ensuring at least a minimal level of existence), but it should not encroach on the market. The redistribution necessary for this aim (Leo XIII 1991: 47) was not one of the state's tasks, as it must guarantee the rights of property, not the contradictory correct *use* of property. Redistribution should rather be one of the harmonizing effects of the actions of the members of society (employers and employees), if they were to realize their duties of supporting the common good, the virtuous lives of themselves and their fellow beings, and the mere maintenance of their social and political union (Leo XIII 1991: 49 ff.). Consequently, Leo was opposed to both *laissez-faire* and trade-unionism, which he held to be subversive – especially the latter, based as it was on an ideology that did not recognize the social whole as an organism. The only acceptable alternative in his eyes was found in the now well known theory of corporatism.

That general justice is still the dominant interpretation of social justice among Thomists is indicated by, for example, Paul Weithman's essay on international distributive justice. A large part of this text, in which Weithman tries to harmonize Thomism and the Rawlsian principles of justice, is devoted to a defence of his unorthodox focus on distributive rather than general justice (Weithman 1992: 181–6). In circles of Marxists, anarchists and utopian socialists, social justice is a more holistic concept. Here, general justice is directly related to distributive justice and vice versa, in the sense that they are seen as necessary conditions for one another. Although the most outspoken proponents of this view are utopian novelists, perhaps the most convincing proof of the existence of a Marxist paradigm can be found in the works of Karl Marx himself.

Marx's views on justice are generally interpreted in two ways: either he is supposed to have dismissed talk about justice as 'twaddle' (McBride 1975: 205; cf. Lock 1989), ideological rhetoric, or he is presented as a champion of social justice, defending the maxim (from his *Critique of the Gotha programme*) 'from each according to his capacity, to each according to his needs'. The first interpretation, obviously, does not allow other than 'contextual' (Nielsen 1986: 107) maxims of justice, that is prescriptions based on the rationality of actions in the light of the liberation of the exploited (see e.g. Hook 1976: 75; Brown 1992; Hübner 1992). In this view, a moral understanding of social justice is impossible: there can be no question of reasoning towards a common truth, as there *is* no such truth where diverging classes and opposite interests exist (cf. Fisk 1975: 59 ff.). Now it seems unlikely that Marx completely banned moral motives from his mind and work (cf. Lukes 1985). Even if the first interpretation is correct, even if to Marx justice was a positive and not a normative concept, he still had views about 'the un-named' (i.e. justice), views that account for much of his social critique, including his once-only adherence to a maxim of social justice. Even on a rationalistic inter-pretation, the Gotha maxim implies that social justice meant both general and distributive justice. They could not be separated.[7] Justice was a matter of how the goods of society were produced as much as of how they were distributed. Both depended on the actual division of economic power in society and not on the social conscience of individuals, which is but an expression and product of a society's productive relations. Hence, social justice is ultimately not a question of abstract rationality or morality, but one of concrete power.

It is only the currently dominant liberal paradigm of social justice that under-stands social justice as, and sometimes completely reduces it to, distributive justice. Note that 'liberal' in this context does not refer to liberalism as a political ideology. Liberal philosophers have neither party nor country. I use it as a shorthand de-scription of a long list of authors who, to varying degrees, share the same liberal values, political philosophers who are heirs of the Enlightenment and the French Revolution: libertarians and near-anarchists, egalitarian liberals, liberal and demo-cratic socialists. It also applies to many communitarians, the most influential and loudest critics of mainstream social justice theory who stress the importance of general justice relative to distributive justice – people like Alasdair MacIntyre, Michael Sandel, Michael Walzer, Michael Jackson, William Galston and Charles Taylor. And the label 'liberal' can even be used to include an Anglo-Saxon Marxist like Gerald Cohen.

Liberalism as a political ideology, as we all know, is divided over the issue of social justice. Hard-liners like Friedrich Hayek (Hayek 1976a, 1976b) and to some extent Karl Popper (Popper 1960, 1986a, 1986b) did not see it as a task of governments to intrude in the private sphere and plan peoples' lives in the name of just distribution and fair shares. Yet inspired by nineteenth-century social liberals like John Stuart Mill and Thomas H. Green, 'liberalism with a human face' has been at least partly responsible for the first intrusions on the night-watchman state and hence for the birth of the welfare state (cf. Mill 1969; Wempe 1986). It is this tradition that resurfaced around 1970 with the publica-tion of John Rawls's *A Theory of Justice* (1971), followed by, among many others (for more see Cullen (1992)), Robert Nozick's (1974) libertarian theory, Bruce Ackerman's (1980) liberal, Michael Walzer's (1983) communitarian, Brian Barry's (1989, 1995) impartialist and Hillel Steiner's (1994) libertarian theories.

Earlier I remarked that the liberal theory of social justice typically focuses on two things: distributive justice and impartiality. Some insiders might find it difficult to accept the first point. It has been argued that neither Rawls, nor Nozick, nor Walzer, three of the main representatives of liberal justice, identify

SOCIAL JUSTICE AND OTHER VIRTUES

social justice with liberal justice. Hans Bedau, for instance, argued that Rawls sees social justice 'in contrast' to distributive justice (Bedau 1982: 85) – but the fact of the matter is that to Rawls distributive justice still is the foundation stone of a just society (cf. Rawls 1971: 4, 5, 8). Robert Nozick may deny that states have any right to *re*distribute individual citizens' properties, but he is nevertheless concerned about distribution: the distribution of absolute property rights over individuals, and its effects on the structure of society. Michael Walzer, finally, argues that things like honour, salvation, sex, security and consumer goods are and should be distributed in separate social spheres according to separate principles of distribution.

The existence of a second point of interest for liberal social justice theorists, impartiality or neutrality (I shall distinguish these often promiscuously used terms in the next section), is less contentious. (For a similar claim see e.g. Kley 1989: 400 ff.) Informally put, impartiality requires that (the basic structure of) a society should not be biased in favour of or against certain theories of the good life. It demands that principles of justice be unbiased, that procedures for the justification of principles of justice be unbiased, and finally that this justification itself be based on non-problematical ethical principles. For many writers, impartiality implies distributive equality, for which an impartial yardstick, the equalisandum ('that which is to be equalized') is needed. Much of the debate has, therefore, focused on the analysis of measures of equality as diverse as welfare, opportunity, resources or Rawls's social primary goods. Even Robert Nozick defends an equalisandum, of sorts: the inviolability of natural rights. However, what we do with these rights, whether we sell them or use them to run naked through the streets or to go on a diet of fugu and sake, is our private and no one else's business. Nozick is a rabid opponent of enforced patterns of substantive equality.

One final thing to note about the liberal conception of social justice and the debate on the subject is that both are inescapably academic and, within the academic world, highly theoretical. The flood of books and articles that started with Rawls consisted from the very start of conjectures, refutations, reformulations and amendments of philosophical theories (see e.g. collections like Daniels 1975, Jeffrey 1981 and Kelly 1998). Over the years, an exchange of arguments with another quite theoretical area, the formal theory of rational choice, has taken place in texts like Barry (1989), Brandt (1979), Elster (1987), Harsanyi (1982), Sen (1975) and more recently in Binmore's impressive *Playing Fair* (1993). But it seems that this is where the influence of social justice theory stops being distinguishable. Philosophers of justice hardly ever use data from empirical research on the issue – Dryzek and Goodin (1984) and Freeden (1978) are rare exceptions. Social psychologists, sociologists and other empirical scientists involved in social justice research, on the other hand, seldom or never use philosophical material.[8] The reason is simple: whereas social justice theory deals with what people *should* believe, social justice research deals with what people *actually* believe (cf. Wegener 1990: 67). And although I would not want to argue that the twain shall never meet, one can legitimately doubt whether it is the mission of philosophy to enlighten science, or that of science to bring philosophers back to earth.[9]

There is no evident reason why the liberal paradigm should have a monopoly on the term social justice. However, in the remainder of this book I shall identify social justice with the liberal interpretation of social justice as distributive impartial justice. In principle, such a limited approach needs no defence: in the first place one has to limit oneself; secondly, the liberal approach is flourishing and as such is at least as interesting as competing models; and thirdly, I simply have personal reasons for preferring a liberal over any other approach to political issues. Yet I think there is more to be said in favour of the liberal programme, even though it may only mean preaching to the converted. An approach to justice that takes impartiality as its guiding light is more viable in pluralistic societies than any alternative – and it is a misconception to believe that there is or can be any society with just one uniform morality. The more substantive a theory of justice becomes, that is, the more it promotes one view of the good over others, the more it becomes a recipe for oppression, persecution and civil war.[10] The liberal theory of justice at least takes moral pluralism seriously, not as a temporary or contingent phenomenon but as a basic fact of life. The ultimate virtue of liberal social justice is that it is humanistic, in the original sense of the word: it places the needs of concrete human beings, here and now, at the centre of attention.

The limits of impartiality

In the previous section I compared the liberal understanding of social justice with two other perspectives. In this section I want to take a closer look at a concept that I claimed is central to the liberal perspective: that of neutrality or impartiality with regard to ideas of the good or the good life. My aims are to determine, first, what second order impartiality means to liberal theorists, in particular Ackerman, Nozick, Rawls and Walzer; secondly, what its abstract meaning is in any liberal theory of justice: and thirdly, what the implications of adhering to this general idea of impartiality are for an attempt to justify principles of justice.

Let me begin in this section by explaining what impartiality does not mean: the complete absence of all moral or ethical convictions. Ethical judgements, including those on justice, are impossible in a total absence of prior normative ideas. Moral judgements presuppose that there is something *on which* to judge and something *with which* to judge – in other words, that there are sides to be chosen.

An obvious consequence of the impossibility of complete impartiality is that the principles or procedures used in defending theories of justice cannot themselves be defended with an appeal to their impartiality; they need a different kind of underpinning. As Ronald Dworkin remarked about the procedure Rawls followed to sustain his principles of justice:

> The device of the original position ... cannot plausibly be taken as the starting point for political philosophy. It requires a deeper theory beneath it, a theory that explains why the original position has the features that it does and why the fact that people would choose particular principles in that position, if they would, certifies those principles as principles of justice. (Dworkin 1981: 345)

Dworkin's remark applies exceptionally well to Rawls's version of the state of nature:[11] it took Rawls more than 20 years and at least three attempts (Rawls 1958, 1967, 1971; cf. Min 1984: 17) to design, test, demolish and rebuild his original position. And he is still not fully satisfied with it (Rawls 1993a: 23 ff.; Rawls 1995: 140). But it also applies to Bruce Ackerman's *Social Justice in the Liberal State* (1980), where principles of distributive justice are defended with an appeal to the plausibility of the contract situation Ackerman sketches (a bunch of colonists occupying a new planet) in the light of higher-order rules for the legitimacy of arguments in bargaining processes. The need for a higher (or deeper) theory is equally obvious in non-contractarian theories like Nozick's: the reader who does not from the very first moment accept his premise that 'Individuals have rights, and there are things no person or group may do to them' (Nozick 1974: ix) is immediately lost for the truth of all that would follow from this assumption. Even in communitarian circles, the need for ever deeper arguments is felt. Michael Walzer, according to whom the choice for one or more rules of distribution for all spheres of social action depends on the shared understandings of individuals in society, writes: 'Even if we choose pluralism, as I shall do, that choice requires a coherent defence' (Walzer 1983: 5). Unfortunately Walzer did not give such a defence: he limited himself to a vague and general critique of the universal, abstract and artificial principles of justice the philosophical tradition had produced, and to a purely descriptive presentation of spheres of social intercourse. To cut a long story short: whatever the impartiality of liberal theories of justice may be, it is not unconditional, complete impartiality. Nor could it be: if we want to prefer one principle to another, or want to defend it, or abstain from preferring, we need *reasons* to do so – including ethical reasons, at least if we want to convince ourselves of the justice of principles, and not merely of their empirical (in)evitability. Notice, by the way, that no particular *type* of deeper justification is excluded from this problem. The problem of defending moral choices is relevant even to relativistic theories of justice: the claim that deeper justifications are impossible or superfluous must itself be sustained.

Now how can a theory of justice be impartial if it is the result of choices based on ever deeper (substantive, partial) arguments? What exactly is the role of impartiality in such theories? There are two answers to these questions. The first one is trivial: justification procedures should be impartial or neutral or non-biased to ensure that they measure (or justify) what they are supposed to measure. In this sense, original positions and the like must be technically 'fair', logically consistent with their aim. If they should measure justice, they should measure justice and not the temperature.

The second answer is in line with the last part of Dworkin's hypothesis. There are *reasons* why particular principles are preferred to others and why they are preferred as *just* principles. Instead of being neutral in all possible respects (complete impartiality), the justification procedure should be justified by neutral reasons or ideals, and it should be scrupulously neutral with regard to the plans of life that are allowed or promoted by the principles it justifies. This is what I define as the material role of impartiality in this context. The notion of impartiality is used here to restrict the discussion, to restrict the set of possible arguments to those deemed 'proper' in matters of social justice. In the remainder of this section, I shall discuss the two means used to ensure impartiality: the formulation of self-evident ethical principles and their translation into impartial decision procedures for the choice of principles of justice. But first, let us introduce a bit of terminological clarity.

As said before, political theorists often use the terms impartiality and neutrality as synonyms, though neutrality is the most popular of the two. Up to this point, I more or less trusted on a tacit common understanding of both as 'giving equal weight to ideas about the good life'. However, a description like that is vague enough to be interpreted in an infinite number of ways – and as a matter of fact, that is precisely what has happened. William Galston, for instance, described four interpretations of neutrality (Galston 1991: 100 ff.); Joseph Raz (1986: 111–15) distinguished no fewer than nine (and perhaps more, if subtleties are included), and in social choice theory another distinct understanding of neutrality is used (Kelly 1988: 9; Sen 1970: 72). What we need is a bit of order. To that purpose, I define neutrality as a scheme containing four variables: *Neutrality* consists in the [subject's] giving equal [relevance] to the [scope] of the [object]. This defines a set of all meanings that can be given to neutrality. We can fill in nearly anything we want between the square brackets – for instance 'the [state] [actively endorsing] [equal opportunities] for [all rational plans of life]' or '[rational beings] [refraining from judgement] on [the weight attached to] [past conceptions of the good]'. I define impartiality in terms of the permutations this definition of neutrality allows: *Impartiality* is each element of the set of all conceptions of neutrality and all combinations of conceptions of neutrality.

To the comfort of reader and author alike, there is no need to go through the whole 'set of impartialities'. We can restrict ourselves to one version of impartiality, one that is characteristic of and central to liberal theories of justice. It is made up of the already mentioned idea of technical neutrality and, for want of better words, objective and subjective neutrality:

Technical neutrality: the decision procedure should actively endorse the promotion (i.e. detection and selection) of neutral principles of justice.
Objective neutrality: rational human beings should all equally endorse the principles or reasons behind the justification procedure, by virtue of their already being endorsed in their plans of life.
Subjective neutrality: the justification procedure and the reasons behind it should give equal relevance to individual plans of life or constituent parts thereof.

Notice that in the definition of objective neutrality the scope remains undefined, whereas in that of subjective neutrality relevance, scope, and – in fact – object are all undefined.

Taken out of the straight-jacket of the definition scheme, and seen in the light of their actual *role* in liberal theories of justice, we can describe these three notions of neutrality in a more informal way. Technical neutrality means, as above, that the justification procedure should measure what it is supposed to measure, that is, justice. Objective and subjective neutrality demand that the reasons behind justification procedures are (objectively, rationally) uncontestable, and that both reasons and procedures are – within limits – not biased, either directly or indirectly, in favour of or against individual plans of life or vital parts thereof. As this is still a rather complex description I shall discuss it in parts.

Objective neutrality

Somehow all liberal theories of justice contain references to intuitive, a priori or shared understandings of basic moral notions. We have already seen some of these notions at work in Rawls's, Nozick's and Walzer's theories. In the case of Ronald Dworkin it is equality of respect as moral persons for moral persons (e.g. Dworkin 1978, 1981, 1985b, 1985c). Bruce Ackerman's basic moral notions are the criteria by which he measures a valid claim to a part of the social stock: rationality, proclaiming the moral priority of legitimacy over power; consistency, doing the same for logic and (for instance) intuition; and neutrality, postulating the rationality of the equal worth given to 'conceptions of the good' (Ackerman 1983: 4, 7, 11).

A theory of justice necessarily needs prior principles: there must be some point of reference from which to evaluate alternative applied or applicable principles of distribution in societies. Without such a basic understanding of the good or the moral, there would be no reason to believe that the principles chosen in an original position or by an impartial observer are certified as principles of *justice* – to quote Dworkin again. Whether such principles can be uncontestable is an open question; that they should be is, on the other hand, generally accepted. As William Galston puts it, 'justified belief, then, is opinion that has survived the most rigorous process of dialectical testing in contestation with the available contrary views' (Galston 1991: 33). As (mostly) Anglo-Saxon philosophers, liberal theorists of justice have been deeply influenced by the critique of intuitionism of early analytical philosophers like – notably – Henry Sidgwick. In his *Methods of Ethics* (1874), Sidgwick rejected intuitionism in favour of teleological methods of ethics (in particular utilitarianism), yet claimed that there is a necessarily intuitive idea of the final aim in each method of ethics, and that there are some very general intuitive truths in ethics as such. Sidgwick also formulated some criteria for these first principles: they must be clear and precise (the Cartesian clear and distinct, cf. Broad 1930: 216), continually self-evident, mutually consistent, and supported by a clear consensus of opinion (Sidgwick 1962: 338 ff.).

In short: Sidgwick was of the opinion that the incontestability of basic intuitions as well as intuition itself are inseparable parts of all ethical theories, including theories of distributive justice. We shall return to Sidgwick's analysis of intuition shortly.

Subjective neutrality

Liberal theorists of justice assume that there is a qualitative difference between the private and public spheres, or, as Dworkin expressed it, between preferences about one's own life, internal preferences, and preferences about the (lives and) preferences of others, external preferences (Dworkin 1985b: 196). We may agree on certain basic values (the objectively neutral ones) but these only give us very general rules. If we know that we should treat one another with equal respect, there may still be innumerable ways in which we can do so. Worse: the neutral values are only rules of conduct for relations with others. They do not tell us how we should treat ourselves. In this last field, liberals accept neither general rules nor authoritative sources of rules. Authorities like the state should be as neutral as possible towards individual conceptions of the (individual's) good life – either because they do not have the right to interfere (cf. Nozick 1974, in whose theory only the individual can have natural rights), or because there are no reasons to assume that authorities are by definition more fit than any individual to determine what is good for that particular individual (cf. Barry 1995: 76, 89).

Individual autonomy, freedom of choice and of life, are – for whatever reasons – of overall importance for liberal theorists of justice. Nevertheless few of them – not even David Gauthier – accept the autonomy of individual preferences for the full 100 per cent. Some preferences are seen as less true than others, as more perverse, less rational, less informed, less authentic or less autonomous. Perfectionists like Joseph Raz disapprove of self-destructive lifestyles. They would not want a state to encourage a life of sex, drugs, and too loud rock 'n' roll, a life leading (in reverse order) to a deaf, dumb, and blind dead end. Some utilitarians would rather base their calculations of total utility on 'true' preferences than on the preferences fallible individuals perceive to be more beneficial. Other more lenient liberals, Rawls for one, at least demand that there is some rationale behind a person's desires, that is, that desires are ordered in rational life-plans.

Individual plans of life or vital parts thereof

There is something about individuals that is sacred, something that makes them morally relevant in ways a rock or a plant is not, if we may believe theorists of social justice. They ascribe it to individuals (rather than to mammals, life, the universe or everything), and they agree that it has something to do with the human capacity to have a private conception of the good. They disagree on the details. For some, that which really matters about persons is an ordered and rational plan of life, for others the underlying conception of the good or the good life, the authenticity or self-determination of convictions, or the ultimate reasons behind plans of life. If we look for a common denominator in all this, the phrase 'individual plans of life or vital parts thereof' will do as well as any other, provided that we do not demand the 'vital parts' to be necessarily ordered in a plan.

No indirect or direct bias

A rule is biased if, without good reasons, it favours something above something else. In theories of social justice this would mean that a principle favours or disfavours ('for or against') certain conceptions of the good life – which is, for lack of reasons or rights, by definition unjust. But principles can be biased in at least two ways: they can openly favour the life-plans of artists over those of philosophers, or they can be unbiased in this direct procedural sense and still produce biased results. If a state valued the life-plans of Nazis as much as those of Jews, negroes, homosexuals, Freemasons, socialists, invalids and women, the result would probably be rather nasty for all life-plans except those of Nazis. There are, in other words, *limits* to the equal relevance given to plans of life.

Within limits

Ronald Dworkin distinguished between internal and external, rather than between private and public, preferences. Obviously, allowing personal freedom to include the freedom of promoting external preferences may lead to a contradiction: if we do not have the same preferences, my freedom will be your oppression.

Dworkin is not alone in signalling this typically liberal dilemma. Robert Nozick acknowledged its existence in stressing the minimal night-watchman state as an absolute side-constraint on the relation between utopian communities (Nozick 1974: 333). His minimal state guarantees both the freedom of individuals to live in accordance with their internal and external preferences *within* communities, and the freedom from interference by *other* communities. Clearly, Nozick's solution is only partly satisfactory; external preferences have the bad habit of extending beyond community borders.

Bruce Ackerman deals with the dilemma when he introduces a Nazi among the participants in his social contract (Ackerman 1980: 97), but he only succeeds in defeating the Nazi by denying the rationality of his opinions and by – tacitly – threatening with the ultimate argument, violence.

John Rawls's first principle limits the execution of person X's life-plans in denying the justice of restricting the liberties of others for the sake of person X. In general, his original position limits the equal weight given to plans of life by supposing that its members are 'mutually disinterested . . . they are conceived as not taking an interest in one another's interests' (Rawls 1971: 13). He thus not only excludes envy as a motivational force from his theory, as was his intention (cf. Rawls 1971: 143), but also a priori excludes external preferences from the realm of justice, which can hardly be called a solution for the dilemma. Moreover, he restricts the 'basic consensus' on which agreement in society should be built, and by means of which the shape of the original position is justified, to one amongst 'reasonable individuals' (Rawls 1993a, 1995).

Finally, Michael Walzer has his own peculiar way of looking at the limits of equal relevance: his just society is one in which 'no social good serves or can serve as a means of domination', it is 'an egalitarianism that is consistent with liberty', based on 'our shared understandings of social goods' (Walzer 1983: xiv). His main premise is that these, our 'own' (read: American?), understandings are the product of harmonious relations between consenting adults – a precondition that, like Rawls', a priori excludes the possibility of (at least) an unwanted bias.

Objectively neutral prior principles

A moment ago, I postulated the existence of a list of objectively neutral (in other words, self-evident) prior principles characteristic of the liberal conception of impartiality. Now according to Henry Sidgwick, self-evident moral axioms have to meet four conditions. First of all, the terms of the proposition must be clear and precise (Sidgwick 1962: 338) – but neither Sidgwick nor Descartes have clearly and precisely specified what the terms 'clear' and 'precise' mean. To clarify this a bit, we could demand of an axiom that it must be possible to define its terms in new terms that are as much as possible not part of the original proposition, but are part of our ordinary vocabulary.

Sidgwick's second criterion is *continued* self-evidence on reflection, so as to avoid, for one, the extreme of 'mere impressions or impulses, which on careful observation do not present themselves as claiming to be dictates of Reason' (Sidgwick 1962: 339) and, for another, that of mere opinion, in the non-problematical truth of which we start to believe simply because we hear an opinion so often. Intuitions thus cannot be presented as unquestionable beliefs (dogmas); they must be tested in such a way that we are maximally tempted to reject them.

Thirdly, self-evident axioms must be mutually consistent, as 'it is obvious that any collision between two intuitions is a proof that there is error in one or the other, or both' (Sidgwick 1962: 341). Note that mutual consistency does not prove the truth of either of two axioms. Note, furthermore, that this condition can be interpreted in two ways. It may presuppose that intuitions *qua* propositions cannot be at the same time true and contradictory, which in our case presumes the existence of some kind of standard of ethical truth – a dubious assumption. I prefer a second interpretation, which avoids (not solves) these problems: intuitions cannot at the same time be applicable and contradictory. This interpretation does not yet require that a moral axiom be applicable (that ought implies can) but it does require that axioms should not be contradictory if they are meant to be applied somewhere and somehow.

Sidgwick's fourth and last condition is universal or general consent: an axiom can only be self-evident if it is intersubjectively self-evident. The experiment of self-evidence must be repeated on other subjects. It stands to reason that an axiom is not *self*-evident if one must force oneself to accept it, instead of being forced by the axiom it*self* to accept it. General consent is thus an extra guarantee for the integrity of an intuition, a necessary but by no means sufficient warrant against subjectivity. The following story can illustrate the importance of testing intuitions, especially for general consent. In *Justice and the Human Good*, William Galston argues for the basic importance of three human goods: life, development and happiness. He also invites us to rank these goods by imagining that:

> You are a healthy, talented young adult forced into a booth with three buttons on a panel. The first will bring you instant death; the second, lifelong imbecility; the third, wretchedness that increases with the duration of your life and the development of your powers. If you fail to push any button within a specified interval, a computer will select and execute one of the alternatives, at random. (Galston 1980: 94)

Galston expected that we would select the third button and that we would be almost indifferent between life and development – 'almost' meaning a slight bias in favour of life. Feeling excluded from humanity – I would have chosen death rather than a life not worth living – I pestered friends, colleagues, family and students with Galston's booth, but found no clear pattern. Some chose death, others a life of possibly happy imbecility, still others would give up happiness – and a small group would let the computer decide. Clearly not every appeal to intuition can be taken for granted.

If we accept Sidgwick's four conditions, we must also accept a paradoxical conclusion: self-evident moral axioms cannot be all that self-evident if they are to be accepted as axioms. They can be self-evident in the sense that we have tried everything to falsify them, or our belief in them or the grounds for our belief – and yet failed to refute them. They cannot be self-evident in the sense that they are somehow revealed to us and need not be questioned.[12] This will lead us to another interesting conclusion at the end of this section, namely that the prior principles in liberal theories of social justice are self-evident in the latter rather than in the earlier sense.

Prior principles

In contributions to the debate on social justice, we find up to seven candidates for the status of self-evident prior principles: liberty, equality and fraternity (the classical liberal ideals), subjective neutrality, rationality, fairness, and finally the abstract notion of justice itself. Unfortunately, they do not pass the Sidgwick test. It is true that they are supported by a general consensus of opinion, but the consensus is limited to a very small community of like-minded philosophers in the Anglo-Saxon tradition. It is true that they are self-evident, but not on reflection; in fact, we often find that authors treat one or more of them as postulates that require no further defence, no reflection. Finally, whether these seven principles meet Sidgwick's demand for mutual consistency cannot be determined because they do not meet his first demand of being clear and precise. What little consensus there really is among philosophers of liberal justice seems to be based on very minimal definitions of the ideals in question, definitions to which each individual author adds his or her bit. I cannot but do the same: I shall formulate the minimal form of these ideals as clearly and precisely as I can, and add, in the rest of this book, my own bit.

First, *liberty* stands for negative liberty, for each person's not being hindered in the pursuit of whatever he or she prefers to do. This is where the agreement on its meaning stops. Many a theorist, but certainly not Nozick or Steiner, would argue that there is more to liberty, that liberty should at times and in some ways be actively promoted, thus transforming it into positive liberty, the capability to realize one's preferences. Others (e.g. Rawls 1971: 4; Dworkin 1985b: 192–3; Ackerman 1980: 43 ff.) will argue that liberty, whether positive or negative, should only apply to certain preferences – plans of life, rational plans of life, or only vital parts of these.

Equality is short for: each person is of equal intrinsical worth. This axiom allows two interpretations, a negative and a positive one. For some authors (Ackerman, Nozick, Walzer) equality means that there is no authoritative source of knowledge for determining a person's worth *qua* person; for others, like Rawls and Dworkin, liberty implies and justifies equality. For all, distributive principles must be established without reference to a person's worth.

By *fraternity* I mean nothing more than mutual concern. There is no consensus even on the subject of concern. In Rawls's theory, for instance, the people in the original position are mutually disinterested in the interests of others and their only mutual concern seems to be to reach an agreement on moral principles that will keep society together and thus protect their private interests. Then again, Rawls's demand that impartiality requires mutually disinterested individuals plus a veil of ignorance that hides all knowledge about their own persons, personality and interests from them also reflects Rawls's belief that our plans of life all matter and matter equally to all of us.

I shall let *subjective neutrality* pass by silently, since I have already discussed this notion above.

Rationality, perhaps the most used, abused and complex concept in philosophy, here means attempting to give good reasons for one's ideas and the behaviour based on them. Since there is little agreement on what exactly constitutes a good reason, an attempt is all we can ask in a minimum definition. Note that some authors refer to 'the reasonable' rather than the rational (e.g. Rawls 1993a), to prevent confusion with the conception of rationality used in the field of social choice, where it means acting to satisfy one's preferences best.

Like rationality, *fairness* is a procedural rather than a substantive ideal. It simply demands that like cases be treated alike. Again, there are more saturated versions of fairness. In John Rawls's theory, for instance, fairness as applied to rules also demands voluntary acceptance of that rule (cf. Rawls 1971: 13, 112).

34

Justice, the idea of giving each person his due (*suum cuique tribuere*) has already been introduced earlier in this chapter. Note that, for reasons which will become obvious later, I shall refer to both 'treating like cases alike' (fairness) and 'giving each his due' as definitions of justice.

On conceptions of justice as impartiality

By convention, theorists often make a distinction between the concept and various conceptions of justice.[13] A concept is abstract and general, and it is made up of the elements common to all (e.g. a society's) conceptions of justice, whereas a conception reflects an individual's views on justice. Rawls, for example, humbly presented his views on justice as a conception, but of course hoped to offer the best possible way to represent the concept of justice; just as I shall try to convince the reader that my conception is in fact a better representation of the concept. Rawls (1971: 130 ff.) characterizes the concept of justice in terms of some very general criteria like generality and universality. Yet the consensus among liberal theorists is broader and deeper: they may share Rawls's criteria but they certainly share certain ethical ideals – and these, rather than the general Rawlsian criteria, form their concept of social justice, that is the hard core of the liberal paradigm of social justice.

Up to now we have tried to map the borders of a concept of social justice that defines a certain community of liberal-minded theorists. Justice as impartiality, we saw, includes or permits a wide range of possible conceptions, those satisfying the conditions of technical, subjective and objective neutrality; but it excludes others, and it is good to keep this in mind. For one, justice excludes aesthetical principles. If it is possible to represent the distribution of goods over a society as symmetrical, there may be reason to say that the distribution is beautiful but none to assume that it is also just. Nor can questions of justice be answered by a simple appeal to convention. Although there is an important element of conventionalism in theories of distributive justice, since they assume that a scheme of justice must be supported by actual people to be viable, conventions are not sacred. They must first be confronted with a conception of justice, and if the two conflict, maybe both need to be adjusted. Rawls's strategy of balancing convictions and ideal theory until a reflective equilibrium has been found is probably the best known example of this convention-critical approach.

But to return to the conceptions that the liberal theory of justice can include: let us recapitulate for a moment. I have looked in some detail at the meaning of a notion central to liberal theories of justice: impartiality. I have argued that these theories of justice cannot be completely impartial, and have identified the sense in which they nevertheless aim to be impartial. I analyzed two substantial elements of this liberal conception of impartiality: objective and subjective neutrality. In short, I have tried to show *why* there must be principles prior to justification procedures and *what* these principles are, roughly. The question we now face is this: *how* are these principles integrated in justification procedures? How exactly is impartiality embodied in the justification of principles of justice? To answer this question, we have to look beyond the form, beyond the justificatory contraptions used by theorists – contract theories, ideal observers, invisible hands – for the substance, the ultimate grounds to which theorists of justice appeal when they introduce their principles of justice, the conception of impartiality upon which they would be based, and the argumentation in favour of impartiality itself.

To judge and justify principles we seem to have, in essence, only two alternatives: the low road of moral relativism in all its subtly differing forms (e.g. nihilism, scepticism, pluralism, subjectivism, conventionalism), and the high road of moral absolutism, again in many forms (naturalism, realism, revelation, historicism, etc.). The archetypical examples of these views can be found in Plato's *Republic*, where Thrasymachus and Socrates argue about the nature of justice and morality in general (Plato 1974: 338c ff.). The view that moral theory is ultimately an either/or matter, either absolutism or relativism, is shared by many.[14] Of course, in the real world of moral theorizing the extremes are, to say the least, rare. The interesting thing about liberal theories of social justice, despite their variety of positions, is that they try to build on a third way next to, rather than a mixture of, the high and the low road to morality. In this third view, the source of valid moral arguments is the human capacity to be impartial.

This role of impartiality can be described both negatively and positively. Negatively, it differs fundamentally from absolutism in denying the moral relevance of the natural order of the universe, divine commandments and so forth, whether such an objective order exists or not (cf. Rawls 1995: 134). Michael Walzer illustrated this point in a Tanner Lecture with a story from the Talmud: Rabbi Eliezer stood alone in his interpretation of the law, and after failing to convince his colleagues on his own, he asked for divine help. But a tree lifted high in the air could not convince his opponents, nor could a river flowing backwards, nor the tumbling down of the walls of the school, nor, in the end, a thundering voice from heaven. Eliezer's greatest opponent, Rabbi Joshua, only commented that the law was not in heaven (Walzer 1988: 29–30).

Impartiality must also be distinguished from relativism. Parallel to the fact that a judgement from the point of view of impartiality will only accidentally agree with one from nature,[15] it will also only accidentally agree with the judgement of ordinary persons in actual, non-reflective circumstances. Impartiality is independent of whatever makes a moral view 'relative': our present culture at this or any point in time and space and the social, political, economic or personal circumstances in which we actually live, work and act.

A positive statement of what impartiality is about is more difficult, as it is essentially a negative concept: *non*-partiality. It can only be done if, first of all, absolutism is so defined as to exclude general characteristics of man or human nature (e.g. equality, freedom, a sense of morality or most of all rationality) from the realm of natural law, the kingdom of ends – and if, secondly, relativism is so defined as to exclude that same area of what is common to humans. Positively stated then, the point of impartiality is to transcend the imperfection of contingent societies, persons and personal views, and thereby take a detached view on man *sub specie aeternitatis* – Spinoza's phrase, taken over by Rawls (Rawls 1971: 587). Impartiality contains elements of both relativism and absolutism. On the one hand it is still the human mind and not some kind of absolute universal Reason that dictates the moral law, but on the other hand this is man at his most absolute. On one hand, the outer world of facts is irrelevant, in the sense that no *is* outside the human mind can ever justify an *ought* within, yet on the other hand it is nothing like universal voluntarism: the physical laws cannot be and are not transcended – *should* is limited by *could*.

To detach oneself from contingency, from all that is accidental about our life and way of life, is one thing, but to decide what is accidental and what is not is another. Although theorists of liberal social justice agree in principle that the construction of principles of justice requires an impartial justification procedure, they disagree profoundly about the border between the realms of the impartial and the partial. The veil of ignorance in John Rawls's original position is one such attempt at creating an impartial justification procedure,[16] and also the best illustration of a contested solution to that problem. Nearly every part of it has been subjected to severe criticism: the fact that people in the original position are partially omniscient and partially suffer from amnesia, the idea that real-life individuals can be represented by 'unencumbered selves' detached from any social environment, the precise lists of things they know and do not know, the rules according to which they select principles of justice, and so forth.[17]

The appeal to the human capacity for impartiality, and on occasion the use of counterfactual situations as vehicles of transcendence, inspired William Galston (Galston 1980: 15) to apply one of the most radical term in politics, utopianism, to theories of social justice and to Rawls in particular. In one sense, the epitaph is misplaced. If we follow the convention on the meaning of the term utopianism,[18] theorists of social justice can hardly be called utopians. They are reformers rather than revolutionaries, they do not sketch blueprints for complete societies, and they believe in impartiality rather than in any substantive idea of the good life. The most radical deed one can accuse them of is that some of them operate as spokesmen and women for certain pressure groups (cf. Matson 1983).

In another sense, though, it is not only correct to describe liberal theorists of social justice as utopians, but also inevitable. Theories of liberal social justice must and should be utopian – in a methodological sense. Their attempts to transcend the interests and prejudices of ordinary human beings in the real world lead them to the use of counterfactual worlds as instruments of justification. First, the appeal to impartiality is presented as an appeal to extract an idea of the essence of man and society from the 'real' world by eliminating contingency. From there on, it is a small step towards translating this abstract idea into a more appealing illusion: the original position, the state of nature, godlike ideal observers, a desert island or a funny new planet where all resources fall from the sky. The last step is one that makes a crucial difference between justice theories and conventional utopianism: rather than living happily ever after, the inhabitants of the imaginary world of essentials start negotiating principles to rule the world of contingency to which they intend to return. Methodological utopianism has its disadvantages. First, a theory of justice of this sort must constantly keep the middle between, on the one hand, credibility in the real world, hence a basis in shared understandings, in an accidental social convention, and on the other hand, credibility as presenting an 'objective', 'no particular', point of view that will only appeal to the beliefs of the brainwashed contracting parties in the theorist's version of the state of nature. Secondly, abstracting from real-world conditions may well result in a theory of justice for a simpler and more perfect world than ours – a fact that cannot add to the credibility of the theory.

Despite these disadvantages, theorists of social justice are prepared to pay the price of transcendence for at least two reasons: one tactical, the other meta-ethical. Tactically speaking, procedures to justify political theories depend for their success on their veracity as well as on their appeal. To appeal to most if not all points of view – as the participants in the justice debate intend to – a balance has to be reached between what is true (according to the philosopher) and what can be legitimized in the minds of humans, between ideal decision rules for making up one's mind, and the imperfect rules followed by imperfect people in everyday life. There is no other solution for this problem but walking the tight rope.

From a meta-ethical point of view, principles of justice must be as absolute as possible to avoid the existence of two or more incompatible moral standards, which would in practice make blame, guilt, praise and pride meaningless and the worst sort of relativism – anything goes – true. Yet since we are not omniscient, absolutism cannot mean more here than the most definite possible agreement on moral standards. A theory of justice must be as absolute as possible – but it cannot be else than human-made, it cannot be anything but a general will. How the impartial point of view, which we need in order to determine this general will, can be constructed is another matter – the subject of the following chapters.

3

Between community and nature

Social justice: temporal, substantial and impartial

The liberal theory of social justice focuses on distributive justice within societies, and it is deeply committed to social ideals like liberty, equality, and impartiality, as we saw in the previous chapter. These basic ideas, however, do not in themselves constitute a meaningful theory of social justice. For that purpose we also need intermediate premises: premises defining a justification procedure that is consistent with the prior principles mentioned in the previous chapter and premises delineating distribution rules consistent with the justification procedure. In the next three chapters, I shall be concerned with the first kind of premises.

Chapter 4 discusses one of the most disturbing problems for theorists of impartiality: how to prefer one distributive scheme over others without preferring one morality over others. This is known, with a mind-boggling metaphor, as the search for an Archimedean point, the point from which any reasonable moral theory or plan of life can be 'lifted' and included in the theory of a just and impartial society. My version of the Archimedean point will simply be called archpoint, or, more precisely, archpoint of view.

At the basis of this search for an Archimedean point lies another question, often referred to as the (Rawlsian) problem of the thin theory of the good. It is said that, in choosing principles of justice that do not unjustifiably promote some reasonable plans of life more than others, people in the original position must have something like a minimal ('thin') notion of the human good, that is, a theory of what matters about a person and for a person regardless of so-called contingent circumstances like class, culture, sex, race, history, or innate capacities. The solution I propose in Chapter 4 is based on a notion similar to the classical idea of virtue: full reasons. Full reasons are fundamental reasons for behaviour, reasons that cannot be denied without also denying that being a person matters from a moral point of view. Denying (or 'neutralizing', or 'impartializing') them reduces personality to a status of moral irrelevancy.

A related issue deeply dividing liberal justice theorists is that of the shape of the Archimedean point. Impartiality must be warranted, either (1) by specifying the special circumstances under which an individual must take an impartial point of view, or (2) by defining a procedure through which individuals can collectively generate the same results as would have been reached from an impartial point of view, or finally (3) by doing both, that is by ensuring both individual rational behaviour and collectively rational results – as Rawls proposed. Among all the different shapes currently in vogue – auction schemes, bargaining, cognitive psychotherapy, ideal observers, invisible hands, shared understandings, and so forth – a Rawlsian type of contract theory seems to offer the best way of securing impartiality.

The crucial question for any contract theory, the knowledge available to the contracting parties, will be addressed in Chapter 5. I shall hold on to the categories of knowledge as Rawls distinguished them, but change their content. Speaking in broad terms, I shall defend the view that 'archpointers', my equivalent of people in the original position, can be allowed to know a good deal more about themselves than a Rawlsian theory would allow, simply because knowledge about one's self need not prejudice a person. Generally speaking, I follow Barry (Barry 1995: 67 ff.) on this point in the choice for a Scanlonian contract made by self-conscious individuals rather than Rawls's contract made by amnesiacs. My position on so-called objective knowledge, that is knowledge about the real world for which the archpointers are to design principles of justice, is less easy to express in a few strokes. It involves redefinitions of self-interest, of equality of power, of scarcity, of the idea of full scientific knowledge and of the related 'facts about the world' known to the archpointers.

Before we can turn to all this, however, Chapter 3 addresses the role or roles which the concept of society should *not* play 'below the surface' of an impartial theory of social justice. It is obvious that judgements of justice can be made about an infinite range of states: one unique event, a whole society, a type or set of societies, society as such, and so forth. A theory of justice may well be expressly designed to allow only propositions about a limited range of states. In other words: what we may hold to be just on such a theory for an impoverished society need not be just under other, more fortunate circumstances.

This is still more a question of applying than one of designing the justification procedure that underlies a theory of justice. A theorist of justice can choose any range he or she likes; the real difference lies below the surface, in the view of the society with which he or she works. Unsurprisingly, the point of view of a British Conservative MP will differ from that of a Finnish communist worker. And so will their judgements – in everyday life. The question then arises, on which conception of society should a liberal theory of justice be founded?

The communitarian theorist of justice, Charles Taylor (Taylor 1986: 35, 39 ff.), has suggested a distinction between three views on justice and society. In the first place, one could distinguish between minimal or natural justice, the code of behaviour for extra-social life (e.g. strangers meeting in the desert), and distributive justice, which applies to life in social settings. Secondly, distributive justice can itself be looked upon from two different angles. The first perspective is absolute justice, a conception presupposing no (specific) type of society whatsoever. Communitarian justice, on the other hand, recognizes (1) that the ideal underlying justice is social equality, and (2) that equality can only be understood – and defended – in the terms of a specific society. Based on these distinctions, and with a few essential changes in the names to protect consistency in the use of terms, I shall describe four views on justice in society: eternal justice, natural justice, minimal justice and communitarian justice. I shall eliminate three of these. Liberal social justice, I argue, must be conceived of as minimal justice.

In most contexts, in most language games, it makes sense to say that life is a woman of ill repute, or to cry out that you cannot appreciate playing Job. Statements like these suggest a strong belief in a point of view outside time and life: eternal justice. If ethical absolutism were true, justice and eternal justice would be perfectly synonymous. If it is not, eternal justice still incorporates a point of view beyond that of humans: it is justice as seen through the eyes of the gods or God, or justice as the natural order of the universe. Either way it can do without our consent. It could even directly conflict with our personal sense of justice, and we may nevertheless accept it as the final word on justice. Larry Temkin's example of a conversation between God and the Devil on God's treatment of Job1 and Job2 illustrates this well. Both Jobs are equally deserving, but Job1 has had a perfectly successful life for his first 40 years, and Job2 has suffered every curse imaginable in the same period. To reward them equally – as they deserve – God decides to turn their fates around: during their last 40 years, Job1's life will be miserable and Job2 will be blessed. To which the Devil comments: 'Bravo! You really *are* the Master. I couldn't have given a better answer myself' (Temkin 1993: 235–6).

For our purposes, eternal justice must be considered an irrelevant hypothetical category. Discussing distributive questions in terms of eternal justice means looking at the supply-side of the issue. Like the supply-side solution to distribution problems, that is enlarging the cake to satisfy all rather than dividing it fairly (cf. Goodin 1984: 1), a supply-side critique is not a solution to the *distribution* question. It comes down to ducking the question – to foul play. Secondly, appealing to eternal justice is also begging the question. Whereas eternal justice does not need our consent to be put in practice – it simply *exists* or does not – principles of social justice *must* be supported, typically by rational argument. 'The law is not in heaven.'

Natural, minimal and communitarian justice offer three perspectives on the mobilization of rational support. What differentiates the three is the kind of constraints they pose on a justification procedure. As already explained, ontological, ethical and epistemological premises are always built into justification procedures, premises which are again reflected in the outcome of the process.

The most fundamental kind of rational agreement is that on the idea of justice itself, on the form without the content, on categorical imperatives. These will be valid regardless of the presence or absence of community or of social bonds: they encompass both the state of nature and anything 'after' that. I shall call this the category of *natural justice*. The category entails three constraints: (1) a demand that we reach an agreement (either a negative 'no answer possible' or a positive 'we hold these truths to be self-evident'), (2) a demand that this be an agreement on what the idea of justice requires, and (3) a demand that we are rational in a minimal sense, that is, that we conform to the rules of logic.

The next kind of agreement concerns *minimal justice*, the realm of the liberal approach to social justice. Once we start to think about the content of justice rather than its nature, about what is and what is not 'due', a new constraint has to be introduced: impartiality with regard to the good or the good life. For reasons discussed earlier, we cannot suppose that either absolutism or relativism are true, nor, therefore, that any theory of the good is true or that it is as good as any other. A meaningful theory of social justice must then correspond with the demands of impartiality, even if there happens to be accidental agreement on one view of the good in the real world. Impartiality is a complex notion; to embody it in a justification procedure, other and more precise constraints than those of natural justice are required. Together, these constraints will form an Archimedean point.

The fourth and last category is that of *communitarian justice*. We can drop the impartiality condition at this stage because it has become superfluous. Community is defined as sincere consensus on what constitutes the good (life).[19] In theory, conceptions of communitarian justice may or may not be consistent with the principles of natural and minimal justice. Yet if we want a conception of social justice to be supported by rational agreement, the last two, 'higher', forms of justice put severe limits on communitarian justice. If some act is to be labelled as just in one particular community, it cannot at the same time be unjust in all societies, that is in society as such, when seen from the point of view of minimal justice. For equally obvious reasons, that same act cannot be unjust in one community and just in itself, that is from the point of view of natural justice. Still, the limits posed by more abstract conceptions of justice allow the existence of mutually incompatible communitarian principles of justice. Thus, an action, a rule or a system may be just in one community and unjust in another – just as long as it is not unjust when measured by a higher standard.

Communitarian justice is also limited by itself. It is predicated on the existence of a common view of the good. Consequently, it is only valid as long as there is a community: as long as, in so far as, and where two or more individuals agree on the good life and on its translation into principles of justice for those agreeing. In the absence of community, in a society where there is little or no consensus on the good life, the best we can do is remain impartial between individual conceptions of the good – and thus limit social justice to principles of minimal justice.

Marilyn: Hold it! You can't do that!

Albert: What? Spit on the pavement?

M: No. That's illegal in this country.

A: Nonsense. It's natural, it's biodegradable, it's manly, it's OK.

M: It's also considered distasteful, disgraceful and offensive.

A: Not on my home planet! Why are people so unreasonable here? I don't harm anyone, so why can't I? It's simply unjust.

M: They're not unreasonable and it's not unjust. It's their interpretation of decency. And it could only be unjust if you were treated unequally for no good reason, that is if your behaviour were totally irrelevant from any possible point of view.

A: We'll see about that.

M: We will.

Communitarian and natural justice

Evidently, the four kinds of justice just described are subordinated: eternal justice, or so one hopes, embraces natural justice; natural justice overarches and limits minimal justice; and minimal justice stands in the same relation to communitarian justice. The separation between especially minimal and communitarian justice is not as rigid in practice as it is in theory. One need only recall a point made earlier, to wit, that liberal theories of justice are never completely impartial. This might be taken to imply that these theories are in fact communitarian rather than minimal, that the validity of the theories is limited to those individuals who share the same, however thin, conception of the good – the community of like-minded liberals. And this would, in turn, mean that justice cannot actually be conceived of as anything but the expression of a community's deepest and most sincere convictions. Because such convictions will by definition reflect a particular culture, a subjective social consciousness, we would end up with Thrasymachos's conception of justice: the will of the ruling class. Which is a far cry from anything we intuitively expect a theory of justice to be.

The job of constructing an impartial point of view, the archpoint, will be a tough job. Before I turn to that task, however, I must first answer some of the questions that were implicitly posed but not addressed by the introduction of this justice quartet. In the next section I shall ask what the principles of natural justice are and what their implications for justice under conditions of impartiality are. In the last section, the concept of communitarian justice and its relation to minimal justice will be investigated. I shall in particular try to demonstrate that, and why, we would not want a liberal theory of justice to be a communitarian theory. Hence, both sections only describe what lies beyond the borders of minimal justice, not what lies within. The latter job is one for the following chapters.

Natural justice

Principles of natural justice are derived from the formal idea of justice only, with no mention of the possible subjects or areas to which the principles will be applied. There are no more than three constraints to be reckoned with: a demand that we reach an agreement, a demand that it be an agreement on what the bare notion of justice implies, and a demand that we be rational. The last constraint is very weak: it amounts to nothing more than the acceptance of logical arguments and the rejection of fallacies. The 'we' in these demands need not be determined too exactly. Let us say that 'we' can be everyone who is capable of meeting these demands, that is every rational being capable of imagining and communicating the idea of justice.

Principles of natural justice are, by definition, categorical imperatives. The main difference with Kant's categorical imperatives[20] is that our imperatives refer to justice and not to duty, but the two types are identical in expressing what Kant called *das moralische Gesetz in mir*, the moral law in me. Like Kant's imperatives, the imperatives that express the nature of justice are universal and general: their validity does not depend on time, place and culture, nor on the nature of the case to which they are applied. Ideally, a categorical imperative is true regardless of whether or not anyone believes in it or accepts it or adheres to it. They are – or should be – nothing but a more extensive description of the idea for which justice (or duty) is the short expression.

It might look as if the allusion to 'the moral law in me' puts a further constraint on the concept of natural justice, namely that we should also want to be just, or at least 'naturally' just. Perhaps this is true for the inventor of the categorical imperative. For Kant, the categorical imperative was no more a joke than anything else in life. In his eyes, being convinced of the truth of the imperative necessarily implied the urge – not even desire – to act accordingly. Yet there is no necessary link between believing in a principle and wanting to act (let alone acting) upon it. It takes an additional theory of the self and the will to mediate between conviction and action. I may sincerely believe that killing is wrong, always and everywhere, and that I should do anything to prevent at least myself from killing. Yet it does not seem to be inconsistent that my will may be tempted if I were left alone for some time with my worst enemy or my suffering and irreversibly ill best friend. I might also allow your death if that meant saving my own life. And I used to risk my own life nearly every day by bicycling between my home and the university (I stopped after a few accidents). To avoid all the intricacies of weakness of will (*akrasia*), of pure moral dilemmas and of duress, I shall simply assume that our interest in natural justice is academic: we only want to *know* what justice requires. Whether we will act upon that idea is another question.

But what then is justice? There are two definitions of justice – both established by convention – that have often been taken to be general and universal enough to constitute categorical imperatives. One of them, Justinian's, defines justice as giving each his due, the other, Aristotle's, as treating equal cases equally and unequal cases unequally. Neither of these is very informative. Principles of natural justice, we shall see, are products of rationality and semantical convention; without some reference to the world in which they are to be applied, they are empty, meaningless.

The first definition, it seems, presupposes a more substantial concept of justice – minimal justice, at the least. It is true that the term 'due', which gives rise to that suspicion, does not directly imply that desert is the only basis of justice. It is rather a way of expressing that whatever the basis be, if X satisfies its criteria, X should get his due. If need were the basis of justice instead of desert, X should get what he or she needs; if contribution were, X should get her proportion of the profit; if equality were, we would all get an equal share. But, as Brian Barry argued, following Hume (Barry 1989: 149), the problem lies in what a term like 'due' itself apparently takes for granted: the existence of an indubitable or universally acknowledged norm. Thus, if we were to transform the Justinian maxim into an Aristotelian formula it would tell us that cases should be treated according to an objective ethical standard – but at this moment we lack such a standard. It may not even exist, for all we know. The bare notion of justice does not contain that kind of information.

One could say that this is no more than a terminological point, which can be solved by simply defining justice as treating cases according to a moral standard if we can somehow agree on one. But if we cannot presuppose anything, there should also be a standard defining cases, a standard which cannot be presupposed in the natural justice imperative. The Justinian imperative is then reduced to something like the demand that the appropriate thing be the case (cf. Cupit 1996). It cannot be easy to be less informative.

The Aristotelian interpretation of justice, on the other hand, does give us some relevant and admissible information. We cannot agree, with the information we have, on standards defining cases and rules of treatment. But we do have enough information to decide that, if there are cases to which principles of justice ought to be applied, and if these cases are equal, then they should be treated equally. This is simply a demand of rationality. There can be no reasons – no rationally acceptable arguments – for treating two equal cases unequally. If there were, there would be a significant difference between the cases; they would no longer be equal – which is a contradiction. It follows that unequal cases should be treated in proportion to their inequality. There can be no reasons for unequal treatment but those given by the differences between cases; if there were other reasons, there would also be other significant differences, which again leads us into a contradiction. Other imaginable imperatives will be logical implications of these two, for instance the implication that if one case was treated (un)justly and an 'equal' case was treated similarly, then this last case must also have been treated (un)justly.

These two basic imperatives, for equal and unequal cases respectively, may be admissible, but they are still quite uninformative. They do not indicate what will make two cases equal or different, for which reason we cannot in any way apply them to the real world. Consider a group of ten persons that is open to everyone with a trait or capacity X. The group consists of three women and seven men, one person white, the others all black, six rich, four poor, eight with a beard and two without. There are lots of differences in this example, differences both inside the group and between the group and the outside world. But are these differences relevant? Is there injustice in this distribution, and if so, for what reason?

Stretching the idea of a categorical imperative a bit, we could argue for the existence of a third imperative: that good reasons be given for claims about (un)just treatment. Lacking a conception of what constitutes 'a case', let alone a similar/different or (un)equal case, a reference to the notion of equal or unequal treatment is just not enough. The categorical imperatives of natural justice are simply too uninformative to judge the justice of anything. An adequate theory of justice will need more than formal principles, and to develop such principles we need more than a bare convention on the meaning of the term justice. We cannot do without the more substantial (i.e. minimal and communitarian) conceptions of justice.

Communitarian justice

Social justice depends *ex hypothesi* on an impartial agreement on principles. An impartial conception of social justice allows the existence of a communitarian view on justice within the limits posed by impartiality, but it does not allow that the principles of social justice are based upon one and only one substantial theory of the good. This implies a rejection of the communitarians's claims about having unique or privileged access to the grounds of moral justification. In this section I shall consider the reasons for this veto.

Note that I take community to be a state of mind rather than a state of affairs. Community is a, let us say honest or sincere, consensus on the good life; it exists in so far as, and only in so far as, two or more persons agree on a conception of the good. Perfect community equals full identity of conceptions, imperfect community exists where there is only a partial consensus. The latter type of community can look surprisingly liberal and democratic, and will by any normal standard actually be liberal and democratic. It is the kind of society where agreement on conceptions of the good is limited to formal procedures and a few substantive ideas. Equivalents of such imperfect communities in political theory are Rawls's just society based on a basic consensus (Rawls 1993a) and the society Barry sketched as built on an impartial agreement among its members (Barry 1995: 7, 11, 67, 76). The fundamental difference between these theories and imperfect communities on the one hand, and minimal justice on the other, is that the former are supported by some common denominator and the latter by a truly impartial foundation. More precisely, Rawlsian and Barryan just societies are called just because they operate on rules that are acceptable to the reasonable persons who happen to live in them at a certain moment, whereas a minimally just society is just *regardless* of the set of reasonable theories of the good that happen to be around at the time, regardless of the plans of life pursued and regardless of the composition of the set of individuals pursuing them.

For reasons of simplicity I shall suppose that we only have to deal with perfect communities. Communitarian theorists are sometimes inclined to think the liberally and democratically unthinkable, that is, that belief in the truth of a substantial theory of the good alone is enough to justify its imposition on others, thereby imprisoning dissenters in the social structure of a 'community' – a community understood as a state of affairs, of course. By assuming the existence of perfect communities, we can avoid the issue of the legitimacy of a communitarian *coup d'état*: if it turns out that community is in itself an insufficient and therefore undesirable basis for a just society, there is no reason to even consider imposing a communitarian way of life on dissenters, strangers or outsiders.

As I said, I presume the existence of an impartial agreement on justice, that is, of an acceptable conception of minimal justice. It is important to see the main difference between communitarian and minimal theories of justice. A communitarian theory is justified by (and viable because of) its consistency with the opinion of the enfranchised members of a social group. In essence, communitarian social critique asks whether a society lives up to its own ideals; it compares the theory and practice of a society. Mainstream liberals, proponents of minimal justice, go one step beyond this by questioning not just the institutions of a society – as a communitarian does – but also the ideals behind them. For liberals, the essence of social criticism is to discover what can be said about standards, institutions and societies from a point of view beyond that of any particular society or person – *pace* Walzer (Walzer 1988). Mainstream theorists also claim that their theories are practical and viable – but only under certain conditions: the members of society are to be susceptible to reasonable and reasoned arguments, and they should agree with the theorist's idea of what an impartial point of view is and demands, because and only because of their reasonableness.

A common point of reference for most communitarians is their critique of mainstream justice theories, in particular Rawls's. With regard to their conception of the Archimedean point, Rawls and like-minded liberal theorists have been criticized from two sides. One strand of critique held that Rawls was in fact 'going' conservative if not communitarian, despite Rawls's own denial in his Kantian period, the early 1970s. His original position would include a theory of the good that was not thin enough to be impartial. Parallel theses, it has been argued, were true for other liberal theories like Ackerman's, Dworkin's and Nozick's. I shall discuss this critique elsewhere. The second school insisted that Rawls was, in fact, no communitarian at all. Rawls would have proposed a theory of justice that had no relevance to real and ordinary human beings, to political beings in the Aristotelian sense. Rawls made no attempt to legitimize his theory in the context of a genuine society (read: community). Nor could he: no political animal in its right mind would agree to a constitution that might very well restrict opportunities to live the good life as he or she saw it. Instead, Rawls fell back on the notion of a counterfactual discourse about considered opinions and on an equally hypothetical contract situation from which all kinds of relevant information, including theories of the good, had been excluded.

Between the lines, in his book, *Political Liberalism*, Rawls (1993a) implicitly bows to the critics of both schools: he now situates his theory somewhere in a twilight zone between pure communitarianism and unmitigated liberalism. His thin theory of the good, he admits, is too thick to be called impartial. It presupposes the existence of so-called reasonable persons, people accepting the burdens of reason, the causes of the impossibility to definitely solve moral disputes. John Gray, reviewing the book, feels that the appeal of Rawls's whole theory is even more limited than that – it would only correspond with the intuitions of American East Coast liberals (Gray 1993: 35). On the other hand, the thin theory is still too thin to allow the original position to serve as a justification procedure in, or for, a particular community (e.g. Rawls 1993a: 190–95). On at least one fundamental point, the communitarians are right: a theory of justice can only be viable if it takes account of people's conceptions of the good life. In a pluralist society like ours, it may be obvious that we shall never agree on the good (which gives us a strategic reason to look for an impartial account of justice), but there are other, more harmonious societies, and there are niches even in our pluralistic societies where communities exist (Kymlicka 1995). In communities like those it will be politically pointless to try to implement, for instance, Rawls's first principle if (but only as long as!) there exists a deep consensus on the unequal value of liberty for separate members of the community. In those circumstances, the members of the community will quite certainly resist any such attempt, first of all by claiming that Rawls's first principle may be theoretically correct (provided that this community accepts the conditions of the original position), but that it will not work in practice. A theory of justice thus has to be either viable, that is open to substantial views of the good and communitarian conceptions of justice, or, in so far as it contradicts these conceptions, merely evaluative. In these terms, mainstream theories are often academic rather than practical, evaluative rather than viable. At first sight, they fail to get their message through (cf. Kukathas and Pettit 1990: 112 on Rawls).

However, this pragmatical critique of liberalism's anti-communitarian inclinations is founded on a misconception of what exactly liberal theorists of social justice are looking for – a misconception to which many a mainstreamer has unfortunately contributed. What interests mainstream theorists is *not* primarily the viability 'here and now' of a conception of justice, but the viability of justice as a measure to judge the here and now *by*. The intention of non-communitarian, 'abstract', theory is to steer clear of justifying or rationalizing the particular conception of justice of a particular society at a particular point in time, whether that be the dominant ideology of an imperfect community, or the theory of the good defining a perfect community. The reasons for this are simple: the harmony on which a communitarian account of justice rests does not exist, and even if it did, the existence of perfect community could not guarantee that the principles adhered to are genuine principles of justice (cf. Barry 1989: 265–71, esp. 268).

Communitarian justice is legitimized, if at all, by a community's honest and unanimous consensus on what constitutes the good life. This consensus need not be explicitly voiced; it can also be 'lived' in practices and institutions, in, one could imagine, a unity of social consciousness and political reality. In so far as such a consensus is absent, as is the case in modern pluralistic societies, communitarian justice loses its legitimacy by definition. This is in itself a reason to turn to the more basic conception of minimal justice. But there are more, better and less opportunistic reasons for challenging the privileges of communitarian justice. Liberal theorists of social justice deeply doubt both the actual and the theoretical possibility of a stable moral consensus. The four reasons I am about to give for this conviction hardly exhaust the list of complaints against communitarianism, nor are they conclusive, but they should suffice to shed some doubt on it.

In the first place, consensus may be a deception. Though this critique of the basis of the idea of communitarian justice can be expressed in more liberal terms, it is perhaps clearer when given a Marxist wording – which is ironic, as some communitarians are Marxists. In this view, there can be no genuinely shared and accepted conception of the good as long as there is class struggle, or, in updated versions of the faith, as long as there are fundamental conflicts of interest. As long as the goods to satisfy fundamental needs are scarce, there will be fundamental conflict. In short, as long as there is scarcity, there can be no community. In the current circumstances of scarcity (which we assume to exist), any attempt to formulate a common substantial view of the good or to clarify our considered judgements on this must necessarily reflect existing power relations. A communitarian theory of justice must then be a biased theory – biased in favour of one party or another. It follows that it cannot be valid by its own standards: whereas it claims validity for a whole society, not all of society's members can honestly and sincerely assent to it.

Yet – still thinking along Marxist lines – we could imagine the existence of a kind of academic agreement on a common good, on an end or principle to which we should adhere but cannot or will not in a society of conflict. We can all agree that honesty is a virtue and redistribution a good and still interpret reality idiosyncratically on our income tax forms. Let us call this general agreement the Enlightened View. The situation resembles a society-wide prisoners's dilemma (i.e. the good guys lose) with at least this relevant difference that there seems to be no way whatsoever to ascertain the pay-off structure. In clearer terms, it is impossible to determine that the Enlightened View of the common good *really* expresses our deepest and most sincere convictions. By implication, it is also impossible to determine that it does so as well as or better than the views currently ruling our actions, views that are based on private or class interests (call these the Current Views). The reason for all this is that we may think that we fundamentally agree on what constitutes the good life, but we cannot be sure that we really do. If our Current View gave us reason to believe in the Enlightened View, then why do we still act upon our Current View – or vice versa?[21] We need a prior principle to account for the priority given to the common good over particular interests. To defend such a principle or refute any opposite principle we cannot, at least not without circularity, appeal to the Enlightened View or to Current Views. So we need a pre-prior principle which, to be defended, requires its own prior principle. *Et cetera ad infinitum.*

Finally, suppose that we do live in a world of abundance. Still following the Marxist view, we are now in ideal circumstances to agree on a common view of the good life. Unfortunately, we now no longer need that view to support a theory of justice, as we no longer need a theory of (at least distributive) justice. By definition, abundance implies the redundancy of distribution schemes.

As a second line of critique, next to Marxism, there is a sociological or anthropological argument against communitarian justice. Historically, any culture, social consciousness, or system of fetishes and taboos is situated: it is partly a product of consciously guided action and partly of tradition, yet it will always be a product of specific historical circumstances. The system could be different and it could be changed, but unless we can transcend it (which goes against the very soul of communitarianism), all *reasons* (not) to change will be either (1) accidental, that is imposed from the outside, or (2) internal to the system, rationalized but not justified by a society's culture, its language game or its shared understandings. 'It should be like this because that is the way it was meant to be' is no more of an argument in a debate on artefacts than 'it is so because that is the way it is'. Yet these are exactly the kinds of arguments communitarian justice would have to be built upon, arguments referring to a basic consensus which is itself little more than an historical accident. Unless we can transcend actual cultures, of course, but then we would no longer be communitarians.

Beyond the Marxist and sociological critiques, we encounter a meta-ethical argument. Communitarianism carries the risk of undermining itself by allowing two types of relativism: moral solipsism and moral nihilism. If there are no sound reasons to support a particular community's theory of the good except those internal to its culture or language game, any individual's theory of the good is just as good, provided it can be fitted into a language game. Ethically speaking then, anything goes. If, on the other hand, it is not *what* a community believes that justifies their consensus, but the fact *that* a community believes in some theory and can live by it, then any theory of the good will do, as long as the almost unlimited potential of people to convince themselves of the improbable is not overstretched. Thus, again, anything goes.

Finally, communitarianism does not only not have an answer to, but even implicitly condones, intuitively immoral notions of the good life. (I shall, for the sake of argument, assume that we share the same intuitive sense of immorality.) A community is free to define 'strangers' on its own terms and draw any line it likes between strangers and the in-crowd. A community is, by definition, deaf to arguments derived from other views on society. To use a Walzerian frame, such

> **Albert:** These people are insane! They throw their grannies off the rocks just because they're 70.
>
> **Marilyn:** They are. I agree. Have you noticed they never talk about this habit, never make jokes about it, only when they're really tired and emotional?
>
> **A:** Yes. Funny. Must be fear. I suppose they realize the same fate awaits them in due course.
>
> **M:** Odd. I can understand it, they don't have the means to take care of both the young and the aged, but it's still disgusting. And even they find it repulsive, apparently, yet it seems they can't do anything about it.
>
> **A:** They can, of course. All they need do is have fewer children. Or produce more food. Or eat less, but on an equal basis.
>
> **M:** It's almost like a prisoner's game – if no-one from outside intervenes, nothing will change, they'll keep on throwing each other off the rocks. And if some do-gooder on the inside tries to do some good everyone else will take advantage of him.
>
> **A:** Reminds me of school.

Gut feelings

arguments could be seen as attempts at colonization. Thus, if a community decides that anyone who speaks a foreign language, wears glasses or lives in a town should be treated as a stranger and sent off to be starved or tortured to death, no outsider can offer the in-crowd a convincing counter-argument. Nor can any insider – critique of that kind immediately labels one as a stranger. Picturesque as the idea of community may sound, we cannot at the same time think that communitarianism is a complete moral theory and hold that the Pol Pots of this world should not be allowed to roam about, whether inside or outside our own community. (Note that this is not only a condemnation of communitarianism based on a 'gut feeling'. It is also the mirror image of our third point: how to choose between two normative views if both are equally (in)defensible?)

Neither these four arguments nor any others can prove that the notion of communitarian justice is superfluous or that principles of justice based on a consensus on the good are by definition immoral, worthless and offensive. In so far as communities actually exist, communitarian theories of justice exist, and their existence is relevant to any theorist of justice, whether communitarian or liberal. In this respect, mainstream theorists of justice might try to reverse the communitarian critique on their hypothetical status: it is communitarianism that is evaluative and academic, and liberal social justice that is practical and viable. A communitarian analysis of justice amounts to a description of – with a Husserlian term – the historicity of a community's or society's conception of justice, an attempt to reconstruct the way in which a social consensus logically *must* have evolved rather than one of how it accidentally *did* evolve. In this light, a communitarian analysis of justice may contain valuable sociological information.

This is not to say that we (assuming we are liberal-minded) should dismiss ideas about liberal social justice 'here and now' simply because they are not in line with the deepest convictions of an existing community, nor that we should give up the first in favour of the latter, nor (least of all) that, on finding no communities at all, we should join a monastic order, the last refuge of the communitarian. We should accept a part of the communitarian critique of liberal justification procedures: these procedures need a sound basis in everyday life. But it does not follow that we should also accept the more fundamental critique of liberalism itself, as expressed by communitarians like Alasdair MacIntyre (1985) and Michael Jackson (1988), who claim that a moral view without a foundational substantive theory of the good is built on quicksand. (We shall, indirectly, address this view in the following chapter.)

Apart from its practical uses, there is another reason not to throw communitarianism overboard too quickly. What the arguments expounded above show is that communitarian theories of justice, in so far as they are defended with an appeal to the idea of community, are insufficiently sustained. The defence is incomplete: one cannot simply jostle questions about the legitimacy of theories of the good off the agenda. It has not been said that *any* defence of *a* communitarian conception of justice is necessarily impossible. If such a theory were compatible with and enclosed in a conception of minimal justice, this could count as an argument in favour of it: it would imply that from a higher, impartial point of view, this particular theory of the good is not despicable in principle. Or, in stronger terms: even a community needs minimal justice.

As a matter of fact, communitarian justice is not only in principle compatible with, it is also an almost indispensable supplement to, minimal justice. A community needs to affirm the principles of minimal justice, but a minimally just society is not necessarily the most desirable society. If a liberal theory of justice takes its devotion to impartiality seriously, it will not be able to answer all questions of justice conclusively (cf. Barry 1995: 143) – as we shall see in Part III. Minimal justice is really very minimal. It can prescribe that fundamental needs be answered whenever physically possible; it cannot command that welfare benefits allow their recipients more than bread and water. It cannot prescribe that 40 years of service to a society's culture be rewarded with a knighthood; it will demand that honours, if admissible in this form, be given to those who deserve them according to relevant criteria, and it will determine what makes certain criteria relevant.

Minimal justice does not exclude the possibility of a society's having a shared conception of the good life and a substantial theory of justice. It only puts limits on the kinds of acts, intentions and states of affairs that can be called (minimally) just. Hence, there is a legitimate role for communitarian justice in a liberal view on society. Where minimal justice is incapable of more precision, where it is indifferent between particular distribution patterns, it is up to the members of a community to decide or, in the absence of community, up to politics. Whereas minimal justice defines the minimal standards of justice, the political will defines the upper limit. This makes justice, like politics, an art rather than a technique.

4

The archpoint

The possibility of impartiality

I have defined minimal justice as the conception of justice that will be chosen or endorsed under conditions of impartiality, and have given a very broad definition of impartiality, one that appears to be the common denominator of liberal conceptions of justice. In this chapter, I shall defend a more precise and concise notion of impartiality.

How should we conceive of impartiality, given the impossibility of ethical absolutism? It cannot be 'anything goes'; under such circumstances there would no longer be moral or immoral ideas – only evaluative or normative fancies. Allowing each and every evaluative view leaves us with no point of view at all, not even one from which we can account for the 'anything goes' rule itself. Because anything goes, nothing goes: both the idea that every moral or immoral or amoral code is allowed, and the idea that none can be allowed as none can be justified, would be equally valid or – since anything goes – equally invalid.

I shall argue instead that impartiality is a negative although not a nihilistic notion. We are morally and intellectually situated, like it or not. We all have an evaluative point of view, even Camus's *étranger*. The intention behind introducing impartiality in theories of justice is to step away, as far as possible, from these particular points of view, without excluding their existence or without denying partiality and contingency.[22]

One way *not* to do this is by simply asking real human beings to be impartial and to judge principles of justice. We might trust them to be impartial, but in this respect it is more secure to control them. In this chapter I shall discuss the side-constraints that should be posed on a justification procedure to ensure its impartiality, and the form best fit for representing such a procedure. As to the first part, this comes down to defining impartiality as, among other things, the point of view (the archpoint) at which one postpones judgement on the most basic human motives. With regard to the form of the justification procedure, I shall argue that the collection of contract theories, general observer theories, insurance games, choice and bargaining theories and like constructions can be compared to the emperor's wardrobe in one important respect. These are all ways to dress up real, naked arguments and thereby to add to the authority of argument that of imaginability. Both the emperor's wardrobe and the collection of justification styles are, in a way, heuristic devices: both are chosen for representational purposes to camouflage something more substantial, and both can be seen through, given the appropriate attitude. The difference is that not all justification devices will fit impartiality.

In Chapter 5 I shall ask what kind of beings we would want to judge on principles of justice (e.g. their psychological and moral make-up), by which rules they ought to judge, and which knowledge they should have at their disposal.

First, however, let us discuss the following questions: is impartiality possible at all in the context of minimal justice? If so, in what form? And is this form a desirable interpretation of impartiality?

There are three reasons in the present context to examine whether impartiality can exist. As remarked above, the separation between minimal justice, or justice under conditions of impartiality, and communitarian justice, which is characterized by the presence of a substantive theory of the good, is not as rigid in practice as it is in theory. No liberal theory of justice goes without some kind of theory of the good. But if the initial distinction between minimal and communitarian justice is blurred in this way, it would seem that liberal social justice is simply a hybrid form of communitarianism – and we found communitarianism to be undesirable. In that case, the one remaining difference between communitarian and minimal justice is the absence or presence of the impartiality constraint. To know if this really makes a difference, we have to know what impartiality entails – and whether it can exist.

A second reason, connected to the 'anything goes' problem discussed above, concerns a possible inconsistency between the micro- and macro-levels of morality. If there can be no sound foundation for conceptions of the good for societies (which was one of the reasons why liberals embraced impartiality), then what about the foundations of the individual's convictions? Why adhere to a private theory of the good, or to a plan of life, or to a Nietzschean or nihilistic view on life? Why would any of these, or all, be legitimate? It seems that if we reject a society's adhering to a theory of the good, we imply that *individuals* should not have one either. Under those conditions, there would not be anything to be impartial to; impartiality would be non-existent.

A third reason is inspired by Marx (cf. Lock 1989: 3) and by Karl Popper's critique of utopian planning (Popper 1986a: 160–61): preferences not only change *in* a society, but also as a result of the *transformation* of a society. This thesis confronts us, first of all, with the problem of distinguishing between persons and their contingent attributes – talents as well as attitudes. I shall deal with that later

> **Marilyn:** So how do *you* determine whether something is unjust?
> **Albert:** I go out in the wild, take off my clothes, bathe in a cold stream, sacrifice a goat under a tree and go home.
> **M:** And then?
> **A:** And then I'll start to think about your question.

Technical neutrality

in this chapter. Further, it raises questions about impartiality itself. How can this idea be reconciled with a revolutionary *Umwertung aller Werte*? Will the archpoint itself be the product of an ideology rather than stand above ideologies?

Earlier, I introduced a series of ideas representative of liberal justice theories, a cluster of three very indefinite types of neutrality to which I attached the collective label 'impartiality'. Taking these as a starting point, we shall see that a defence of impartiality requires a further specification of this concept, especially with regard to the theory of the good. Let's recap:

Technical neutrality: the decision procedure should actively endorse the promotion (i.e. detection and selection) of neutral principles of justice. In ordinary English: the justification procedure should measure what it is supposed to measure.

Objective neutrality: rational human beings should all equally endorse the principles or reasons behind the justification procedure, by virtue of their already being endorsed in their plans of life. In Rawlsian words: the thin theory of the good should be reasonable.

Subjective neutrality: the justification procedure, and the reasons behind it, should give equal relevance to individual plans of life or constituent parts thereof.

I shall take the demand of technical neutrality to be either trivial or, if it cannot be that simple (few things in philosophy are), as a postulate.

Objective neutrality is quite a strong demand in postmodern times. By insisting on universal approval, it apparently excludes all moral notions and ideals except those that are never denied by rational beings, nor ever in history were, nor ever will be. This also implies – but now I am running ahead of things a little – the exclusion on grounds of insufficient evidence of most current liberal theories about the justification of conceptions of justice, in particular Ackerman's belief in a societal *modus vivendi*, and probably Rawls's belief in a basic consensus as well. I shall discuss the details of objective neutrality in a moment.

Prior to that, however, let us consider the condition of subjective neutrality, which appears to be at least as demanding as objective neutrality. At the political macro-level, it seems to exclude virtually every conception of society as a system of rules – for how can rules give equal relevance to the plans of life of anarchists, libertarians, liberals and other rule-sceptics on the one hand, and those of rule-disciples on the other? Also, it apparently allows, at the micro-level, virtually every individual morality, even sadism, nihilism, terrorism and other codes containing so-called perverse preferences. The latter problem reflects one of the central dilemmas of democracy, that is the danger of a democratic aboli- tion of democracy. Its solution is also the same – and equally dissatisfying: sub- jective neutrality can only be guaranteed by the exclusion of preferences that, if rewarded, would systematically and structurally hinder the expression of all deviat- ing preferences.

The greatest obstacle to our defence of impartiality lies in the realm of object- ive rather than subjective neutrality. Ultimately, neither the democratic paradox nor that of subjective neutrality can be solved or dissolved without reference to a meta-theory. In the case of subjective neutrality, its possibility depends primarily on the way we interpret the phrase 'individual plans of life or constituent parts thereof'. If, for some reason, we must give equal relevance to all aspects of all plans of life, then the paradox cannot be solved or evaded. However, if there are good reasons to limit the ban on political biases to *parts* of plans of life only, then perhaps the paradox will not arise, ergo subjective neutrality will be possible, ergo impartiality will be possible, ergo liberal social justice will be possible. It all depends on one thing: whether all rational human beings will equally endorse the principles or reasons behind the justification procedure, and this for the right reason, namely by virtue of their already being endorsed in their plans of life – as the definition of objective neutrality runs. In the Rawlsian vocabulary, this is described as the problem of the thin theory of the good. If, in questions of justice, all rational beings would have to agree that what matters to and about persons is that their lives go as planned, then we have a problem. If what matters is only that *some* things go right, then the paradox may not arise, in which case everything else follows.

The best known, though unsatisfactory, solution to this problem is Rawls's. In his latest exegeses of his own theory, Rawls has argued that his two principles of justice are reasonable (read: realistic or feasible) while acceptable for everyone, *assuming* that there is a 'basic consensus' on fundamental values among us (or US citizens). It is the purpose of the dialogue between our considered judgements and the judgements of people in the original position to let us develop a rational reconstruction of this consensus (Rawls 1993a: 28, 38–9, etc.). At the moment when both views on justice are in agreement and the basic consensus becomes visible, we have reached a state known as reflective equilibrium. Now Rawls has done a lot of this work for us. The basic consensus, as he sees it, is already embodied partly in the structure of the original position itself (for instance in the freedom and equality of the people in that position), and partly in the thin theory of the good as applied in the original position. In essence, Brian Barry follows the same course when he describes justice as impartiality as an agreement on principles of justice among the reasonable members of concrete societies (Barry 1995: 11, 67 ff.).

It will be clear why Rawls's solution is not satisfactory for anyone who – like us – is looking for a universally acceptable Archimedean point. In this new interpretation, Rawls explicitly allows for the possibility of a society, even a just society, based on a basic consensus other than the one he discerns in his own society.[23] Consequently, dissenting societies can neither accept Rawls's version of the Archimedean point, nor that which follows from an exchange with this original position: the famous two principles. This is what gives Rawls's theory its republican[24] and conservative twist: it no longer has universal pretensions. Rawls now allows justice to depend on a contingent feature, the culture of a particular society at a particular moment. Justice as fairness has become the *alter ego* of *a* rather than *any* society.

Rawls himself saw Bruce Ackerman's *modus vivendi* conception of the social contract as the antithesis of the notion of a basic consensus (Rawls 1993a: 147; cf. Kymlicka 1995: 14). In Ackerman's theory, the aim of constructing an Archimedean point is not to generate a consensus but to do exactly the reverse: to avoid and exclude moral disagreements, contradictions and conflicts (Ackerman 1983: 375). Ackerman believes that the contemporary disagreement on the most basic values determining our plans of life is insurmountable. He therefore denies the legitimacy and authenticity of a Rawlsian basic consensus. However, assuming that we are rational and that we would appreciate a debate on the reasons for our behaviour over a war of all against all, we can still reach a viable live-and-let-live agreement in the form of a social contract. We would need some rules of debate – rules Ackerman defends (Ackerman 1980: 4–11) – and we would have to assume that we all need resources (manna). Apart from that, there would be no need for any thin theory of the good, nor for that which it necessitates: an evaluation of private conceptions of the good. All we would need is a good debate on what can count as a neutrally defensible reason for action, regardless of the underlying private conception of the good. Nevertheless, one can find traces of a thin theory of the good in Ackerman's theory as well: his purely formal tests of the rationality or neutrality of reasons still incorporates a range of (contestable) ethical presumptions, beginning with the idea that no conception of the good can be said to be better than any other.

The Ackerman–Rawls controversy illustrates, once more, the problem confronting all attempts at designing an impartial justification device. Rawls's choice for one particular culture as he perceives it to be is one example; the substantial ethical assumptions both he and Ackerman made in presupposing the value of (physical) resources – assumptions that many will not share in every detail, and few of the contemplatively living in general – is another. It is a problem relevant to every theorist subscribing, in some form or other, to the seven ideals that we earlier identified as the core values of liberal theories of justice. It is even relevant to more liberal-minded communitarians like Walzer. All of them deny at least the relevance if not the existence of a 'true' basis of morality (read: of ethical absolutism). They thereby create the impression that their theories are ideologies: *partial* or *biased* theories offering political liberalism a philosophical disguise. Now there is nothing wrong with being an ideologue, except if, by your own standards, you should be able to convince everyone of your *im*partiality.

We are then, once again, slipping over the catch-22 dilemma of impartiality. Denying (the relevance of) ethical truth, rejecting ethical absolutism, will lead to theories that can be branded ideological, but we want to certify that we are *im*partial. Accepting ethical absolutism, on the other hand, will lead to theories that cannot be accepted as impartial by those who do not share our privileged knowledge of and access to the Truth. There is no impartiality without a theory of the good, and there is no impartial theory of the good. Or is there?

Returning to the roots of liberalism, I think we can find a way to save objective neutrality and impartiality without committing ourselves to a too substantial theory of the good. My argumentation on this point seems to concur with Barry's appeal to scepsis (Barry 1995: 169, 173 ff.).

Step one on this way takes us back to David Hume's distinction between fact and value. Hume's Law holds that ethical judgements cannot be derived from empirical premises – though of course meaningful judgements can only be passed on empirical facts or on (possible) counterfactuals. The law can be applied in two ways. For one, we may start to believe that there is an ethical truth independent of facts and try to discover it; this is the road to ethical absolutism, which has already been rejected in previous sections. Alternatively, we may give up the search for an absolute ethical truth independent of the world of positive facts – for instance because we come to believe that ethical propositions and convictions are, as states of mind, simply another type of empirical fact. In the latter case, we open up roads to conventionalism, relativism, nihilism and so forth, none of which are very helpful if we want moral arguments to have any independent significance.

Step two is a tentative denial of Hume's Law. Let us assume for a moment that ethical propositions can in fact be derived from states of affairs. This is not an uncommon view, although a bit out of fashion nowadays and in places – it belongs more to Platonists and Neoplatonists. Were views like these correct, it could be quite well possible to formulate (or rather, discover) an absolute ethical truth acceptable to all rational beings, all beings capable of knowing and understanding. This would give us a very sound basis for objective neutrality. One of the inconveniences of life, however, is the existence of people who are firmly convinced of the truth of Hume's Law.

Step three takes us to the Far East, where we encounter yet another surprising view on morality: Zen or Ch'an Buddhism. One day, the honourable Shui-lao appeared before Ma-tsu, asking the Master to teach him wisdom. Ma-tsu told him to bow, and gave him a fierce kick on a painful place. 'Oh wonder, oh wonder!', and the student had his moment of Enlightenment (Ma-tsu 1981: 107).

Step four is an observation: the possibility and shape of objective neutrality depends on our metaphysical conception of the world, that is on the way we relate facts and morals. If we were all Humeians, objective neutrality might be possible but it would always rest on shaky foundations. If we were Spinozists or Neoplatonists, formulating the objectively neutral archpoint is only a matter of sound thinking. If we were Ch'an Buddhists, objective neutrality would be unthinkable, namely the idea of the Absolute Nothing, or possible but perhaps a bit painful – who knows? And, obviously, we have no guarantee that the Humeian conception of objective neutrality is congruent with the Neoplatonic, Ch'an, or other versions of that idea.

Step five is an educated guess: given the actual plentitude and imaginable infinitude of metaphysical theories, given our limited intellectual capacities and the suspicion that it may not even be possible to have a meaningful debate on metaphysics, and barring the appearance of an angel with a solution, there is little hope that we will shortly formulate the definitive metaphysics (cf. Barry 1995: 173). Hence, there is also little hope for an objectively neutral theory of the good so long as it is predicated on one or more, but not all, imaginable metaphysical theories.

This leaves us two options. We could give up, deciding that any attempt at formulating a universally inoffensive theory of the good is fruitless. This means taking a very radical Wittgensteinian or postmodern stand, and interpreting justice talk as providing us with an interesting opportunity to clarify or analyze the understanding of language games, perhaps even without any pretention of contributing to the understanding of justice as such. On the other hand, and without denying the validity of the first alternative, we could try to turn the tables in our favour and look for a minimally offensive theory: a theory that cannot be rejected by any reasonable individual, or in other words, one that is reasonable from the point of view of all individuals with a reasonable plan of life.[25] I shall argue that there is such a theory.

Objective neutrality at the archpoint can be conceived of as a combination of three ideas: the revived sceptic idea of postponing judgement, a set of things to postpone judgement on, and a super-thin theory of the good. As for the last idea, this is mainly a restatement of one of the constraints posed earlier on natural justice. It consists of one simple axiom: that it is good to be, and that in fact we are, reasonable, or rational in a weak sense, that is we reject fallacies and accept logically sound arguments.[26] There is, to my mind, no rational way to account for rationality; that would require circular reasoning. Perhaps we could give a negative defence by pointing – as Karl Popper did – to the undesirable consequences of a rejection of rationality and rational argument (Popper 1986b: 232), but even such an argument seems to presuppose rationality if it is to hit home. On the other hand, perhaps the burden of proof does not rest on us but on anyone questioning that this super-thin theory of the good is equally endorsed by all rational human beings. Even though we do not know what exactly logic is, or why we resent illogicality and uncertainty so much, the fact is that we all work with it (i.e. first order predicate logic) and deeply resent working without it. Hardly anyone ever questions the rules of logic; in everyday life, we only question premises and conclusions.

In the absence of a thin theory of the good, we shall have to work without a particular point of view on the good life (as we intended to), and even without a view on meta-ethics or metaphysics. This means that we shall have to pretend:

we must postpone any judgement on right and wrong *as if* one day it may or will be possible to make a final judgement. As any theory of the good can legitimately be rejected, and any theory of justice without an ethical starting point will lack authority, this seems to be the only option left. Thinking a few steps ahead, one might expect such more-than-Humeian scepticism (it is also sceptical with regard to Hume's Law) to lead once more to an 'anything goes' approach towards justice. But it does not, as I hope to show.

Full reasons

Of course there must be something on which to postpone judgements. I shall introduce my object for the postponement of judgement, full reasons, in four steps. First, they will be described and defined. Next, I shall give some reasons for 'believing in their existence', that is, for accepting full reasons as a fruitful concept. Then I shall defend the thesis that full reasons are of fundamental importance in every reasonable theory of or about morality, that is that they are – depending on one's vocabulary – morally relevant, valid, or the truth about morality. Finally, I shall discuss the relevance of full reasons for liberalism in particular.

In the real world, we are often uncertain about the way we should act, about the quality of our actions, about the reasons for our judgements on both, in short: about morality. If we were not, it would be hard to explain why there are so many ethical and moral theories to pick from. There may be two reasons for this uncertainty. In the first place, experience may at times contradict our intentions: if we do not feel too happy about (the consequences of) our actions, we may start to doubt the rules we were following – or the wisdom of not following any. Secondly, contradictions between intentions or rules themselves may arise, both in an interpersonal context and in personal moral conflicts. It is this second kind of uncertainty, connected to conflicting intentions, in which I am interested.

Some of the intentions we have, some of our reasons for acting or judging as we do, are basic (cf. Sen 1970: 59 ff.; see also Brandt 1979: 149 ff.). They cannot be reduced to other, more fundamental moral propositions, nor to empirical propositions. Of course there are bound to be psychological or sociological *explanations* for their occurrence, but explaining and justifying are two different things. Other reasons are, to abuse a Kantian term, hypothetical. They can be partly reduced to basic moral propositions, and for the remainder depend on non-moral, empirical observations, estimates and rules. Being hypothetical, they can be criticized, accepted, rejected or improved. Hence, there is no need to remain neutral or sceptical about them.

There is a deeper distinction within the category of basic reasons. Some of them are what I call *full* reasons. Full reasons function as the foundations upon which other reasons and convictions rest; they are the ultimate grounds for those reasons and the last resort in their defence. They are also purely local, even

---

Albert: I believe unemployment benefits should be made available for everyone, regardless of the reasons for unemployment. It's what I want for myself, and if I want it for myself I can't deny it to others. Equal cases, you know.

Marilyn: So why do *you* want unconditional unemployment benefits?

A: In the end, because it's all about autonomy – because I want to live life the way I want to and not be forced to give in to a necessity to work for even one single moment.

M: Since when does a desire for autonomy directly imply that you should have a free lunch? First of all, you don't need that funny benefits system of yours to follow all the courses in life you could possibly pursue; secondly, I don't see why the course of life you've just described would make you autonomous – you'd still depend on others; thirdly, what if everyone did it – who would pay for it?; and last, why is your autonomy so important that others would have to pay for it?

A: Are you going to say that to any social security proposal I make?

M: Yes.

A: So in your opinion, social justice does not imply social security?

M: I didn't say that – all I say is: no social security on the kind of grounds you're offering. They're questionable, and you don't have an answer to my questions.

Questionable reasons

purely personal, in that they form a person's subset of the culturally and intellectually available 'virtues'. (I shall return to the relation with virtues in a moment.)

Full reasons are constant, stable and undeniable – that is one cannot think of any good excuse (in one's own eyes) when acting against them. We can think of them as private categorical imperatives. They are part of our selves, our psychological make-up, our nature – or rather, in view of the fact that they probably have a social origin,[27] they constitute our second nature. They can operate in our consciousness, in our conscience, or, like virtues, subconsciously. Full reasons are, as I shall argue below, the final reasons beyond which we cannot and should not reason, at least not in so far as justice and politics are concerned. They determine what things in life are and what are not *crucial* in making our lives go well (cf. Barry 1995: 84). Examples of full reasons are honesty, authenticity, reciprocity, mercy, obligation, fraternity, patience, honour, humour, humility, fullness, growth, harmony as well as justice. (Compare in this context Robert Nozick's essay on 'evaluative dimensions' (Nozick 1989: 182 ff.).) Full reasons do not need to be virtues or potentially 'substantial' ethical ideals, though – more typically liberal full reasons could be described as Kantian categorical imperatives, or as the desire to do the moral thing or discover what the morally correct course of action should be.

About other basic reasons our conscience is more lenient. As compared to full reasons, they are conditional. We may, for instance, sincerely believe that every human life is inviolable, and that therefore killing is wrong, no matter why, by whom or in whatever circumstances. Yet in a kill-or-risk-being-killed situation, and given ample opportunity to consider the alternatives, we will soon find out how lenient or firm we are.

Note that I do not pose any further conditions on full reasons. They may be characterized as ethical, egoistic, perverse or decent – all in the eyes of others – and they can, as a set, be internally inconsistent, intransitive, cyclical or whatever. Full reasons are not distinguished by their moral stature (we have to postpone any judgement on that issue) or their practicability, but by the firmness and stability, the basicness, of our belief in them. We can compare them to plans of life, a category that has often been proposed as a reasonable basis for objective neutrality. Plans of life depend on, and often change with, the flow of circumstances – war, marriage, divorce, pregnancy, the death of others, changing economic prospects, new social mores, religious conversion, mental or physical illness, and so on. Full reasons, on the other hand, have been purged of references to the contingencies of life, and thus delineate the way we would like to live *regardless* of changing or changeable circumstances (cf. Nozick 1989). We need not trade the concept of life-plans for full reasons, however; the two are perfectly compatible. Adapting to convention, one can define (1) a person's set of full reasons as that person's *full* plan of life or plan of a *full* life ('full', for want of a better word, also in the sense of being basically good or satisfactory or successful), and (2) his or her plan of life in the regular sense as an *extended* plan of life or as a plan of a *complete* life. It is possible to have as many extended plans of life as life itself allows: having full reasons does not (or not necessarily) commit a person to one and no more than one way of putting them into practice.

Do full reasons exist? Any answer would contain an empirical claim and raise the question of its verification (or falsification). A first step towards sustaining or refuting my claim would be to apply a modified version of Richard Brandt's cognitive psychotherapy (Brandt 1979: 16 ff.) to our desires and motives, eliminating the hypothetical imperatives. In so far as our reasons for action turn out to be sensitive to arguments of truth with regard to facts or to consistency arguments with regard to more fundamental principles, they are obviously not basic. Assuming the reliability of our eliminative therapy, the reasons that survive must be basic reasons. Whether these are full reasons depends on their stability, and to determine if they are, we need a test to identify private categorical imperatives, principles that we could want to be laws of our own part of nature. If there is at least one human being with at least one private categorical imperative, full reasons exist. Now we can ask ourselves to judge real-life moral dilemmas and find out if we value (for instance) our own life or self more than that of others. We can even extend the test procedure to include the type of counterfactual

Albert: I've been thinking. I still want an unconditional unemployment benefit, at least for myself.

Marilyn: Under all circumstances? We've just decided that won't work.

A: No, not under all circumstances. But listen to this. When I die, I want to know I haven't wasted my life, I want to know that I've tried everything I could, regardless of whether I failed or not. And right now, my life would be wasted if I couldn't sit back for a couple of months to see if I can disprove that gravity is an autosuggestion. I wake up with the idea, I go to bed with it, I can't get rid of it, I can't eat, I can't drink, I've lost twenty pounds, and my shrink says it's perfectly normal for a genius of my magnitude. Only my university won't pay for it because it doesn't fit in with their Astrophysics, Technology and Breakfast Improvement research programme, and other universities are in the exact same position, and all they can offer are bureaucratic excuses. It's a matter of life and death to me to do this thing, I can't do it without that particular benefit, and society won't miss it.

M: What if everyone did it? Wouldn't the money run out? Would you then settle for less, or accept as unavoidable that you don't get any money?

A: I'd have to.

M: But here comes a man who says he can't live without a harem. And he wants the state to pay for it. And furnish him with women. What do you say?

A: Women aren't a commodity. Please be serious. Let's imagine a man who needs a moon base to live a life worth living. If we can pay for it, I'd have to accept it. The criterion is: would it create the same kind of life and death dilemma for others? If it doesn't, I'd have to pay. We'd have to pay. Equal cases and that stuff.

M: I'll admit you've got a full reason but I still can't agree with it.

A: Nor can you reject it on any grounds. Show me that it's not a basic reason, show me that you can argue against it, and then I might reconsider.

M: OK. Well, at least it seems like we're getting somewhere at least.

Full reasons

dilemma Derek Parfit (1984) is famous for: 'Would you kill a perfect copy of yourself, one made five minutes ago, to survive? Even if you were not really sure that you were the original and that the other was the copy?' Or we can simply try to violate a basic reason and find out if we can still look into the mirror. But as with every inductive or deductive argument, we can never completely trust any answer or result. Full reasons are, like every concept in science, a theoretical construction of which the validity can never be completely confirmed.

Still, we can make the notion of full reasons more acceptable by understanding them in terms of another, more conventional and less controversial concept: virtue. Full reasons are very much akin to virtues. Both terms describe our dispositions, our, in Aristotelian terms, second nature. Both are the most basic reasons we can give for doing what we do; both are character features in which we can excel. We believe in their value not because of any ulterior motive, any accidental fact, or any deeper reason, but because we hold them to be good *as such*, good in themselves (cf. e.g. Brandt's description of virtues, Brandt 1988: 64).

What distinguishes full reasons from the traditional conception of virtues is that full reasons are self-defined and that we can be conscious of them. As to the first aspect: virtues derive their meaning in ordinary life and language from their relation to either a universal theory of the human good, or a particular society's conception of the good and the appropriate (Nussbaum 1988: 33). Full reasons, on the other hand, may have but do not require this contingent social background; we consider them, for all practical purposes, to be disconnected from any setting they may originate in. Hence, virtues have opposites: vices. Full reasons do not – there is no higher standard to measure them by. As to the second difference: a virtue is a rule or reason upon which we act without thinking, without reflection, as if the virtuous act comes instinctively. I do not demand this of full reasons. I assume that we can, if necessary, be conscious of them and even consciously (at a price) act against them. Virtues are, in these two respects, a special case of full reasons.

Full reasons and virtues have more in common. For instance, neither one can be evaluated in terms of the modern distinction between inadmissible egocentric behaviour and admissible, unbiased, moral behaviour (in Anglo-Saxon political philosophy known as rationality versus morality). Each and every one of the virtues – or full reasons – we can think of, can be accounted for both in terms of what is best for me and in terms of what is best overall. Many virtues – such as modesty, sincerity, authenticity and prudence – are definitely self-regarding (cf. Galston 1991: 230), and at least one of them, the classic mean between egoism and altruism, explicitly acknowledges the moral importance of the self.

A further resemblance between full reasons and virtues is their stability. Both are stable in two senses. First of all, at a personal level, they are like all dispositions, hard to come by and hard to change. Most often, they are the product of education and socialization, and sometimes the result of dramatic experiences[28] that shock or evoke belief in a full reason – but again, where they actually come from does not actually matter. Secondly, at a cultural level, full reasons and virtues have a very long life. A person's full reasons may evolve or occasionally change, and different cultures may know and esteem different virtues, yet full reasons in themselves are much more stable. Basic moral ideas that have often served as personal full reasons are not limited to unique persons, times, societies or cultures (cf. MacIntyre 1985: 187). Finally, virtues and full reasons share one destabilizing characteristic: they can be rationally criticized, they can be doubted, discussed, evaluated, acknowledged and rejected. The kind of critique meant here does not touch upon the appropriateness of some full reason in particular circumstances or a particular society, but on the legitimacy of a virtue or full reason itself, *sub specie aeternitatis*. Although we do not have moral criteria for virtues, we can ask whether a virtue is a virtue at all, or a full reason a full reason, or whether it is a kind of collective or individual prejudice (cf. Kley 1989: 339). From time to time, counting in centuries, critique of this kind leads to the discovery of new virtues or the rejection of an old one. Admittedly, such a slowly changing and fundamentally open list of full reasons is not the most stable and indubitable basis for an Archimedean point – but it is the best we have.

Before we go on discussing this paradoxical conclusion, we should recapitulate what we have established so far. If we believe that virtues exist, we must also believe that full reasons exist. Comparing full reasons to virtues, we saw that they share all important characteristics except one: unlike full reasons, virtues derive their meaning, their moral import, from a social context. Virtues, or supposed virtues, can be criticized within a society by relating them to a local or universal conception of the good; full reasons are exempted from that kind of critique. Consequently, we cannot but postpone judgement on the latter, that is, remain objectively neutral. Nevertheless, both virtues and full reasons can be criticized from another point of view, or so we just claimed. In a meta-social discourse, it would be possible to assess the, let us say extra-temporal, virtuousness of a virtue or the full-ness of a full reason.

Yet this is a genuine problem. If such a meta-social critique is impossible, full reasons are arbitrary; we would have no reason to value them, or to value anything, for that matter. If it is not, there *seems* to be a higher standard, and thus no reason to postpone judgement, no sense in demanding objective neutrality, no future for impartiality or for minimal liberal justice. The way out of this possible contradiction is indicated by the word *seems*. We can, without contradiction, claim both that there is a meta-social discourse, and that there are no higher standards.

The discourse in question resembles the discourse of philosophy and the hermeneutic sciences, albeit applied at the level of individual friends or sympathetic minds. We cannot be certain that we fully understand the Greeks of antiquity, and we are even less certain that we would understand a lion if it could talk (cf. also Nagel 1974: 438–42) – but we can interpret the symbols of other cultures, other language games, other people's full reasons, and clarify that which we cannot help but believe. We cannot be sure of the (in)correctness of our interpretations, unless perhaps serious inconsistencies come to light. Our interpretations are always ours, not theirs; there is no hope of certainty in understanding them. All we have is, as a Dutch expression says, the courage of desperation: the conviction that there is no other way of learning and understanding than interpreting, again and again. Perhaps at times an appeal can be made to mutually shared understandings, to the apparent coherence of two individuals'

Albert: I put it to you that society should create room for the recognition of excellence again. Room for honour. Excellence should be rewarded, not because people's qualities are put to 'use', whatever they may be, but because excellence is good in itself, and because honour is what people ultimately strive for. The good ones, at least. Society should be a place where men of honour live – and women, if you insist.

Marilyn: Honour is dead. Brutus was an honourable man, remember? You can't even say that it's a full reason – it's not something anyone can let his or her life be directed by. It's not even an independent value – it's supposedly a judgement on excellence in more basic qualities, virtues to be exact. But it's not even that. Honour is given by 'people who matter', based on their perception of you, based on what you manage to make them perceive. It's a judgement on the appearance of virtue. And it's circular – who are the people who matter? Shouldn't they be honourable as well? And how, unless you already consider yourself honourable, can you decide which people matter?

A: So you say honour exists only in one's perception of oneself?

M: Quite. And that reduces it to sincerity, or to *noblesse* perhaps.

A: No decorations then? No titles? No rewards? No public recognition?

M: That's not what I said. There may well be room for 'honours', just not for honour. If there's any sense in the idea of honour it's at a deeper level – excellence in socially important qualities, perhaps. But certainly not excellence in appearance. Honour is dead.

A: O tempora, o mores.

A meta-social discourse

interpretations of one another's beliefs, resulting in a reappraisal or redefinition of one's full reasons. Yet two conclusions must be drawn: first, that the limited criticizability of full reasons does not necessarily lead to their rejection, and secondly, that there can be no authoritative standard, least of all one imposed by political authorities, for the reasonableness of one person's belief in a full reason – except for the judgement of that person herself.

Disenchanting as this answer may be, it is probably the only way we can ever hope to substantiate claims to truth in moral matters. Full reasons are, furthermore, an adequate if not always satisfactory answer to some of the other problems encountered earlier. For one thing, we can now partly solve the paradox of subjective neutrality that surfaced earlier: it is perfectly simple to postpone judgement on this category of *reasons* and give equal relevance to their exhibition, without giving equal relevance to all the *ways* in which they can be exhibited. Consequently, both objective and subjective neutrality are possible, as is impartiality, as is – ultimately – a liberal conception of social justice.

Secondly, we can now conclude that the possibly pseudo-communitarian character of mainstream liberalism signalled above is no longer an issue. We have dropped as much of the idea of thin theories of the good as possible, including all ties with the 'shared understandings' and language games of particular cultures. Likewise, the legitimacy of individual moral convictions, including nihilistic and Nietzschean 'moralities', has been principally affirmed by our defence of full reasons. We reject a society's adherence to a theory of the good *precisely because* we have no other basis for attitudes than the individual's conscience – or the absence thereof, in the case of nihilists.

The Marx–Popper problem, however, cannot be solved. Even if a theory of justice would not reflect a political ideology, it will still reflect a certain culture or social consciousness. In other words, the justification procedure for a liberal theory of social justice may be impartial regarding ideologies and conventions, predicated as it is on the equal relevance shown to full reasons, but it nevertheless reflects *our* conviction that full reasons matter. Any attempt to claim meta–social validity for this view is bound to run up against the limits of interpretation.

I have defined and described full reasons, and given arguments to believe in their existence and in the practical advantages of making them the basis of an impartial theory of justice. But obviously any theory of justice will be prohibitive in some respects and prescriptive in others. Theoretically, full reasons are attractive – but is that enough reason to accept the practical consequences of impartiality?

A first step towards answering this is to establish that if we accept full reasons as a basis for justice, we must also accept the results of a reliable justification procedure based on these reasons – and act accordingly. The second and last step will be to prove that we must affirm the universal validity of full reasons, their fundamental role in every reasonable morality.

As for the first step, there can be no rational reason to reject the conclusion of a valid argument based on true premises. Yet believing an argument, especially one that incites us to act, and actually acting upon it are two different things. The latter requires an answer to a deeper question: why should I be moral and do that which is best overall rather than, say, be rational and do that which is best for me (cf. e.g. Parfit 1984: 3, 24; Brandt 1979: 14 ff.; Gauthier 1986: 7)? There is no need to dwell here on traditional responses to this question; I refer the reader to a good introduction to moral philosophy (e.g. Frankena 1963; Raphael 1981) or to the more recent debate on the rationality for rational egoists of being moral and recognizing that (other people's) demand for morally responsible behaviour is a fundamental and irreducible human motive, the denial of which would imply disregarding relevant facts needed for a rational decision (cf. Parfit 1984: 45 ff.; Barry 1989: 363–6). The point to note about the 'why be moral' dispute is that no resolution strategy will be persuasive if it is not a *clearly* logically sound argument – *and* if it is not based on premises acceptable to each and every one who may be obliged by the conclusion. The cardinal premise of our impartial justification device, the archpoint, is that full reasons have overall moral importance in every reasonable theory of morality. So far, my claim has been that full reasons are the legitimate primordial material on the basis of which an archpoint must be erected. Yet provided that the justification procedure is reliable, why should we trust this elementary assumption?

A first reason for accepting the legitimacy of full reasons is plainly negative and similar to Rawls's recent defence of his conception of impartiality (Rawls 1995: 134). There is no guarantee that anyone's conscience reflects the, or an, ultimate ethical truth, but we have excluded all alternative foundations for justice as questionable. Full reasons are the only, or at least last, thing for which we have – theoretically – good reasons. They are the only part of plans of life that are really beyond critique. Note that Brian Barry seems to hold a similar view when he distinguishes things that are 'crucial' to plans of life (Barry 1995: 84) and parts of those plans that are criticizable and subject to negotiation (Barry 1995: 6).

A second reason is more positive: we can trust full reasons to be a universally valid and universally fundamental concept of any moral theory, because (1) full reasons are an integral part of human nature, and because (2) ignoring that part implies denying human freedom and renouncing the existence of (im)morality.

Before I elaborate on this, two remarks are in order. First, to be precise, it is the *capacity* for having full reasons that is part of our nature, part of what makes us human. The set of *specific* full reasons that makes an individual out of a human being is part of our second, artificial, nature, the dispositions and character traits acquired through education and socialization. We are necessarily equipped with a capacity for full reasons but whether and in what way this capacity is developed depends on circumstances. Secondly, it should be noted that the term 'nature' is not meant as a symbol for some kind of philosophical realism, essentialism, determinism or naturalism. Whether or not things like human nature, or, altern-atively, the human condition, the platonic Form, or the ideal-type of the human being exists is of no consequence to us. Using terms like nature or essence is merely a matter of convenience. In due course, I shall adapt my small exegesis of human nature to non-essentialistic vocabularies.

What defines the human being? It has been said that the human is *animal implume bipes*, or a plucked chicken. More serious attempts to define human nature are variations on classical phrases like Boethius's *animal rationale*. The phrase indicates that humans are thought of as being capable of giving reasons for their actions, and (consequently) that they are self-conscious. Now we must assume that neither physical and mental determinism, nor chaos, are true, or that even if one of these theories were true this would still be irrelevant for moral discourse. There is no sense in talking about right and wrong if every bit of this universe, including our ideas, deliberations and decisions, follows an inescapable law of nature. The same is true in the other extreme case, chaos, where there is no relation whatsoever between ideas, decisions, actions, results, perception, and so forth – where there is only happenstance.

On this assumption, rationality implies both freedom of mind (autonomy) and freedom of action (agency).[29] Autonomy and agency have been incorporated in numerous broader ideas on human nature, including concepts like the good life, plan of life, theory of the good, virtue – and full reasons. Among these, and notwithstanding the relevance of other concepts, full reasons are the most economic and therefore most indispensable means of representing human freedom. Without them, we cannot be Boethian-rational; we would be incomplete, merely potentially human.

If we think of action as being caused by external forces, instinct and other uncontrollable inclinations, and reasons, then agency is only possible if the sole controllable factor, reasons, is to some degree autonomously caused. To the degree that our reasons are caused by, once more, external circumstances and internal predispositions, they cannot be autonomously determined. Hence we must think of reasons as being caused somehow and to some degree by other reasons, so that autonomous behaviour must ultimately have its source in basic reasons. If at least part of these basic reasons are not full reasons but reasons of a more wavering kind, our agency will be erratic and unaccountable, even and especially to ourselves. In that case it would be a practical joke to ascribe agency, autonomy or rationality to man. If there were no basic reasons at all, the reasons we do have would show a cyclical character: we would believe in *A* because of *B*, in *B* because of *C*, in *C* because of *D*, and in *D* because of *A*. In this case, our actions may not be erratic, but they are still ultimately inexplicable and uncontrolled. If, finally, we do not think of reasons in causal terms, all reasons will be equal, none would be stronger or weaker than any other, and the same problem of unaccountability would recur, only on a larger scale. Our actions would now be fully unaccountable, and agency, autonomy and rationality would be altogether meaningless. In the words of Joseph Raz, 'The ideal of autonomy, if you like, makes a virtue out of necessity' (Raz 1986: 390).

This, I think, establishes the indispensable role of full reasons as part of man's rational nature – if we use an essentialist vocabulary. To establish the same from a non-essentialistic perspective, we need only change the wording a bit. Instead of being part of our nature, we must now think of full reasons as part of our self-image, part of what we would like our nature to be if we had one. We do not have one – in this view – but we still need to imagine one, similar to what in the essentialistic view is called a second nature. Not having anything like an essence, we enter life and the world naked, stripped of everything but blood, skin, nerves and brains, an undetermined near-abstract entity. Without rules and reasons we cannot in any way be autonomous (self-ruling), let alone rational. There is no option but to re-create oneself, or create *a* self, and become a concrete being. If we do this perfectly, we will in the end find in ourselves rules and reasons, basic reasons, and full reasons. Identifying the process that brings this re-creation about is not important right now. It may be a social or solipsistic process, a combination of both, or it may have any other source. What counts is that there must be *some* kind of self-creation entailing the formulation of rules, values and reasons.

Whether humans have a nature or imagine or create one is therefore of no consequence. The heart and soul of the argument remains unaffected: the capacity for developing full reasons is inherently part of what defines a person as a potentially free and rational being; their actual occurrence makes a being genuinely free, rational – and morally responsible.

If there is any decisive argument for believing in the moral relevancy of full reasons and, provided that the rest of the justification procedure is found reliable, for adhering to principles of justice derived from that idea – it must be one along the lines just sketched. To summarize Timmons's lucid catalogue of views on ethical foundationalism (Timmons 1987: 602): even if fundamental ethical propositions do not need justification, a more reasoned defence than an appeal to intuition will not harm; if, on the other hand, they do need a defence, an appeal to a theory of the person will not harm either (after all, ethics is supposed to affect persons); and if that theory could also be one about the person's necessary rather than contingent features, we would come as near to an ultimate proof as imaginable.

Let me finish this section – as promised in the beginning – with a few special reasons for liberals to accept the postponement of judgement on full reasons (i.e. our version of objective neutrality) as a basis for impartiality. Earlier, in Chapter 2, I described seven ideals that were typically reflected in the thin theories of the good at the heart of liberal theories of justice. For liberals, the charm of this new conception of objective neutrality lies in its compatibility with these seven ideals.

We have already seen above that full reasons and subjective neutrality were quite compatible – indeed, that the first was vitally important for the existence of the other. It is, secondly, easy to see that postponing judgements on full reasons is compatible with the ideal of rationality in the sense given to the word in Chapter 3, that of the attempt to give good reasons for behaviour and principles. Objective neutrality exempts no act, no argument, and no reason from analysis – with an exception only for the most basic, irreducible and irrefutable reasons. In accounting for ideas and actions, we cannot go any further or deeper than full reasons; they are ultimate arguments. Postponing judgement on full reasons may also be compatible with fairness (the willing acceptance of rules for the equal treatment of equal cases); we have at least discussed some arguments for the 'willing acceptance' part. However, it is as yet impossible to say whether an impartial justification procedure based on full reasons will be valid with regard to the equal treatment of equal cases. The same can be said with regard to a fourth liberal ideal, the demand that each be given his due. As long as we have not indicated what the grounds of desert are, or how a relevant difference between cases can be discovered – we simply do not have any argument pro or con objective impartiality.

Probably the most persuasive arguments, as far as liberals are concerned, can be found in the correspondence between objective neutrality and the classic liberal ideals of liberty, equality and fraternity.

Objective neutrality satisfies the demand for liberty in a much broader sense than not being hindered in the pursuit of whatever one wants to do. There is an important element of negative freedom in it, freedom from interference. Being obliged to postpone judgement on the most fundamental and sincere convictions a person can have, we may personally think that X is wrong to believe, or a fool for believing, what X believes – but no creature or institution can be given the authority to correct X's error. But next to this, objective neutrality incorporates the aspect of freedom that Sir Isaiah Berlin once passionately described as follows:

> I wish my life and decisions to depend upon myself, not on external forces of whatever kind. I wish to be the instrument of my own, not of other men's, acts of will. I wish to be a subject, not an object; to be moved by reasons, by conscious purposes, which are my own, not by causes which affect me, as it were, from outside. I wish to be somebody, not nobody; a doer – deciding, not being decided for, self-directed and not acted upon by external nature or by other men as if I were a thing, or an animal, or a slave incapable of playing a human role, that is, of conceiving goals and policies of my own and realizing them. (Berlin 1969: 131)[30]

Positive freedom, the freedom of which Berlin spoke and to which Kymlicka refers as 'living one's life from inside' (Kymlicka 1995: 80), demands respect for individual autonomy, for the development of individuality. Objective neutrality, with its postponement of judgement on the roots of individuality, expresses this respect at the most fundamental level.

The choice to postpone judgement on full reasons does not imply that critique on less fundamental reasons has become impossible. To judge the latter, we still have standards like rationality, appropriateness or consistency with known facts, as well as methods to incorporate those standards (for instance a modified version of cognitive psychotherapy). Which brings me to the second of liberalism's cardinal virtues: equality.

Objective neutrality as sketched above supports the demand that each person should be considered as being equally worthy of moral consideration. It takes the good of the individual as its background, rather than that of the collective (cf. Galston 1991: 120 ff.), and it does so without judging and discriminating the individual's most sincere convictions. Hence, it avoids Bruce Ackerman's critique on Rawls's concept of a thin theory of the good (see above): truly impartial principles of justice cannot distribute goods, rights and freedoms on the basis of the correspondence between an individual's aspirations and a society's, however thin, theory of the good.

Impartiality based on respect for full reasons commits us to a kind of perfectionism that is still compatible with equality, but not to the more authoritarian kind that measures the claims of people by their moral worth, and their moral worth by the value of their convictions and plans. We may agree with Joseph Raz that an autonomous life 'is valuable only if it is spent in the pursuit of acceptable and valuable projects and relationships' (Raz 1986: 417). Objective neutrality obliges us to accept that we can blame or praise ourselves and others for our or their projects, and that we can criticize their views or our own. In doing so, in helping to perfect lives, we express our respect for the autonomous life. Yet this is as far as we can go. Encouraging autonomy is one thing; actively discriminating between agents is something else. Neither we nor a government can be the *judge* of anyone's conscience. We can doubt and discuss full reasons either indefinitely or until the courage of desperation leaves us. There is no other end imaginable because there simply is no yardstick for the morality of full reasons.

Finally, impartiality as it has been described here supports fraternity, the desire to maintain and reproduce the social bond. Full reasons do not entail claims to ethical truth, let alone to the truth of ethical absolutism, at least not beyond the body and mind of the person believing in them. In this, full reasons are typically liberal: they tell us that we have reached a point where a sensible debate becomes impossible, where, in the words of Rawls, the burdens of reason allow no further polemics, and where only the original principle of liberalism remains: tolerance. Albeit a negative motivation, the awareness that one's deepest convictions will be tolerated is a strong reason to support the instruments of toleration.

On forms and contents

Let me recapitulate once more. I set out to investigate the notion of impartiality because, as indicated in Chapter 3, any attempt to take justice seriously, in particular communitarian justice, must be based on an adequate conception of minimal justice, justice under conditions of impartiality. I then argued that such an adequate understanding required technical, subjective and objective neutrality. Finally, I analyzed the concept of objective neutrality, to find that this demand is best satisfied by (1) a very thin theory of the good, axiomatizing the merit of everyday logic, in combination with (2) the sceptical postponement of judgements on full reasons. Together, these three forms of neutrality constitute the impartial point of view on distributive justice, the archpoint. My next concern will be to give this conception of impartiality a representative look.

Earlier I claimed that justification devices serve a heuristic end, that of wrapping up the ethical propositions demarcating an Archimedean point enough to bridge the gap between justification and legitimation, between being right and being put in the right. In the last twenty-odd years, the justice debate has sired an impressive family of justification devices. Not all of these are equally fit to represent the archpoint. A specific type of contract theory, the single-mind contract pattern, turns out to be most suitable. So as not to waste time, I shall only discuss a few of the more popular but less appropriate justification models, and this only in so far as required to show why they are less appropriate.

Richard Brandt's cognitive psychotherapy, for example, focuses on the rationality of desires. It satisfies our super-thin theory of the good, but falls short in some other respects. First of all, it only operates in the sphere of truth, subsuming morality to rationality. Brandt is convinced that the first question we should ask regarding a person's moral code is: 'What kind of social moral code, if any, would you most tend to support for a society in which you expected to live, if you were fully rational?' (Brandt 1979: 185). This is, to a large extent, a fruitful strategy – as explained in the previous section. It can be used to distinguish hypothetical from basic reasons, or to analyze and criticize both empirically and/ or in terms of rationality. But this is where cognitive psychotherapy stops being useful: it results in the exclusion or transformation of illogical (irrational) reasons, and what remains are 'rational' reasons and their justifying basic moral reasons. There is no certainty that cognitive psychotherapy leaves us with one and no more than one moral code. In other words, it is inconclusive. Even if cognitive psychotherapy would result in the choice of (only) one moral code, we would have no reason to assume that this one code was impartial. Cognitive psycho-therapy demands that even full reasons be subjected to criticism – which is in itself a quite legitimate demand. Now any set of full reasons can be internally inconsistent: justice and mercy, mercy and prudence, or prudence and honesty, may at times conflict with one another. If we were true to Brandt's rationalistic intentions, we would have to 'purify' our full reasons until they formed a consist-ent system. If luck were on our side, we might in the end all share the same system of ultimate reasons and desires, the same moral code, the same theory of justice. However, such a code would no longer be *our* code; it would be one for people with whom someone had been meddling. Now, notwithstanding other possible good reasons in favour of accommodating basic motives in *specific* (e.g. psychiatric) cases, this is not a good idea where an impartial theory of justice is at stake – for at least two reasons.

Any theory of justice that answers to the adjusted full reasons of people is no longer an answer to their original desires and convictions; it is a supply-side solution, based on changing the parameters of the problem, rather than a solution to the original problem. Desires or at least basic desires cannot be criticized without a sound theory of rational and good desires (Daniels 1985: 127). But there is no defensible way of criticizing full reasons, nor consequently one of correcting or calibrating them, not even on grounds of internal inconsistency, for the simple reason that there is no higher moral point of view from which to judge full reasons. There is, in particular, no higher judge able to determine whether rationality should overrule (other) full reasons because doing so would require a (rational) defence of rationality itself, which, as we also saw before, is quite infeasible. Finally, it is hard to see how coercive interference with some-one's basic motives, the core of his or her personality, can be harmonized with the basic respect due to persons and with the condition of subjective neutrality.

A second justification device, Robert Nozick's (1974) invisible hand explana-tion of the minimal state, is based on the axiom that there are natural rights (rather than natural might) and that these rights are inviolable. If we support this axiom, the model makes sense. But we cannot. Nozick somehow turns nature, an *is*, into nature, an *ought*, and subsequently into justice, another *ought*. An impartial theory of justice cannot take sides on such issues as whether (let alone which) natural rights exist, whether any fact can in any way result in any norm, or what the metaphysical qualities are that apparently make nature so exception-ally fit for service in ethics. All it can do is make archpointers *recognize* rights. The fact that such recognized rights can coincide with natural rights is irrelevant.

Yet the invisible hand is nothing more than a black (or rather translucent) contraption changing input into output. We could fill it with a substance other than natural rights – say, objective neutrality. Instead of primitive libertarians who, fighting over their own and other persons' rights, one day wake up to find themselves in a minimal state, we could try to imagine primitive impartialists who, in the process of executing their own and respecting other people's full reasons, create a minimally just society. There is, I think, only one objection to using Nozick's contraption in this way: it could turn the whole justification procedure into determinism of a rather crude sort. Whatever the results of an invisible hand process be, they will come about despite rather than because of voluntary actions aimed at those results. The results of individual actions may follow logically and rationally from anything that precedes them, but they need not be what we want. At best, the description of an invisible hand guiding the actions of impartialists will convince us – or the impartialists – that the output *had* to be the way it is, not that it is what it *should* be. In short, the invisible hand procedure lacks a property that is essential for any justification procedure: it leaves no room for the creation of consent. (I shall say more about the import-ance of consent for justification in a moment.)

A third model, highly popular especially among utilitarians, is that of the ideal observer, an imaginary person or perhaps computer capable of seeing the whole world and taking in all available or relevant information, including that which behaviourists cannot see: our true convictions and desires. As this god-like figure has no ideas or emotions of its own, only a purely rational brain, it can be trusted to give an impartial solution for any moral problem with which we challenge it. Or so the story goes. For our purposes, we could inform this creature that it is to follow the rules of the game as we see them, in particular, that it is to post-pone its judgement on full reasons.

Again, we have to reject a model. The ideal observer, despite its divinity, lacks two characteristics that are highly desirable in justification procedures: participa-tion and consent. It is one of the virtues of the invisible hand procedure that it at least allows for participation instead of the ideal observer's sublime deliberation, and as we shall soon find out, the advantages of contract and bargaining theories are that they have, respectively can have, both traits. Now participation is a psychological feature. For a justification procedure to be effective, it seems to be more important that one can voluntarily affirm the principles of justice it gener-ates than that one actually contributes, or can imagine oneself as contributing, to the formulation of those principles. To use an analogy, if we can trust our lawyer there is no need to defend ourselves in court. For the moment then, I shall neglect this trait.

Consent is a more serious problem. The standard objection to an ideal observer's judgement on justice is that there are no independent reasons for me to act in accordance with its decrees, *unless* it has been made clear that its judgement is based on ethical premises to which I already subscribe. Only then can I consent to the ideal observer's decisions. In this view, the ideal observer device becomes a kind of contract theory, that is a contract between the observer and me – though unlike an ordinary contract, this one establishes little more than a common understanding. Contract theories themselves, on the other hand, do not necessarily need the fiction of a contract: the unanimous decision in Rawls's original position, it has been argued, could very well have been taken by one and only one person behind a veil of ignorance, as Rawls's model leaves no room for disagreement on either moral or empirical premises. What Rawls's contract theory really needs, what in fact every contract theory and every impartial observer needs, is consent. In the case of Rawls's theory of justice, consent is guaranteed by the reader's considered judgements in reflective equilibrium on what it is reasonable to require from an original position (cf. Rawls 1995: 140). Thus it seems that this model is uneconomical. If an ideal observer's judgement is to be convincing, we must be certain – in advance – that its point of view will be one we share. However, we will want our observer to be impartial, and once we have ensured that it is, we find that we no longer need it. The reason for this is simply that there is something else we need even more, a necessary ingredient of justification, namely consent. We need *real* people in the *real* world to take the impartial point of view and agree on principles of justice.

I shall call the fourth justification device, a bit inappropriately, the bargaining theory model. Bargaining theories, of which David Gauthier's social choice version (1986), James Buchanan's game theory version (1975), and Ronald Dworkin's auction scheme (1981) are the most widely known examples, should be well distinguished from formal political theory as such, or the application of the rational choice apparatus to questions of political philosophy. The latter is nothing more (and certainly nothing less) than a set of new ways or formats, as their wielders would say, that allow us to test the purely formal consistency and coherence of political theories and principles. Formal political theory is simply ordinary political theory, translated into symbols and subjected to the insurpassable scrutiny of mathematics and logic. A classic example of pure formal analysis is Amartya Sen's liberal or libertarian paradox (Sen 1970: 87–8), which suggests that it is impossible for a society to combine an unlimited political agenda and Pareto-optimality with unrestricted respect for individual liberty.

A bargaining theory – the name is a *pars pro toto* label – is a representation of the problems that are involved in social co-operation and distribution. Without committing myself to any specific rational choice format, I suggest that we think of a bargaining theory as, for instance and for the moment, a complicated process of negotiations about claims to a co-operative surplus. We start by presupposing the existence of two persons x and y who, purely on their own, would be able to produce amounts a and b of useful goods. Co-operating, they would be able to produce more: $a + b + c$. A bargaining theory then looks at possible answers to the question how c should be distributed, one of which could be 'rational'. In our example, a 50:50 division seems intuitively rational, but once we have more information our criteria for an equilibrium and hence our answer may change. Suppose, for instance, that y can force x to work for y without any repercussion. If y were a complete egoist, the rational division from y's point of view would be 0:100. If x can survive on less than a, y could even seize part of x's original production. Or suppose that c can only be produced if x brings in his 500 resources and y her 1,000; the rational proportions can now arguably be set at 33:66. Obviously, the model can be refined by introducing n persons, more resources and other bargaining advantages, a variable co-operation surplus – or, of course, by giving more adequate information about the individuals' preferences and about (e.g. moral) co-operation rules.

Now there is a difference between what bargaining theories – as rational choice theories – can do in principle, and what bargaining theorists actually did. Formal theory assesses the validity of propositions. It can only presume, not decide on, the truth of basic moral propositions or the morality of preferences. Hence, it can establish the logical possibility or impossibility of theories. The claims of bargaining theorists have gone far beyond such modest (im)possibility results; they have claimed truth, or at least *direct* relevance, for the real world when showing that justice is possible if certain (only at first sight innocent) conditions are met. Unfortunately, precisely these conditions are the reason why bargaining theories have – so far – failed to convince. Of course, this is not an a priori reason for rejecting a formal approach to justice. We would have no reason at all to mistrust an impartial bargaining theory, a theory predicated on the conditions of subjective, objective and technical neutrality as described in the last section. But if we try to develop such a theory, we soon find that we need more 'innocent' conditions than we can allow – if we are to remain impartial. Consequently, this model cannot be used to represent impartiality.

Some of the problems involved in adapting the bargaining structure to impartiality are merely technical; they do not constitute fundamental objections to our attempt. For instance, one of the standard assumptions in bargaining theories is that the members of a co-operative venture will each want as large a part in the surplus production as possible. In an impartial version of the bargaining device, this assumption would have to be changed to account for the strange preferences genuine persons can have. Consider the Franciscan friar, whose only interests are the possession of a pair of sandals, a habit and something to eat; or consider his seducible brother, whose preferences are the same up to a point where he starts to give in to seduction, whence he becomes an ordinary rational egoist; or consider a caricatural version of the Benedictine friar, who eats and drinks and enjoys all the pleasures of life, never having heard of the law of diminishing marginal utility, till death make him part; or a split personality, who cannot decide for herself where her best interests lie. Another assumption that would need revision concerns the measure for the social product. Usually this is welfare or utility. In an impartial bargaining theory, however, we cannot use such a measure unless we know in advance that it is acting upon full reasons that count, rather than the opportunity to act upon them, or anything else. At this point, we encounter a real obstacle for the application of the bargaining theory device: where do such hidden assumptions come from? For a lot of those assumptions are needed: we must know in advance who, in a real society, can and cannot claim or deserve part of the social (surplus) product; we must know how to measure the social product; we must know what preferences, tastes, desires and arguments are allowed in the negotiating process (that is what are the relevant differences between persons that determine the size of shares); and so on and so forth. These are, without exception, substantial questions of justice, the kind of questions that we wanted to answer – from an impartial point of view. Obviously, a bargaining device can at best represent only that part of the process of formulating principles of justice that comes after the basic principles.

Nevertheless, the bargaining model also has certain advantages, most notably that of being a radically democratic device: the decision on distribution principles is made by the interested parties themselves. For them to be both genuine persons defending their own interests, and impartial judges of claims, they must be schizophrenic. Their position thus equates to that of any reader of Rawls's *A Theory of Justice* or any other theory of liberal social justice, who is asked to place herself in a position of impartiality and at the same time consider the implications of impartiality for her own life. In this respect, the bargaining device is a sincere reflection of reality.

Of course, there is no reason to suppose that a bargaining theory, enveloped in a more general formal framework explaining the formulation of the theory's assumptions, cannot represent impartiality – on the contrary (cf. Roemer 1996). Such an extended translation of impartiality into symbols would have enormous advantages in terms of precision, making its composition a worthwhile enterprise for any formal theorist. Unfortunately all this may well go at the cost of immense complication.

When we turn to the various types of contract theories, again we find that most versions of the contract cannot represent the archpoint of view. The basic idea of a contract is that a certain group of people, reasonable representatives of the reading public, agree to arrange certain public affairs in certain ways, that they feel the obligation to respect the agreement, and that their adherence to the agreement is stable over a considerable period of time. We will have to be more subtle than that: a contract based on a comfortably vague description like this contains no details about the range and legitimacy of the obligation, nor about the way it embodies the archpoint. The contract might very well be the result of a plebiscite, valid only because, in so far as, and so long as the contracting parties feel the same way about its content – for whatever reason. It derives its validity from the existence of community. A contract like this will only accident-ally duplicate the impartial solution that would be reached at the archpoint of view.

Michael Walzer has taken one step away from the plebiscite by introducing 'shared understandings' as the source of legitimation for a social contract. His solution, however, lacks something we would want a social contract to have, that is stability. Walzer claims that his conception of a constant redefinition of principles and spheres of interaction, by means of which the 'shared understandings in society' are mirrored in the actual structure of society, constitutes a social contract (Walzer 1983: 82–3).[31] Yet it is not a social contract at all, nor is it contractarian enough to warrant representation of the key principles of the archpoint. For example, building a social contract on shared understandings *in society* is a contradiction in terms; the idea of a social contact is to create a society *ex nihilo* rather than reform one that already exists. Unlike the contract as we know it, Walzer's contract is based on perhaps coincidental and certainly for the main part subconscious opinions. Of course, Walzer rejects all talk of justification based on would-be impartial reasons; arguments of that type would lack the necessary force to convince people living in a community and sharing a communitarian social consciousness – but that is exactly what distinguishes a justifying contract theory from a legitimizing consensus. Transporting a term like social contract from one language game (contractarianism) to another (communitarianism) necessarily results in a change of meaning for that term. If we still want to call Walzer's theory a contract theory, we will have to stretch the meaning of the term beyond recognition – and call even Nozick a contractarian. After all, his theory is no less one of agreements guided by an invisible hand.

Additionally, Walzer's contract lacks stability. It is not a foundational contract, merely an agreement to stick to certain rules for the time being, until someone changes his or her mind. Consequently, it is not even a fundamental contract, in the sense that it is based on tacit consent rather than on an explicit agreement acknowledging whatever may be tacitly believed. Not resulting from a conscious act, Walzer's contract does not serve any purpose that is not already served by the community's shared understandings. In sum: any reference by Walzer to a social contract is superfluous in a communitarian, and misplaced in a contractarian, context.

Even if Walzer's doctrine could be called a contract theory, the structure of his contract would still not do for the archpoint. Shared understandings, whatever they may be, are not necessarily full reasons; indiscriminately 'living' those understandings is therefore quite the opposite of objective neutrality, that is postponing judgement on the validity of full reasons without excluding other motives from rational investigation.

We are, then, left with two types of contract theory: the multi-person contract represented by Bruce Ackerman (Ackerman 1980), Thomas Scanlon (Scanlon 1982) and Brian Barry (Barry 1995), and the single-mind contract as introduced by John Rawls (Rawls 1971). The (analytical) difference between the two is obvious: in the first theory, the contract derives its legitimacy from the support it gets from individuals, people as differing from one another as possible, whereas the force of the single-mind contract lies in its being backed by (separate but) equal minds, representative of the rational nature that unites us, rather than the whimsies that divide us.

Of these two, only the single-mind contract turns out to be able to represent impartiality. A multi-person contract like Ackerman's appears to violate objective neutrality. After all, Ackerman explicitly demands that the contracting parties hold any conception of the good to be as good as any other; objective neutrality only asks that all sets of full reasons be treated that way. But this, it seems, is more a peculiarity of Ackerman's than a necessary trait of every multi-person contract. We can easily imagine a contract situation in which differing persons with differing views of life and the good are asked to be less neutral than Ackerman asks, that is to be objectively neutral. Doing so, however, means changing the multi-person contract into a single-mind contract: the terms of the contract no longer depend on what divides us. Here then is a more fundamental argument against multi-person contracts – not just Ackerman's, but Scanlon's and Barry's as well: if, and in so far as, the contingent differences between the contracting parties influence the terms of the contract, it no longer embodies an impartial point of view (cf. Horton 1996). It cannot be just from an *impartial* point of view that a person is beheaded, dismembered or stoned in one country for something he could get away with unharmed in another; nor can it be just that one qualifies for the presidency of a country on the basis of the same *curriculum vitae* that would bring one in front of a war tribunal anywhere else. The idea of impartiality is best served if the contracting parties are forced to stand apart both from the current set of values and theories of the good in a definite society and, consequently, from their particular point of view – including their full reasons. Having taken the sting out of the multi-person contract, there seems to be no reason to hold on to what remains, that is the fiction of separate persons. A quasi-multi-person contract is uneconomical: we do not need all the baroque details of profoundly differing persons with all their private points of view to represent an impartial point of view. It may give a bit of flavour and charm to a contract theory, but we really do not need it. The reader will note that this is an inconclusive and purely cosmetic argument: it concerns the question how we can *best* represent impartiality, not whether a quasi-multi-person contract can represent it at all.

We may also note another point: a contract theory without the fiction of separate persons will look suspiciously like an ideal observer theory. It has, in fact, been argued against Rawls that his contract is expendable (M. G. Singer 1976: 239; Sandel 1982: 127 ff.; cf. Barry 1995: 58 ff.); the original position would lead to exactly the same conclusions if there were only one person in it. A contract, Singer argues, is only a contract when there is some kind of negotiation or bargaining going on, even among equals, and that is not what happens in the original position. The people in that situation are basically clones: they have equal talents in the intellectual and rhetorical field, they have the same psychological make-up, the same non-history, the same rights, duties and possessions (none), the same information, and the same task – so of course they will think alike and come to a unanimous decision. Following Singer's line of thought, the job could have been performed as effectively and more efficiently by the *Weltgeist* in meditation.

There is little reason to see a fundamental challenge to Rawls-like (single-mind) contract theories in Singer's objection – or to ideal observer theories, for that matter. Contract theories, whether single-mind or multi-person, are not designed to get the people *in* a fictitious contract situation to disagree, debate, and agree; they are designed to create a moral obligation in the *real world* towards the agreement reached in a fictitious state of grace. The real contract is one between us or you as readers and the person who gets the royalties for the book, the author of the theory.[32] Together, we agree that the author is right, that justice is what he or she calls justice, and that we should act accordingly. Note that this is precisely the same agreement an ideal observer – another *alter ego* of author and reader – hopes to bring about. Note, furthermore, that this makes a single-mind contract as uneconomical as we found the ideal observer to be: once we have ensured that the contracting parties are impartial clones, we no longer need them.

My reasons for opting for a single-mind contract theory rather than an ideal observer theory are, consequently, by no means substantial. The difference between the two is not a matter of being able or unable to satisfy the conditions of the archpoint, the principles of impartiality. It is a psychological difference: even though a single-mind contract is by definition based on unanimous agreement, even though there is no bargaining of whatever kind, and even though the contracting parties are ideal if not angelic beings, the contract results from participation. It is not a divine decree. Still, as none of us, real persons, partake in their feast of reason, there is good reason to ask why this would matter.

For one thing, participation may make a difference for the legitimacy of the contract. The judgement of one is not *obviously* as legitimate as that of a forum. An adequate picture of the archpoint will be more convincing if it reflects the structure of real-world moral discourse. Nevertheless, the difference remains purely aesthetical: real people can criticize a forum as easily as a single observer.

This argument suggests another reason of a different kind based on a tactical consideration: a forum creates its own support, whereas a dictator creates mistrust. But even if this were generally true – and not just true for the enlightened citizens of modern Western democratic societies – it would be the wrong kind of argument. We want to be convinced by reason, not by self-deception.

The idea of a forum might, furthermore, go some way towards dealing with an at least on the Continent highly influential strand of critique of Western moral philosophy, a critique that is inspired by Emanuel Levinas's work. The forum could, to some extent, overcome the difference between an egocentric and a social ethics. Unfortunately, this argument will not work for a single-mind contract. Levinas has always argued that Western philosophy does not take *l'Autre* seriously, the other human being as fundamentally different, fundamentally incomprehensible, fundamentally uncontrollable; whenever philosophers give guidelines for social action, they are based on conceptions of the other (*l'autre*, lower case 'a') as fundamentally alike to oneself. If there is one thing obvious about the single-mind contract, it is that there are no Others present at the archpoint, only others. There is a pleasant note to this, however: the single-mind contract is in good company. There is no device at all that could ever adequately represent an Other – as every attempt at representation must be an attempt to comprehend and control, and as such must therefore fail. Finally then, only the writer's rhetorical argument (inspired by Kley 1989: 268, 274) remains: identification with the heroes. It is simply *easier*, both for authors and their audience, to imagine a multitude (however detached) as representing all the different groups and interests in society, than it is to imagine this being done by an alien from outer space.

The secret of models representing the arguments for a theory of justice – original position, ideal observer, and so forth – is not in the type-casting but in the inescapable logic of the roles (cf. Kley 1989: 289–94 and Rawls 1995: 140). An adequate justification device must satisfy a principle Voltaire once formulated: if the devil were to take God's place, he would soon discover that he must also behave like God.

5

Impartiality and information

Categories of information

As ordinary human beings, we will probably decide not to jump into a deep hole in the side of a mountain if all the information we have is that it looks like a volcano, shakes like a volcano and makes rude noises like a volcano. We may decide otherwise if we know that the smoke and sounds are fake, that there is a safety net and no chance of missing it, and that we will be rewarded generously for jumping. Information, then, is a key factor in making choices.

In the process of developing an impartial theory of justice, it is sometimes better *not* to know certain things; for this reason, Iustitia wears a blindfold. Knowledge of the facts that you have a talent for making the right choices on the stock market and that you deeply enjoy wealth may prejudice you in favour of a free market society with profound differences between rich and poor – unless, of course, you are capable of overcoming prejudice, have no opportunity or incentive to be ruled by prejudice, or are temporarily freed from it. On the other hand, contracting parties must know other things – for one, they must know why they have gathered together at all.

More systematically, the issue looks as follows. In contract theories of justice, seven categories of information can be distinguished. Each of these categories represents a necessary condition for a decision, none of them can be omitted and no other types of information are required. An adequate contract theory of justice must account for the assumptions it makes about each of these seven types of knowledge; an impartial theory will have to do so in terms of impartiality. If we would discard the idea of a contract as a fiction, a vehicle for the imagination, we would still have to explain what kinds and amounts of knowledge are required for an impartial choice of principles of justice. Although there would no longer be contracting parties, we would still want the reader to be able to imagine herself as an impartial being.

Two of the seven categories are necessitated by the fictitious character of a contract theory. The parties designing a contract do not have to be the same parties as those who will have to live under the terms of the contract. In the first respect, the contracting parties are judges or arbiters; in the latter, they are subjects or recipients. The so-called archpoint of view, the set of criteria for the impartiality of a theory of justice formulated in the previous chapter, puts severe restrictions on two aspects of our conception of parties contracting for justice: their knowledge about their characters and about the place they might have in a particular society should not hinder them from being impartial. A contract theory must account for these two constituents; if they were not specified we would have no reason to trust the impartiality of the judgement of our contracting parties – whom, by the way, we shall from now on call archpointers.

Two further constituents run parallel to the factors we just introduced: knowledge about the human self and about the particular society for which a contract is designed. There are two trivial and partly familiar reasons why these categories are indispensable. First, we will want to make sure that whatever the archpointers know cannot hinder their impartiality. Secondly, we cannot imagine archpointers deciding on anything if they do not know that there is anything to decide on, let alone what. What we are interested in is social justice, that is justice for individual entities living in a society. The archpointers should at least be acquainted with the notion of society and its constituent parts. They do not necessarily need to know everything there is to know about either subject – as long as we make sure that they know enough.

The three remaining categories of knowledge are all in a sense end-oriented. To decide on justice, on what should be, archpointers must know more than simply *what is*; they cannot work without information about the possible, either possible facts (from a teleological perspective), or possible dispositions (from a deontological perspective) or both. In the Rawlsian vocabulary, this constituent is known as the category of general (social) scientific knowledge. Next, information is useless without a guiding question. In designing a contract situation, we must also account for the simplest of its constituents: the task posed on the archpointers. Are they to design a theory of justice, the institutions of a state, a criminal system, or a raft? Finally, all these types of information must be mediated in order to produce some kind of output, that is principles of social justice. We will want such mediating decision rules to be assuredly impartial. In the following section I shall discuss real-world information, that is, the knowledge archpointers must have about the human self and about the society or societies for which they are to develop a conception of justice, and the general scientific knowledge available about both. As it turns out, the problem with these three constituents is less to decide how much information can be allowed without endangering impartiality than of how to control the flow of data. Provided the parties establishing principles of justice are archpointers, that is provided they see things from an impartial point of view, only the absence of data can prejudice them. Hence, rather than being barred from real-world information, archpointers must have unrestricted access to all possible data. It is up to them to decide, in second instance, what types of information are relevant and what are not. Only at this point can we put restrictions on the contracting parties' knowledge.

The third section, where the character and social background of the archpointers are discussed, delineates how the contracting parties can be impartial. Obviously, this is an area in which restrictions on knowledge *are* relevant – and also one in which restrictions can endanger the credibility of a contract. It has been argued, notably by Michael Walzer (Walzer 1988: 33), that the less the archpointers' point of view becomes ours, the more reason we have to suspect that their judgements are (too) uninformed. To really understand the sense of justice of a genuine society, one would have to be part of it and judge it from the point of view of its members. I shall argue instead that the omission of a social conscious-ness and of information about one's background will not make the archpointers's decisions uninformed. Archpointers can have any amount of information about particular cultures and specific points of view, they can even be allowed to 'experience' these points of view – as long as the information they have does not give them an *interest* in the choice for one possible conception of justice rather than another. For this last reason, archpointers will essentially have to remain what they are in Rawls's theory: amnesiacs, as far as the relevant aspects of their own identity is concerned.

Finally, the fourth section addresses the remaining types of information: in-formation on the task of the contracting parties and on mediating decision rules. The themes discussed in this section are mainly technical; they concern (1) the so-called formal constraints of justice, that is criteria for the form that an impartial conception of justice should have, and (2) the order in which the different conditions of impartiality should be satisfied.

Knowing the self, society and possibility

First things first: in this section I shall often use terms like 'human' and 'human self' and I shall only refer to humans as recipients of distributive justice. This may seem to indicate the existence on my part of a prejudice against extraterrestrials, animals or other imaginable recipients. The reasons for not (yet) discussing justice towards non-humans are, however, lack of knowledge rather than lack of imagina-tion. The term justice is applied to intentions, acts and results. Not knowing any other self-conscious and self-governing beings like extraterrestrials, we can for now assume that only a human being or a group of humans can *want* to be (un)just, can *act* (un)justly and can *create* just or unjust institutions and circumstances. Animals do not seem to qualify on these points. In a theory of social justice, the only role an animal can play is that of a recipient, a being to which the distributors or the designers of the distribution scheme *owe* something.[33] However, at this point in the development of our theory we cannot yet distribute membership cards, that is we cannot yet determine if and to what degree animals are recipients of social justice. I shall for now simply assume that social justice is an intra-human, intra-social affair only and patch up any holes that may be left later on in Part III of this book.

There is, it seems, no reason not to brief the archpointers on everything there is to know about humans and their societies. The archpointers, we assume, are detached enough to deal with this information without bias, strategic behaviour or premature judgement. What is more, the archpointers would by definition be biased if we withheld any relevant information. Being, unlike the archpointers, ordinary human beings with a subjective point of view, we cannot ourselves decide when information is relevant and when it will be superfluous. Hence, we have a *prima facie* case for full access to all sorts of information – and for not further specifying the contents of this information.

Nevertheless, we cannot escape the question of the relevancy of information that easily. The data archpointers have about the human self, about society and about science is necessarily of *our* making – or, more precisely, they are what the author through his assumptions decides that they are. It is, then, better to be explicit about these assumptions and determine what we must assume that archpointers should *minimally* know: where the border lies between the knowledge that is necessary and sufficient for their impartiality, and additional information that will not or should not alter their judgement.

Let us start with the issue of knowledge on the human self and pose the fundamental question whether knowledge of human nature or the human condition is relevant at all. Now it has been argued by – among many others – Hume, Rawls and to some extent Barry that the need for principles of justice arises because of certain human characteristics (the so-called subjective circumstances of justice) and certain traits of society (the objective circumstances). I intend to treat these circumstances in a somewhat different order and, to bring some consistency in our vocabulary, I shall refer to them as subjective and objective *conditions* of social justice. I shall be concerned with the subjective conditions, circumstances of individuals rather than societies, first: moderate self-interest or, in Rawls's theory, mutual disinterest, and rough equality of power (Barry 1989: 154 ff., 182 ff.). Justice, it is supposed, would be an impossibility and the question of justice would never arise, if humans were slightly egoistical but not approximately equally powerful. In the latter case, a war of all against all would follow in which the strong would win and the weak lose. Justice would also be out of demand if we were not a bit egoistical or at least a bit disinterested in the wellbeing of others. With too much egoism, the question of fair behaviour would never rise – let alone that anyone would want to live up to the possible answer. In a world of altruists on the other hand, a conception of justice would be superfluous. No-one would bother about fair shares: any sign of need or desire would immediately be recognized as valid and, if possible, answered.

These two conditions do indeed necessitate the question of justice, although their exact wording requires some revision. In the first place, as a primitive (i.e.

irreducible) motive, selfishness or its alternatives will not do. Neither selfishness, moderate or boundless, nor mutual disinterest are indisputable and omnipresent facts of life, and neither one necessarily gives rise to questions of justice. As such, selfishness is a most unsophisticated notion, perhaps able to reduce all human behaviour to an ultimate cause but certainly unable to explain any particular act. Taking a cup of coffee can be interpreted as selfish behaviour, raising a child can be understood in similar terms, as can giving presents, sharing feelings, having sex or dying for whatever cause. But why drink vodka at this moment rather than later or not, if these are all selfish acts? Why die for your country if desertion seems more healthy?

To understand human behaviour, motives other than pure selfishness have to be introduced. We can then characterize humans, with Hume, as only *moderately* self-interested or, with Rawls, as neither egoists nor altruists but simply mutually *dis*interested. But if we do so, we soon discover that the need for justice does not arise merely because of the way we think about ourselves as compared to others. The new motives, motives other than our self-image, can as easily incite problems of just behaviour or distribution.

If, for instance, the justice problem arises when Harry Stottle and Cissy Roo, two more or less selfish persons, fight over a penny, the problem will not go away if we turn them into, for example, other-regarding altruists. The single difference this makes is that we reverse their preferences: Harry now has Cissy's best interests in mind and Cissy Harry's. In a world of altruists, the problem of just distribution and fair shares *still* arises, though in a different form; it would not be a matter of keeping people from fighting over shares, but one of getting them to accept any. Of course, we can imagine circumstances in which Harry's and Cissy's self-images would not necessarily lead them to pose questions about justice: we could attribute Harry with perfect egoism and Cissy with perfect altruism or vice versa. But – and this is an argument that we shall encounter on several later occasions – there is a crucial difference between the existence of a problem and its being perceived. The fact that no human being perceives a problem does not mean that it does not exist; we do not directly perceive gamma radiation either. Perhaps one can maintain that, in real life, the question of justice surfaces because and in so far as we are, in whatever sense, self-interested; nevertheless, the problem also exists where and in so far as we have another self-image.

If there is an indisputable and omnipresent fact of life about human motivation at all, it is not that all these reasons for fighting can somehow be brought together under the heading of self-interest or mutual disinterest. It is not selves fighting for themselves that gives rise to questions of justice; they can also fight for others or, as a matter of principle, for an idea rather than a person. The question of justice then arises everywhere where separate beings fight about diverse desires. What matters is the separateness of humans and the diversity of their reasons for acting in itself – a condition that Rawls, by the way, mentions in relation to moderate scarcity (Rawls 1971: 127). I shall call this the first subjective condition of social justice: the presence of separate persons with distinct reasons for acting.

Albert: So we agree that there should be freedom of religion in a just society. We have no way of deciding on the right religion, no way to justify imposing any particular religion, and every reason to fear the effects of imposing a religion.

Marilyn: Hold it. I agree with the principle but not with the arguments. God is not a hypothesis I need – in fact, I think religious people are mildly insane and latent mass murderers. History proves it. There's no arguing with them – no amount of absence of proof or impossibility of proof can give them a reason even to doubt their beliefs in God or gods or that the moon is made of Swiss cheese. Freedom of religion, OK – but only because you can't argue with the faithful.

A: Wow! You've got a temper! But apart from that, what's the difference?

M: The difference is that in your interpretation any faith can be questioned but faith itself is not considered irrational, whereas in mine even that can be questioned. The difference is that I would allow true freedom of religion – even the freedom to be free of religion.

A: Whatever. As long as we agree on the principle.

M: But we don't. Your reasons aren't mine, therefore your acts won't necessarily be mine. I can imagine myself being a religious person, and I would want our rulers to be forced to be the same, but you haven't bothered to imagine yourself the way I am, and I wouldn't want our rulers to be like that.

A: You're moving too fast – we haven't reached the point yet where we being able to stand in other people's shoes becomes a source of justification. Let's discuss other freedoms first. How about freedom of sports?

M: Same story. You're wasting time.

Reasons for acting and principles for acting

A second subjective condition of justice proposed by Hume and the Humeans, an approximately equal distribution of power among humans, is at least equally disputable. The theory connecting rough equality to justice is simple enough: if Harry Stottle and Cissy Roo are roughly equally powerful and they fight about a scarce resource, say a penny, neither of them can win or the costs of winning will more than outweigh the benefits. If Harry and Cissy have friends and relatives, they could form coalitions and raise their dispute to a higher level – without ever really winning. Rawls writes that the members of coalitions 'are vulnerable to attack, and all are subject to having their plans blocked by the united force of others' (Rawls 1971: 127). The rational solution to this dilemma is to co-operate, to agree on certain principles of distributive justice and act accordingly. Thus, the discovery that we are all approximately equally powerful would make justice an issue. However, rough equality of power is not a necessary trait of humans, nor is it the only way in which power can give rise to questions of justice. It is therefore not the best choice for a subjective condition of justice.

It should be noted that the idea of rough equality of power is not very helpful in explaining the existence of questions of justice. Rough equality means that there are slight inequalities – which is, in itself, a plausible thesis. Whether rough equality will lead to the consideration of justice as a solution for a distribution problem depends on circumstances. One of these is the individuals' estimates of the relative costs and benefits, over a longer period of time, of negotiations, limited warfare and adherence to a principle of justice. Evidently, these estimates may differ enough to exclude the justice talk option. But consider also the sense in which real individuals can be near-equals in power: one is smarter than another, who is stronger, and a third is neither strong nor smart but has a talent for making friends with people in high places – and somehow their potentials would have to even out. Thus, the question whether they are roughly equals in the real world does not depend on their potential only, but also on the structure of society – which is seldom fair to all. For rough equality to lead to questions of justice, we must then presuppose the existence of circumstances in which powers more or less even out. Clearly they do not between each individual at every moment in every society, so we must see things in a broader perspective. Things only get worse if we think of rough equality as equality between coalitions or equality between societies. Some coalitions, for example, are more vulnerable than others. The aspiration to prove the existence of equality of power between coalitions will inevitably lead to absurd conclusions: to save this notion, its scope must be widened over time and space – endlessly, so as to make sure that in the end all powers even out, that all winners will also have been losers and all losers winners. Which would make rough equality of power a tautology.

Further, it is cynical to suggest that the question of justice arises only in circumstances of approximate equality of power, when bargaining is preferred to fighting – as if the truly powerless are voiceless. True enough, being a potential loser in the fight between rough equals, maybe everyone has a reason for demanding justice. As Brian Barry once said in another context, the exploited and suppressed demand equality and justice rather than a change of places with the powerful (Barry 1965: 282); perhaps the almost exploited have a similar sense of justice. However, those who stand to win – and in circumstances of rough inequality, everyone has that chance – have quite different motives for opening negotiations. Under circumstances, the slightest inequality in power can be and often has been exploited to rob, rape, torture and subject others. If potential winners start to negotiate, their reasons will have little to do with justice, morality or kindness, but more with efficiency and greed. For them, agreeing to reasonable distribution principles may simply be a better bargain than open warfare.

Now if the question of justice arose only under circumstances of rough equality, it would be an issue introduced by the bargaining parties in their quality as potential losers; as potential winners, they must be interested in quite other things.

> **Albert:** Back to atheism. Yours is really a minority opinion, isn't it?
> **Marilyn:** Depends on where you're living, depends on class, education, culture, many things.
> **A:** But listen: if you're a minority, on a world scale, why should the majority care?
> **M:** First of all, any coalition can be countered. Remember the Pilgrim Fathers – they simply set up shop elsewhere; it's a game you can keep up for a long time. This whole minority, majority, equality, inequality of power talk, I don't really understand it. And apart from that, might still doesn't make right.

Rough equality of power

By the same logic, if the distribution of power were a little more unequal, justice would not be an issue – the winners, if rational, would simply exploit their advantage and take what they want. In other words, the implication seems to be that questions of justice are out of place where people are plainly unequal with respect to their power. Again, the fact that no human being perceives a problem – in this case, the fact that no greedy self-regarding rational winner is willing to listen to the losers' grievances – will not make the problem disappear.

In the political part of the real world, approximate equality of power does in fact have something to do with justice. It can be an incentive both to raise questions of justice and to support the answers, but it is not a necessary condition. In more unequal circumstances, constraints on the use of power such as a sense of morality or the unlimited use of absolute power by a benevolent dictator can do either job just as effectively.

In another part of the real world, the world of morality, I suggest that we look at the connection between justice and power in a different, more lenient way, one that better expresses the moral significance of the conviction – especially Rawls's – that justice can arise only out of a confrontation of free and equal beings (Rawls 1971: 12). Despite their different endowments, humans are in a sense equal regarding power, namely by nature: they are equal in having, storing and on occasion using, power in whatever form or amount. I call this the second subjective condition of social justice.

Apart from one additional premise concerning motivation, these two conditions are practically all the archpointers need to know about the human self. It may seem plausible, however, to include two other conditions, earlier included in the conditions of the archpoint: weak rationality and the existence of full reasons. The advantages would be twofold: it would give manageable proportions to the flow of information with which the archpointers have to deal, and it would limit the information to what is relevant from an impartial point of view. However, neither one is a necessary subjective condition of justice, that is a trait of human nature that necessitates justice. The need for justice and compliance to principles of justice can conceivably originate in reasons other than full reasons or under conditions other than the desire to be weakly rational. Moreover, the desire for justice can be a full reason, but not all full reasons are desires for justice; not every human being may have a deep and sincere desire for justice. Weak rationality is only a mediator between propositions, not a proposition or fact or reason by itself. Finally, neither full reasons nor weak rationality are by definition constitutive of the human self; the *capacity* for either one is.

The one additional premise that we need explains how reasons, persons and power are connected to justice. For questions of justice to arise, it is not enough to presume the existence of separate persons with certain kinds and quantities of power to act upon their distinct reasons. Once the interests of these persons collide, there are two options, not one: voice, that is an appeal to justice, and exit.[34] In the example given before, where Harry and Cissy both want the scarce resource of £0.01, they could start to reason with one another – or they could decide to forego the penny and escape the troubles of dialogue. To explain this choice, we need a theory of motivation. I shall discuss two such explanations and reject both in favour of a more down-to-earth approach.

For a long time, one of the basic suppositions of mainstream philosophy has been that humans, or in fact all components of the universe, have an innate desire to persist in their existence. In Spinoza's metaphysics, for example, this desire defines the individual entity's essence; Spinoza called it the *conatus perseverandi*. In views like these, anything that serves the goal of perpetuating existence must necessarily be the object of desire; under the conditions of justice, that object would be the object of negotiation. Although a persuasive basis for self-interest theories, the desire for continued existence is quite incapable of dealing with antithetic desires, desires that are as common in real life as they are inexplicable from this metaphysical perspective: suicide, paying taxes where free-riding would go unnoticed and so forth. (Clearly, I am assuming that money and death can be resources.)

A second tradition is, in a loose interpretation of the word, hedonistic: it understands action as motivated by a desire to enjoy life, affirm one's existence, realize one's nature or potentials and so forth. Rawls's Aristotelian principle, attributing man with a desire to make the best of his capacities (Rawls 1971: 426), is a good example. In this perspective, the evolution of a need for principles of justice is understood in terms of means and ends: resources furthering self-realization are worth the effort of fighting for – or reasoning about, if the conditions of justice obtain. Like self-perpetuation, the hedonistic approach has its imperfections, one of them being its restriction to purely hedonistic ends. In a hedonistic perspective, actions like suicide, having children or caring for future persons or generations, are or can easily be incomprehensible.[35]

These examples should suffice: even if we momentarily forget our earlier objections to metaphysical theories, metaphysics are still inefficient. 'Deep' theories of the human self like these two tend to be incapable of explaining quite common but by their own standards perverse acts and reasons for acting. On the other hand, any attempt to broaden the scope of concepts like self-perpetuation or hedonism to include deviant behaviour is bound to end in explanations with the same (lack of) subtlety and sophistication that characterize the concept of selfishness.

Instead of designing a new and better metaphysics of the self, I suggest we let Ockham's razor do its work. As long as we do not try to explain *why* exactly people have the reasons they have and why those reasons are as strong as they are, we can avoid the extremes of under- and over-explaining. After all, there is no reason, other than pure curiosity, why we should want to know all this or, specifically, why archpointers should have to know. What matters here is the existence of reasons, not their history. The essential point for us and for archpointers is simply that people sometimes *have* reasons strong enough to hold on to, that they have goals, ends and desires that they consider worth pursuing: 'they are the interests of a self that regards its conception of the good as worthy of recognition and that advances claims in its behalf as deserving satisfaction' (Rawls 1971: 127). Hence I propose, as a third subjective condition of social justice, the presence of a profound identification of persons with their reasons for acting.

These three conditions are all an archpointer needs to know about the human self – *needs* to know, as other information can, but need not, be given. There is, in particular, no need to inform (or not to inform) archpointers about the sets of full reasons to which real persons in a genuine society adhere. By definition of the archpoint, they already know that principles of justice that are based on the actual distribution of full reasons in a given society may generate a bias against persons, societies and especially sets of full reasons that do not yet exist.

As an illustration of this claim: suppose that we live in a society without beggars or anyone else to whom we can show benevolence, as there is no-one to show it to. In fact, no-one can even remember ever having heard of someone deserving benevolence. In this society, benevolence will not be a reason for action, let alone that it ever crossed anyone's mind to turn it into a full reason. A social system based on these data can, however, easily turn out to be prejudiced against benevolence. Suppose there is an action X that can only be performed as an act of benevolence, and that benevolence can only be shown by doing X – say, giving small change to a complete stranger without asking or expecting anything in return, in the knowledge that the money will never be returned anyway. Benevolence does not exist in our society, and as an implication of a rule against bribery, anything that looks like X is forbidden. One day, the first beggar ever to be seen in living history turns up on the steps of the cathedral. You, I, Brian Barry, Harry Stottle and Cissy Roo walk by, and the more humane among us are so deeply shocked by what we see that we (re)discover the concept of benevolence on the spot. In due course, we find that benevolence is or becomes a full reason. Benevolence may conflict with another full reason like prudence, it may sometimes even be wiser to let prudence take precedence (Hardin 1990: 101) – but all this does not change the fact that our social system

Albert: We all have reason inside us. We can all be reasonable. We can all *see* what is reasonable. Why the detour? Why imagine some kind of contract theory where everyone's in some way supposed to imagine every mathematically possible person? Isn't that a bit overdone? Can't you take us humans seriously? I tell you *we are reasonable!*

Marilyn: Sure. Don't get exited. But may I point out that we've chosen for a dialogue between impartiality and imperfection? Please take impartiality seriously as well – we need it exactly because we're human, because we've got a limited imagination and need to ensure that we don't forget those we would want to forget, those we don't know, those we don't understand.

A: So?

M: Imagine we weren't the enlightened, omniscient urban Westerners we are, imagine that we lived in other times, other places, and imagine we do as you, or Brian Barry, would have us do: talk until we've written a social contract for real existing people only. We might end up with a very odd interpretation of the differences between sexes; we might get even homosexuals themselves to agree that their behaviour is against nature because we'd all be Aristotelians; we might end up with obligatory monogamy, polytheism or geronticide. Are you sure that enlightened, omniscient urban Westerners will transcend their particular ideologies, language games, paradigms, *Weltanschauungen*, whatever?

Imperfection

forbids us to do X even when, in conscience, we can do no other. The message is clear: principles of social justice had better not depend on too detailed and in that sense too limited information.

The archpointers are, then, left with two options: that of imagining all possible persons, characters and sets of full reasons, and that of leaving the character and full reasons of possible persons undefined. The first option is unpractical, as it demands the archpointers to work with a probably infinite amount of information; unconvincing, as the archpointer should be our *alter ego* rather than an intelligence beyond imagination (cf. Kley 1989: 389); and improbable, as we inform the archpointers, but to my knowledge do not ourselves possess complete information on all possible humans. In practice, this leaves us and the archpointers with the second option.

Once more, it must be stressed that any data we have on the human self, beyond the information expressed by the three subjective conditions of justice, *can* be passed on to the archpointers – provided we actually *do* have such incontrovertible data. From an archpoint of view however, extra information adds no value to an impartial judgement. At best, it allows archpointers to add the example of one particular society to their treatise on justice in any society.

All in all, the archpointers have to deal with a lot of uncertainties. They know that the persons for whom they design principles of justice are separate beings with separate reasons with which they strongly identify, and they know that these beings are endowed with power to act upon their reasons. They also know that persons and their reasons, including full reasons, may be incompatible. Yet they do not necessarily know what these reasons are and what personalities their clients actually have – nor what persons and full reasons could possibly exist. Moreover, they have to allow for the fact that not all actual reasons for acting are full reasons, and that some of their clients may not even have full reasons or may not want to be weakly rational.

So much for the subjective conditions of justice. The objective conditions, the properties of society necessitating justice, are traditionally twofold: the existence of society and of moderate scarcity. Rawls describes the first as the coexistence of many individuals at the same time on a definite geographical territory (Rawls 1971: 126). I shall for now assume that this is an unproblematical clarification of the first objective condition of social justice: that there is a society.

The second condition poses more difficulties. Ever since Hume, and even more so since Rawls, moderate scarcity has been looked upon as the most important if not in some cases the only objective condition of justice. Hume's argument can be summarized very briefly: there is no problem of justice in circumstances of abundance, and there will not be any support for justice (just distribution) if the stock is too small. (Brian Barry describes the last situation very aptly as universal predation (Barry 1989: 156).) Therefore, Hume concludes, the notion of justice is only relevant in between these extremes, where co-operation is mutually advantageous. Rawls adds nothing essential to this extremely positivistic account (Rawls 1971: 127). There is, admittedly, no need to in so far as moderate scarcity is a condition of the *adherence* to principles of justice. Yet in so far as moderate scarcity would be a necessary condition for the *evolution* of the question of justice, it is not clear at all why scarcity should be relevant (cf. also Galston 1980: 109–20).

Moderate scarcity, in Hume's, Rawls's and Barry's opinion, is a mean between too much (or at least enough) and too little, between abundance and absence. But it is not clear at all what defines enough and what abundance. Enough may be enough for one generation and one society, or for all generations and/or all societies. Enough may be enough to satisfy needs, to satisfy wants or to satisfy the demand on a free market. Moderate scarcity obviously cannot be specified any further until it is clear who exactly can claim a part of whatever stock is available, on what grounds these claims are to be made and by whose authority all these specifications are legitimately introduced. Moreover, there may be distributable goods of which there cannot be more than enough, like Mozart for Mozart-lovers or puppies for kids, or bads of which there cannot be too little, like mosquitos or taxes (both being ineradicable). Such goods will be moderately scarce no matter how great or small the stock is, so that the expression loses any power of discrimination. Finally, genuine abundance does not exist. Plenty is ultimately a plague: too many oranges means a heap of viciously smelling rotting garbage, a good that can and usually is distributed as a burden rather than as a benefit.[36]

Similar arguments apply, *mutatis mutandis*, to the lower limit of moderate scarcity, that is absolute scarcity. But let me add one more. Obviously, there are situations of extreme scarcity in which principles of justice will not stand a test of adherence. Imagine real life: famine in Africa. At the moment that a car with food supplies arrives at a refugee camp, the refugees gather around it and do what they cannot help doing: they fight for their survival. Some of them end up with nothing, some of them end up with more than their immediate need requires and occasionally share it with a few of their unlucky companions, others keep their harvest all to themselves. Next morning, five or fifty or five hundred corpses will be buried – the remains of those who might have made it through the night if the law of the jungle had not been followed. Things like this happen, they are understandable, they can often be excused and forgiven, but all that does not make the law of the jungle a just law or the concept of justice inappropriate. No-one ever promised that justice would not at times be demanding. If we exclude an extreme case like this from consideration at the archpoint, we implicitly bow to a dangerous form of conventionalism: we would let interested parties decide when a resource is too scarce to play by the rules.

Even if the term 'moderate' could be sensibly related to scarcity, the latter term itself should be avoided. Scarcity has a materialistic connotation, even or especially when used in a figurative way of speech. Freedom or equal protection by the law cannot be scarce in the same sense as perfume, caviar or bread. The term scarcity creates the impression that what is important about bread and freedom is that they are rare and hard to come by. They are, but not in the same sense for everyone. If we want to keep an open mind to the possibility that some of us would not want to trade freedom for bread or conscience for money (cf. Rawls 1971: 62), it is perhaps better to avoid the appearance that all these goods can be measured by the same standard and hence exchanged for one another.

Although the term moderate scarcity is not the most fortunate choice for a condition of justice, this changes nothing about the fact that, for the question of justice to come forth, there must be something outside our bodies worth arguing over. Expressing this something in relation to our subjective reasons for wanting it, we obtain a complex second objective condition of social justice: the availability of means of action (regardless of the reasons for acting), over the distribution of which a conflict of interests is possible. Note that this formulation allows archpointers to consider material and immaterial means, as well as things that are considered to be good in themselves – such as art for art's sake or liberty for the sake of liberty. There is no reason why means cannot also be ends.

As with the subjective conditions of justice, these objective conditions do not ban the archpointers from other knowledge, but further details are irrelevant (*pace*

Barry 1995: 7, 11, 67, 76). Suppose that the archpointers had been given all available data on Italy in AD 2025. We want them to design principles of social justice, rather than principles of Italian justice – in fact, we are not interested in Italy at all. Would information on Italy damage their impartiality? In advance, one might suspect that the archpointers' judgement will at least appear to be biased. The structure of a particular society often reflects the values of the happy few in that society, or rather the other way around: time, place and social and natural constellation create the opportunity for some to become the happy few. Others are either unfortunate enough to have their plans of life obstructed by the structure of society, or they have adapted their plans to their limited possibilities – which is known as the sour grapes effect. If all this is the case in Italy, we must assure that the structure of Italian society and the values of Italians do not somehow influence the impartiality of the archpointers.

We could consider taking away the *appearance* of bias by simply withholding all information on particular societies, which would certainly keep the archpointers from favouring or obstructing certain reasons, plans and lives. To prevent a bias from *actually* occurring, such drastic actions are nevertheless unnecessary. The conditions of the archpoint, that is the conditions defining impartiality, should suffice to generate the level of abstraction that we need to assure that the archpointers's principles are as valid for any society as they will be for Italy, AD 2025. The problem is to make sure that the archpointers will stick to those conditions. That, however, is not a problem of information but one of motivation; it will be dealt with in the next section.

The third type of information archpointers can have, general scientific knowledge,[37] is directly related to the types discussed so far. The principal difference between knowledge of the self and society, and scientific knowledge, is that the latter is concerned with – from the point of view of a theorist of justice – more contingent facts. Judgements on social justice in general lead to conclusions about the justice and injustice of particular societies or situations in those societies. Those conclusions may in turn induce political action, either to change an unjust or preserve a just situation. Neither universal judgements on justice, nor political action in particular circumstances, are possible without prior information on the way societies and persons *can* or *could* function – provided, of course, that we want a theory of social justice to be practical. If we believe in, for instance, personal responsibility and retributive justice, we need to know how an instance of tax evasion came about, whether it could have been avoided and who could have avoided it; or if we believe in distributive social justice, we have to know at least whether and how injustice can be cured or prevented.

I should stress that general scientific knowledge is not indispensable for a theory of social justice, even though it is essential if we want the theory to be practical. In moral philosophy, there is an axiom known as *ought implies can*, meaning that an ought-statement is only morally relevant or meaningful if it is possible to act upon it. We can condemn earthquakes, we can say that they ought not happen and that we should do everything to prevent them from happening

– but as long as we cannot control earthquakes, any such statement is pointless. If the *ought implies can* axiom were applied to social justice theory, general scientific knowledge would indeed be indispensable; any theory would be meaningless without it, not to mention impractical. But I hesitate to do so, for at least two reasons.

First, the *can*-part in the *ought implies can* axiom is itself dubitable. Even if it were certain what we 'ought' to be or do, we do not know for certain what can be or what we can do. 'It is certain that machines cannot fly if they are heavier than air.' Or so it was, until the Wright brothers took off. 'It is certain that we cannot fly to the moon.' 'It is certain that we cannot clone and re-create dinosaurs using the DNA retrieved from fossils.' Of one thing we are certain: that the truths of science are of a controversial and all too frequently temporary nature.

Secondly, if the *can*-part becomes controversial, the *ought*-part must follow. If we firmly believe in *ought implies can*, 'we ought to fly to the moon' would not have been a century ago what it now is: a morally meaningful proposition. Today 'you ought to give birth to a frog' is at best a disapproving moral proposition in a fairy tale; tomorrow – who knows? Suppose that it were moral, provided that it were also theoretically possible, to change deserts into coconuts. And suppose we learn that we cannot do so for practical reasons. Should we now believe that 'one ought to turn deserts into coconuts' is a meaningless phrase? Or should we not instead believe that, perhaps, it does have a meaning – that of a commandment to do everything in our power to turn deserts into coconuts, including research to find out if we can do so in the future? If the latter is true, as I believe it is, the borderline between genuine moral propositions and impossible-therefore-amoral propositions starts to blur.

Now this is not an entirely academic issue; it has specific consequences for the liberal theory of justice. For one, it means that scientific knowledge influences its feasibility more than its meaningfulness. For another, it undermines a doctrine that used to be quite popular in rational choice theories: the doctrine of complete information, according to which individuals, in order to make an informed rational choice, should have full knowledge of all the aspects of all the options among which they are to choose. Along with this doctrine, it undermines the role John Rawls assigned to scientific knowledge. In his conception of people in the original position, Rawls wants them to have knowledge of all the

> general facts about human society. They understand political affairs and the prin-
> ciples of economic theory; they know the basis of social organization and the
> laws of human psychology. Indeed, the parties are presumed to know whatever
> general facts affect the choice of the principles of justice. (Rawls 1971: 137)

Obviously, Rawls's contracting parties know a great deal more than any of us do. All in all, complete knowledge is not a very plausible demand. First, scientific knowledge is often controversial: proofs are not always definite. Secondly, it is incomplete – or if it were not, scientists would all be out of a job. Thirdly, to ascribe to archpointers full knowledge of the achievements the natural and social sciences have and (mainly) have not made does not add to the credibility of their status as an impartial jury. Why would anyone, earlier having been asked to be rational, trust the opinion of beings who are supposed to have privileged access to information no rational being can have, let alone verify?

If omniscience is impossible, we can still assume that archpointers have *some* general knowledge on hypotheticals. The kind of general knowledge that is needed for sensible *can*-propositions and *ought*-judgements does exist; the problem is that it is of an incomplete and for the most part hypothetical nature. Without omniscience, all we have are three less attractive options:

(1) We withhold all or part of the available general information from the archpointers, thereby taking the risk of giving definitely unrealistic recommendations;

(2) We credit the archpointers with knowledge of the definite scientific truth in all areas, at the risk of fraud on the side of the author and loss of all credibility on the side of the reader; or

(3) We attribute the contracting parties with all the scanty knowledge on general facts that we actually have.

The first choice is unacceptable: it is impossible to select knowledge on the basis of its relevancy without upgrading one's own and degrading others' views on relevancy, on 'what matters' in the world. It is also unnecessary. Irrelevant facts are, by definition, irrelevant; they cannot influence the opinions of rational archpointers. The second choice is clearly unacceptable for practical reasons, which leaves us with the last: full access to our limited knowledge.

The consequence of this third option is, beyond doubt, uncertainty. It has already been made clear that the credibility of an impartial theory of justice depends on the plausibility of the archpoint. Now we must add a second and equally significant qualification: the more the justification of a theory or principle of social justice depends on empirical scientific knowledge, the more hypothetical it becomes.

As the archpointers are to have access to all general scientific knowledge available in the real world, we can formulate the following first information condition of social justice: scientific knowledge is available but it is, to varying degrees, incomplete and of a hypothetical nature. Two other information conditions are related to the way archpointers treat the knowledge they have (all knowledge, not just the information on hypotheticals), rather than to their knowledge itself.

The second information condition, a direct consequence of the conditions of impartiality, demands that the archpointers have equal access to the available information on general facts, on the human self and on particular societies, lest they cannot manipulate or be manipulated. I am not supposing the existence of ill will at the archpoint, but opportunities for manipulation do not necessarily

Albert: You know what? I just realize egalitarians can't believe in their own ideas. Technology. One guy comes up with a good idea, say television, boom goes your equal distribution of knowledge, power, opportunities, whatever. In fact, boom goes every distributive scheme, not just egalitarianism. Tomorrow we may be able to adapt our genetic make-up to the Martian atmosphere, or discover anti-gravity, or Star Trek-like duplicators – goo goes in, and out comes any first-class meal you can dream of, or a sports jacket, or whatever. You can't make rules for that. You don't even know who'll benefit and who won't.

Marilyn: So justice can't be described in exact rules of distribution. *Tant pis* for all the bureaucrats in the world – now they'll have to use their brains to account for their acts and not another rule book. But who says you can't make rules for rules, general rules for the composition of rules in practice? You don't need to know who exactly will suffer exactly what kind of harm if nothing else happens, to be able to design a general rule for the fair distribution of harm. If you catch my drift. Likewise for any other possible principle of justice. It means you can't always prevent injustice, not that you can't try to control it.

A: Yea – still, it's a disappointment. Wasn't it Frank Sinatra who said justice is a remedial virtue? Can't remember – don't read poetry that much.

A little knowledge

originate in privileged information only. Suppose that individual archpointers were to have different information. How could one of them be certain that the (apparently) privileged information used by another is correct and not made up by that other; or that the aggregate information available to all individuals equals the whole of the information that should be available?

Finally, according to the third information condition, the contracting parties should be equally (weakly) rational. Some logical constructions, and consequently theories in which these are employed, are – as far as we know – incomprehensible for children of a certain age and average intelligence; the more intelligent ones understand them earlier in life, the less intelligent are later (see e.g. Hodges 1977: 181). It seems reasonable to assume that archpointers with differing intellectual dispositions can run into the same problem. Thus, if they do not have equal intellectual capacities, they cannot be equally well (or equally poorly) informed – which would be a violation of the second information condition.

It follows, by the way and probably to no-one's surprise, that if the archpointers are equally motivated, and if the information they have allows for an agreement on principles of social justice, it will necessarily be a unanimous agreement.

Knowing oneself

We now turn to a second cardinal question: that of the motivation of the arch-pointers. What can we allow them to 'know' about themselves, or allow them to feel or to be moved by, if we want them to be convincingly alike to us and at the same time impartial? Can they have a personality, a character, a psychological and physical make-up, convictions, full reasons – and if so, of what kind? Should they, for instance, know or be motivated by the knowledge that they will be part of the society they design?

In answering these questions, three issues must be distinguished. First, knowledge about oneself or one's interests need not by itself keep anyone from being impartial. The danger to impartiality lies rather in being motivated by that knowledge (i.e., being prejudiced; cf. Bell and Schokkaert 1992: 247; Lehning 1980: 101) and in having an interest in the society one is helping to design. These two cases are clearly different, though not mutually exclusive: it is possible to gamble on one's interests in a society without knowing where one will end up in it, and it is equally possible to unconsciously impress the private convictions one has as a Hindu or butcher on principles for a society of vegetarians. Additionally, consciousness must be distinguished from subconscious attitudes, motives, and so forth. To warrant impartiality, it is simply not enough to neutralize the effect of knowledge and experience or the lack thereof. Thirdly, we must ask ourselves how exactly, technically speaking, an impartial person can represent real-life persons and interests.

The last issue is of primary importance: any answer to this determines the degree to which, or the sense in which, archpointers can be 'themselves'. In representing others, impartiality is an ambiguous concept allowing several interpretations.

According to David Gauthier (Gauthier 1985: 260), John Rawls and Thomas Scanlon interpreted impartiality as choosing in ignorance of one's actual endowments and future position in society. However, people in the original position still know something about themselves, knowledge without which they would be vegetables. They know that they are rational, mutually disinterested and so forth. The point is that they have no knowledge that *identifies* them as distinct personalities with private interests. What they know about themselves or we about them only describes the outlines of all reasonable humans; it leaves the details open. As a consequence, they can imagine themselves as standing in anyone else's shoes – anyone, no matter who and in what society – without identifying with them; the contracting parties are merely possible persons. Let us call this interpretation of impartiality omni-partiality.

Other interpretations of impartiality are equally possible – for example, the ecologists's version of impartiality. Green critics of Rawls have accused him of being biased against animals if not against all of non-human nature. In this view, an impartial choice requires ignorance about individualizing endowments, about one's position in society *and* about whether one will be a human. Some of these critics have adapted the veil of ignorance accordingly to include animals (in particular mammals), others have gone so far as to include the possibility that a contracting party wakes up one day to find that he or she is a mountain, the ozone layer or a biosphere (cf. B. Singer 1988; VanDerVeer 1977). Let us label this collection of conceptions of impartiality, in which contracting parties are possibly any (living) thing, super-partiality.

In a third version, Gauthier's, the contracting parties are impartial if their choice for principles of justice is acceptable to everyone in every social position within a society (Gauthier 1985: 261). We could call this set-partiality. The difference with Rawls's omni-partiality is that, in Gauthier's view, principles must be unanimously accepted by a given set of people in society *the way they (i.e. the people) are*. There is no veil of ignorance; according to Gauthier it suffices to let everyone place herself in the position of everyone else.

These three views in no way exhaust the possibilities for interpreting impartiality, but they can serve well enough to illustrate why Rawls's – or a Rawlsian – interpretation is best fit for a contract theory of justice, why more general variants are superfluous and why more specific variants are faulty. Super-partiality, as in the green version, extends the range of application of Rawlsian omni-partiality. It does not challenge the validity of the basic idea of Rawlsian impartiality, which is that impartial judges may collect and use any information available, including the knowledge and experience gathered by imagining to stand in someone else's shoes – but that their decision on principles should not be taken from, or depend on, 'any particular point of view', as Thomas Nagel describes impartiality (Nagel 1986: 61 ff.; Nagel 1991: 10–1). In both theories, the Rawlsian and the green, the impartial point of view differs substantially from any particular point of view, including the sum of particular points of view.

These two theories clearly contrast with Gauthier's, which comes down to giving each and every individual in his or her particular circumstances a veto on the decisions of contracting parties.[38] As claimed before, Gauthier's idea of impartiality is inappropriate. The idea was developed as a critique of Rawls, but is in fact based on a misrepresentation of Rawls's position. Ideally, Rawls's principles, although chosen under a different interpretation of impartial circumstances, should also be acceptable to every real person in every real position – not because a unanimous agreement as such is sacred but because every imperfect real individual would, *in reflective equilibrium*, agree that impartiality is best represented by Rawlsian people behind a veil of ignorance. Gauthier, however, did not extend his critique of Rawls's theory to the core of the argument for omni-partiality, the notion of considered judgements in reflective equilibrium. Hence, he gives us insufficient reason to think of his and Rawls's interpretations of impartiality as alternatives; what remains are simply two descriptions of two *different* things.

A more fundamental objection to Gauthier's interpretation of impartiality was already implicit in my characterization of his views: set-partiality is a result of adding up all particular points of view or of giving each a veto. It is not by itself a point of view, it is 'no point of view' rather than the Nagelian 'no particular' point of view; it is, like Brian Barry's conception of justice as impartiality (Barry

1995: 76), an amalgam of *some* particular points of view. Yet Gauthier-like set-partiality would not be impartial even if we extended the reference set to include all possible persons and societies – for the same reason. In ordinary life, being impartial means that one can stand back from one's own personality, interests and beliefs, look upon things from a distance, and let other interests or persons prevail if they deserve to prevail. This kind of impartiality allows that claims are evaluated, ranked and even rejected – unlike set-partiality, but consistent with the views on impartiality defended in the previous chapter. Gauthier denies that claims can be judged: all claims, all plans of life, all revealed preferences (whether sincere or not), have equal value or relevance. My view of impartiality is different. Up to a point, reasons for acting can be criticized and claims can be evaluated: some are better or more valid than others, and some – but only some – are even beyond judgement. What makes the interests of individuals morally relevant, from the archpoint of view, is not the fact that individuals have interests or reasons, but that some of these reasons are irrefutable basic reasons – full reasons. The respect archpointers show for these reasons over others gives them a point of view which differs from any particular point of view, yet does not leave them without *any* point of view.

It thus seems that omni-partiality, that is judging without self-knowledge and identification, but with a capacity to stand in anyone's shoes, best expresses the spirit of impartiality.[39] Nevertheless, there is no need to be so radical as to demand that archpointers 'be ignorant' about their own and their fellow arch-pointers' characters and places in society (cf. Galston 1982: 501). It is, as we shall see in a moment, enough to demand that they disregard such information, that is, to demand that they cannot or do not identify themselves with any person or place or set of places in society. Ideally, everyone is equal at the archpoint. It makes no difference *who* takes an impartial standpoint, or whether an impartial judge has a personal identity at all, whether he or she is a *who* at all – what matters is that anyone whom we demand to be impartial is manifestly *capable* of doing so.

Turning to the question of the self-knowledge of archpointers, we find that archpointers can know as much or as little about themselves as we care; self-knowledge is not an essential factor for impartiality in the sense of omni-partiality. Having or not having self-knowledge is clearly an irrelevant matter in so far as one's character is concerned; whether such information has any impact at all depends on the motivation of archpointers. A bad temper, paranoia or arrogance may obstruct any negotiation *process*, but they will not influence the *outcome* of negotiations at the archpoint. After all, we have already demanded that the archpointers be equally well informed and equally rational; if a desire to choose rational principles of justice is all that motivates them, the archpointers will merely take one another's shortcomings for granted and negotiate until a satis-factory agreement has been reached.

Something similar is true for knowledge about one's place in society. Clearly, anyone with the least bit of self-interest has a (not: every) reason to prefer a

Hayekian society of freedom of opportunity and freedom from state interference over a Rawlsian social democracy, if she knows herself to have a talent for making the right investments. The reverse is true for a self-interested risk-avoider. Still, not knowing one's place in society is no guarantee for impartiality. Consider the fact that, in most of the societies that exist or have existed, wealth never was on the whole a social disadvantage. Few would bet that the rich consider their wealth a personal disadvantage. Poverty, on the other hand, probably has more, and more often, disadvantages than advantages. Similar arguments could be made regarding the knowledge of being a parent, a prisoner, a prime minister, and so forth. Even when oblivious of their actual place in society (that is when choosing under conditions of uncertainty), the archpointers can have an incentive to promote their private interests – if the incentive attracts and motivates them.

Finally, one might argue for one particular exception to the rule that any kind of self-knowledge is allowed provided that the archpointers are motivated in the right way. Archpointers who are aware of the bare fact that they will be part of the society they design could be prejudiced, no matter what their motivation and no matter how little else they know. Being rational, knowing that the conditions of justice obtain in their future society, and thus knowing that they will have interests and will identify with these, the archpointers cannot help wanting to protect their future interests. Yet even here no exceptions need to be made. It does not matter whether archpointers are informed or not; this very general kind of knowledge is not enough to prejudice them in favour of any particular principle, person or plan of life. In either case they will be omni-partial: all they can do (given the right motivation) is imagine themselves to be in each distinct social position and show equal consideration for all positions. After all, we have assumed that they have the right motivation, so that even if they had full knowledge of their identity they would not take sides with any particular person – including themselves.

Adding all this together, we find that our contracting parties should be immune to 'particularizing' types of information, though they do not need to go without. For the concrete shape of the contract situations and contracting parties, we can choose any of a large number of options, all of which *could* satisfy omni-partiality if our claim about the decisive role of motivation is correct. We could imagine them as Rawls's people in the original position, humans who do not know the society to which they will belong or the capacities they have, but who do know that they satisfy the previously discussed conditions of justice. Some of his critics have argued that by depriving his contracting parties of individual knowledge, Rawls would not take the difference between persons seriously, but obviously that is not the issue. What Rawls disregarded is the difference between the contracting parties themselves, and this (that is the contracting parties not having a personal identity) furthers rather than hinders the cause of taking every *real* person's ideas and plans seriously.

Still, even the appearance of prejudice – Rawls's creatures are not totally disinterested in anyone's fate – can be prevented. A second option is to take one step back and imagine the archpointers as 'self-effacing' beings for whom not even the conditions of justice obtain. They would not just be ignorant of their position in society and of the society in which they are to participate, but they would also know, positively, that they will not belong to a society at all. Angelic as they now are, they look most like an assembly of impartial observers.

We could also move in the opposite direction and enlarge the archpoint with a representative selection of possibly or actually existing persons, with Martians landing on Trafalgar Square, with genetically manipulated dogs with the intelligence of humans, with people with full knowledge but no social bonds (quasi-emigrants), with ordinary people – or ultimately with you and me. The essence of a contract theory is that the parties are representatives, agents for whomever their motivation allows them to represent, whether normal humans, Martians or animals. Which brings us to the third and last issue, one that I have been careful to evade so far: that of motivation. What is it that moves the archpointers to be impartial or that can move any being to be an archpointer?

Part of the answer lies in the *absence* of motivations, the absence of identification with any of their reasons for acting. Thus, the third subjective condition of justice should not obtain for archpointers. In general, the more contracting parties are alike to us, the easier it is to identify with them and to share their conclusions on justice – but we would trust them as replicas of our separate selves and our separate interests, rather than as impartial agents. At least in the area of motivation, archpointers should be *unlike* us: neither greedy nor liberal, neither self-interested nor altruistic, neither progressive nor conservative, neither good nor bad – but beyond all that.[40] There are intuitive and semantical reasons to link impartiality with lack of private interests or motives, but another, technical reason is even more important: impartial agents cannot at the same time have (full) reasons and respect those of others. At best, they can tolerate them if forced to by an external power. Any, or probably any, full reason or reason for acting can come into conflict with impartiality. For example, an archpointer motivated by the deep and sincere desire to be benevolent will not be able to fully respect a political order in which benevolence is limited by prudence, nor can he or she be convinced of the morality of any principle of justice prescribing such an order. An archpointer who would be totally committed to sincerity or honesty would find it extremely difficult to embrace a democratic order, as democracy requires compromise, and political compromises tend to be at odds with the honest and sincere expression of preferences. Allowing archpointers to have full reasons, or allowing them to have any reasons for action at all, will lead to deadlock: their debate would be one about a question that cannot be settled, that of the priority and relative worth of reasons for action.

If we do not want archpointers to be consciously motivated by private reasons, we surely cannot want them to have another typical trait of humans: a subconsciousness. To be unaware of one's reasons for acting and still act upon them contradicts the demands of impartiality even more clearly than conscious partiality.

Albert: Just because I'm a scientist don't mean I'm insensitive. I'm merely impassionate. I don't let feelings control me, but I do have them. You, on the other hand, are oversensitive.

Marilyn: Oh get a life. I tell you, I *have* had a life – and that enables me to feel what others feel, even if I haven't lived through the same experiences. You on the other hand are merely perceiving. You're impartial in a very funny way. You don't care.

A: Well, let's not quibble. In the end, we can both stand in other people's shoes, you because your feet can vary in any dimension, I because mine don't take up space.

M: Just one more thing: doesn't your being dispassionate make you rather than me biased? I can imagine what it's like to be you, but can you really *feel* feelings?

A: But then, can you really know what it's like to be dispassionate? In fact, even though we're creatures of an author's imagination, can either of us transcend our complete social and psychological background? Don't we have or at least act upon an interest in reproducing that background?

M: Now that's exactly what I wanted to say all along. The only society about which you really can't judge impartially is your own. That is, first of all, why you and I won't discuss the USA – we'll do the rest of the world. You could perhaps even do Germany; there's little chance of you going back there or wanting to go back. And that is, secondly, why real existing people would have to imagine us, as people with no direct interest in their fate relative to ours, to make up for their own imperfection.

Conscience and consciousness

In summary: we can allow archpointers to imagine themselves in any social position and to experience everything anyone can experience, from torture and rape to riches and fame, from justice to injustice – provided they do not identify themselves with these experiences, or with these roles or with these persons. We can also allow them to know themselves, their own society, their own motives – provided they do not feel motivated by this. We cannot allow them to have any reason for their interest in the issue of justice without – by definition – motivating them, and we cannot motivate them without running the risk of admitting interests, prejudice and bias at the archpoint. The only motivation we can safely ascribe to archpointers is an entirely impersonal one: an interest in knowledge for its own sake, an intellectual curiosity about the problem of justice – or more precisely, about the task that will be assigned to them in the next section.

Knowing what to do

The mind has a tendency to wander, a tendency that cannot be taken away by choosing an impartial point of view. The archpoint is a point of view like any other; we can try to stand 'on' it, become archpointers, and look in any direction and at any object we happen to like. If we want to motivate the archpointers to stick to the issue, discuss justice and formulate impartial principles of minimal justice, their task has to be circumscribed as precisely as possible.

Up to a point, the definition of this task is an arbitrary affair. The archpointers are asked to formulate a set of rules defining the domain of social justice (that is describing society), the objects of distribution and the basis for comparisons between these objects, the distributor and recipients, the grounds for desert and the rules of distribution. The archpointers will, furthermore, be forced to respect the boundaries of the archpoint, that is the conditions of impartiality, justice and knowledge. I shall refer to the whole set of rules as the metric of social justice or simply as the principles of social justice.

As justice is a predicate both of individuals and of society, and as the just society presumably cannot exist without just citizens, we can also ask our impartial agents to sketch the implications of their metric for individuals and their actions and convictions (cf. Kley 1989: 265). Moreover, justice as seen from the archpoint is minimal justice, justice for a society of strangers. In order to fully assess the consequences of minimal justice, we might therefore want to examine the relation between minimal and communitarian justice. However, we shall discuss these issues only superficially in the last chapter, as I cannot give a complete account of social justice in this book. I have limited myself to *liberal* social justice for a good reason: communitarian justice presupposes a consensus on values and purposes that does not seem to reflect the natural state of man and one that does not seem to be open to grounded support or critique. The detection, description or composition of a conception of justice for a community, no matter what community, is a colossal problem worthy of another book in its own right. The same is true for the question of individual attitudes towards minimal justice: for a serious appraisal of that problem, we need theories of education, of socialization, of personality and so on – issues that are too big to deal with in this context. For this reason, I shall discuss both problems only summarily.

In contrast to the definition of the object of inquiry, the delineation of the output of the archpoint, the contract, is not a simple matter of convenience. John Rawls (Rawls 1971: 130–36) has argued that principles of justice should be *general* (they should not contain proper names or 'definite descriptions'), *universal* in their application (relevant to all moral beings), *public* (known to all members of society), capable of *ordering* conflicting claims and fit to serve as the *final* court of appeal in matters of justice. Rawls hastens to add that these criteria are not innocent. The condition of generality, for instance, demands that principles of justice should not contain proper names; it thus bans egoism. A vindication of these so-called formal constraints of the concept of right can therefore only be given by way of 'the reasonableness of the theory of which they are part' (Rawls 1971: 131). This immediately raises the question of their compatibility with what I hold to be the reasonable theory of impartiality as reflected in the archpoint.

Generality, universality and publicity can pass without comment. If the necessary changes in terminology are made, Rawls's arguments can be transplanted to our contract theory without any problem. Finality, the status of the principles as the last word on and highest resort for justice, must be taken with two grains of salt. First, the finality of principles, both Rawls's and those of the archpointers, actually depends on the 'reasonableness of the theory of which they are part', in other words, on the adequacy of premises – so there may be a higher judge. Secondly, as the archpointers, unlike Rawls's people in the original position, do not have full knowledge of general scientific facts, the finality of principles also depends on the absence of relevant new information (cf. Rawls 1995: 142; Baker 1995: 93).

Under the heading of the demand for an *ordering*, Rawls in fact poses three demands: completeness, transitivity and morally acceptable reasons for the ranking of claims (Rawls 1971: 134). Completeness requires that the principles of justice can be applied to all claims that are likely to arise, a requirement that can again pass without comment. The other two demands need some extra attention.

Transitivity, i.e. $\forall x, y, z: (xRy \land yRz) \rightarrow xRz$, can be demanded without violation of the conditions of the archpoint. It is plain that we may ultimately learn that some alternatives are equally good or just, or even that all are: $\forall x, y: xRy \land yRx$. If this turns out to be the case we have still learned one thing: that principles of distributive justice do not have an answer to all problems of distribution.

It follows that in absence of a unique best element,[41] distribution problems can only be solved by introducing an element of chance. We might flip a coin or rotate the disputed resource, or, if it turns out that nearly all differences between humans are irrelevant, as far as justice is concerned, we might even turn our whole society into one gigantic redistributive lottery, as Barbara Goodwin suggested (Goodwin 1992: 43, 199 ff.). We do not need to restrict ourselves to chance: a rule ranking alternatives by means of irrelevant characteristics, one that can be fully unreasonable or based on something other than justice, for example aesthetics, is equally possible – provided that the additional rule does not involve *wrong*, partial, criteria for the further ordering of claims. It is up to the archpointers to decide whether chance should be introduced, for what reason and in what form. Until they prove the opposite, any rule, even trial by combat (*pace* Rawls 1971: 134), and any result is equally just.

The possibility that no unique best element is chosen may seem to pose a fundamental objection to an impartial conception of justice, as it allows questions of justice to remain unsolved, apparently in contradiction to the demand of finality. Yet such results do not change the finality of principles of justice: they can still be the court of final appeal, the last word *on matters of justice*. The irresoluteness of principles can, in some cases, even be a virtue. In a paragraph on retributive justice, the medieval political theorist, John of Salisbury, confronted a comparable dilemma. He relates how the case of a mother, who had killed her husband and son for vilely slaying another son from an earlier marriage, could not be resolved by any ordinary court.

> Consequently, the matter was referred to the members of the Athenian Areopagus, as the more venerable and more experienced judges. However, upon examination of the case, they ordered the return of the plaintiffs and the woman in a hundred years. (John of Salisbury 1990: 58)

There is one more guideline for the output of the archpointers' deliberations, which unfortunately remained implicit in Rawls's theory: simplicity (cf. Braybrooke 1982: 1). If we want principles of justice to be *legitimate* as well as justified, ordinary beings in real society should be able to discuss and evaluate the reasoning and conclusion of the archpointers. Thus, the principles should be as clear and intelligible as possible for real persons with ordinary intellectual capacities. Like ordering, this is a practical condition rather than a matter of principle.

Next to a task and some requirements for the form of the contract, archpointers need instructions in one last respect. We have described them as ordinary or extraordinary persons with a definitely extraordinary motivation, who are to consider principles of justice for societies characterized by the conditions of justice. They are to do so within the limits of the conception of natural justice, they should be weakly rational, and their point of view should be the impartial point of view described above. Thus, the archpoint contains several rules for the formulation and evaluation of a scale: objective and subjective conditions of justice, demands posed on the contracting parties' self-knowledge and the conditions of impartiality themselves. This last set of conditions in particular could cause trouble. Ideally, archpointers will come up with a conception of justice that satisfies all the criteria for an acceptable conception of minimal justice: it will conform to natural justice, it will be rational, and it will be technically, subjectively and objectively neutral. However, it is obvious that these five demands may conflict. Hence, the final rule for contracting parties at the archpoint will have to be one that determines the relative weight of each of these criteria.

In the first place, we can rank (1) weak rationality over (2) consistency with the principles of natural justice. Without weak rationality there is no sense in talking, let alone in talking about justice. Any principle overruling rationality cannot be accounted for; any evaluation based on such an overruling principle is pure mysticism. The reader may recall that weak rationality was also – and not by coincidence – a prerequisite for natural justice. Secondly, we can rank (3) technical neutrality third. Once the arena for a meaningful debate on minimal justice has been defined – by the conditions ranked first and second – a debate becomes possible, and technical neutrality determines that this debate will be one about minimal justice rather than anything else. Thirdly and obviously, the conditions of subjective and objective neutrality should be ranked below technical neutrality. Finally, (4) objective neutrality should overrule (5) subjective neutrality. As I argued at the beginning of this chapter, we need a definite description of the object of impartiality before we can be subjectively neutral; we cannot give equal relevance to all aspects of all plans of life without getting tangled up in paradoxes.

A further reason for ranking objective neutrality in the fourth place and subjective neutrality fifth is less formal and more controversial, but should not come as a surprise. The archpointers have been obliged to show equal and impartial consideration for all persons and for the ways in which they express their personality, that is their reasons for acting and plans of life. Nevertheless, some reasons behind some plans of life are simply irrational and 'just no good', whereas others are 'mere inclinations' and still others are reasonable but not reasonable enough – the plans lack a foundation or the foundation is itself unstable. Full reasons, on the other hand, are the ultimate foundation; unlike other reasons, they cannot be rejected from an impartial point of view. Under these circumstances, the priority given to objective over subjective neutrality can be defended in two ways. One could claim, or try to claim, that objective neutrality best embodies Dworkin's minimum requirement for a moral theory: that it shows equal respect to, or equal concern for, all persons. Objective neutrality would do this by respecting the integrity of the real, matured person, the rational being with full reasons. An argument like this is probably sensitive to the objection that it only shows respect by insulting those to whom it does not show respect. I rather prefer a second argument: the priority given to objective neutrality expresses our conviction that we should give precedence to good reasons over just any kind of reason.

Part III
Principles of distributive justice

The love of women's over,
And ended is desire,
Men's strife with men is quiet,
And the world lusts no more.
From St Columba's *Dies irae* (Waddell 1968: 78–9)

6

Dies Irae

Premises, premises

In the previous three chapters I gave an outline of the foundations of a liberal theory of social justice. One distinctive feature of this theory is the central role that a particular conception of impartiality plays in it; another is the sheer magnitude of this role. If we recall for a moment the picture of liberal theories of social justice as sketched in Chapter 2, we find that, in comparison, the significance of impartiality in those theories was much more modest. There, impartiality was merely one among several ideals that liberal theorists took as defining marks of a liberal theory of justice. Consequently, impartiality sometimes had to give way to more substantial ideals and views of the good. The conception of liberal justice sketched in this part, on the other hand, gives precedence to impartiality over any notion of the good or any other reason for acting. It starts from the idea that impartiality should be taken extremely seriously – in fact, that the implications of impartiality (tolerance, freedom, equal respect, moderate scepticism) make it the cornerstone of liberalism.

The process of developing said new foundations has led us to the point where we, or our better selves acting on our behalf, should be able to formulate principles of social justice. Before we turn to this our second task, however, I want to complete our picture of the Archimedean point by adding two details. I have so far stacked condition upon condition, requirement upon requirement and level upon level. It seems appropriate to spend a section – this one – on a systematic synopsis of all these premises. I also owe the reader visualizations of archpoint and contract. I shall give these in the next section.

In Chapter 3, I distinguished four views on justice in society:

(1) *Eternal justice*, or justice seen from a point of view outside time and life;
(2) *Natural justice*, or the categorical imperatives of justice;
(3) *Minimal justice*, or justice under conditions of impartiality; and

113

(4)   *Communitarian justice*, justice under circumstances of an honest and sincere consensus on the good life.

I immediately dismissed the notion of eternal justice as irrelevant. Natural justice was specified as a view on justice under three constraints:

(2.1)   The demand that we reach an agreement;
(2.2)   The demand that this agreement be one on what the pure idea of justice requires; and
(2.3)   The demand that we are weakly rational;

which resulted in three rather uninformative imperatives:

(P1)   Treat equal cases equally; and
(P2)   Treat unequal cases in proportion to their inequality.
(P3)   Claims about (un)just treatment need to be sustained by good reasons, other than and in addition to P1 or P2.

Minimal justice, which should generate the good reasons mentioned in P3, contained two new constraints and two that were already part of the natural justice model:

(3.1)   The demand that we reach an agreement;
(3.2)   The demand that this agreement be one on the content of justice;
(3.3)   The demand that we are weakly rational; and
(3.4)   The demand that we are impartial with regard to theories of the good (life).

Finally, I described communitarian justice as minimal justice minus the impartiality constraint. Communitarian justice can exist if and only if there is community, that is as long as, in so far as, and where two or more persons agree on the good life and on its translation into principles of justice for those agreeing. Consequently, it can only exist within the limits of natural and minimal justice.

In Chapter 4, I turned to the notion of minimal justice and thereby entered the realm of the liberal theory of social justice. To satisfy the impartiality constraint (3.4), I designed the *archpoint* or archpoint of view, which stipulates the conditions allowing for an impartial judgement on matters of justice. These conditions specified *impartiality* as follows:

(C1)   *Technical neutrality*, that is the justification device representing impartiality should determine the content of principles of justice rather than that of (principles of) anything else;
(C2)   *Subjective neutrality*, or the absence of bias with regard to the essential parts of plans of life (full reasons); and
(C3)   *Objective neutrality*, that is the principles behind the justification device should be acceptable to all reasonable beings. This condition was found to be satisfied by:

114

(C3.1)   A very thin theory of the good, according to which it is good to be, and we in fact are, weakly rational, that is we accept second order predicate logic; and

(C3.2)   A sceptic postponement of judgements on full reasons.

In Chapter 5, I discussed the formal details of the so-called single-mind type of contract theory, which was earlier found to be the most suitable way of representing the archpoint. I argued that there was no reason to limit the availability of most types of information. Instead, I formulated some minimum standards, requiring (R) that the least contracting parties ought to know about the world outside them was:

(R1)   The *first* subjective condition of social justice: the presence of separate persons with distinct reasons for acting;

(R2)   The *second* subjective condition: humans are equal in respect of having, storing and on occasion using, power in whatever form or amount;

(R3)   The *third* subjective condition: the presence of a profound identification of persons with their reasons for acting;

(R4)   The *first* objective condition of social justice: that there is a society;

(R5)   The *second* objective condition: the availability of means to acting, over the distribution of which a conflict of interests is possible;

(R6)   The *first* information condition of social justice: the contracting parties share all the scientific knowledge available to us in the real world, which implies that it is available in limited amounts and that it is, to varying degrees, of a hypothetical nature;

(R7)   The *second* information condition: the archpointers have equal access to the available information on general facts, on the human self and on particular societies; and

(R8)   The *third* information condition: the archpointers should be equally (weakly) rational.

As for their self-knowledge, I argued that there was no need to keep archpointers ignorant of any *facts* about themselves. The danger to their impartiality, the danger that they identify with any particular interest, comes from the side of their *motivation*. Consequently, I introduced a further requirement:

(R9)   Archpointers are best imagined as (only) having an entirely impersonal motivation: intellectual curiosity about the problem of justice.

Finally, I posed some demands on the form of the contract and on the deliberations of the contracting parties, beginning with the demand that the archpointers stick to their task, which was to formulate principles of distributive social justice, or in other words:

(R10)   The archpointers are asked to define the domain of social justice, the objects of distribution and the basis for comparisons between these objects, the distributor and recipients, the grounds for desert and the rules of distribution. All this is to be done under observance of the conditions of the archpoint (C1–3) and the conditions of knowledge (R1–9, 11–17), and in accordance with the principles of natural justice (P1–3).

The guidelines for the form of the contract, that is for the principles resulting from the archpointers's deliberations were, for the most part, taken over from Rawls:

(R11)   Principles of minimal justice should be general;
(R12)   They should be universal;
(R13)   They should be public;
(R14)   They should be the final court of appeal in matters of justice (This did not mean that their infallibility can be guaranteed; finality still depends on the 'reasonableness' of the rest of the theory of justice and on the absence or presence of relevant new information.);
(R15)   They should allow a complete and transitive ranking (ordering) of alternatives (where the principles are indecisive, an impartial chance rule should be followed);
(R16)   They should be simple.

A last guideline determines the order in which the conditions of the archpoint and the principles of natural justice should be satisfied, if such a rule should be necessary.

(R17)   The constraints posed by natural justice and the conditions of the archpoint should be satisfied in the following order:
(1)   Weak rationality (2.3, 3.3);
(2)   Consistency with the principles of natural justice (P1–3);
(3)   Technical neutrality (C1);
(4)   Objective neutrality (C3);
(5)   Subjective neutrality (C2).

The final position and Philadelphia

With the list of conditions from the last section in hand, we can turn to the matter of designing a credible and convincing contract situation. As established before, there are no fundamental objections to any shape or form that we might want the debate between the contracting parties to have – just as long as the archpointers are equally rational, equally well informed, equally motivated by pure curiosity and not hindered by other motives. Nevertheless, practical objections to experiments with credibility are an altogether different subject, as the debate on Rawls's conception of the original position and in particular his selection of people for the original position has shown. Let us suppose that Rawls's 'heads of families' with emotional ties to at least two future generations (Rawls 1971: 128) are the most restricted population imaginable for any impartial contract theory, any archpoint. I shall call this population A. The first and most straightforward objection that could be raised – and indeed has been raised – is that A is a gender-biased rather than representative selection of real-life humanity. A does not obviously include women – Okin remarks about the average person in the original position that Rawls never reveals 'his' sex but only refers to 'his' ignorance about 'his' place in society, 'his' status, 'his' capacities, 'his' plan of life and so forth (Okin 1989: 91). Secondly, A seems to include a quite peculiar conception of family life, that of the twentieth-century Western ideal of a nuclear family situated in a separate private sphere (Okin 1989: 93–6).

The last of these two arguments *should* not be relevant, even though, as Okin showed, it is relevant for at least Rawls's theory. If archpointers were really impartial, it should not matter who or what they are. But Okin's first argument brings us to an issue that *is* relevant to any contractarian theory: credibility. As far as potentially neglected groups are concerned, it is a matter of politeness that they be nonetheless *visibly* represented.

However, one can easily go too far in these things. If we carefully represent all creeds, colours, sexes and sexual preferences, all age groups and all types and degrees of mental and physical prowess – then why not animals, Martians or, closer to home, future and past generations and foreigners? For one, because this would make it hard to strike a balance between impartiality and imperfection; we do not all agree, even on reflection, that these groups are subjects of social justice. For another, because their presence is simply not required. They are groups that may or may not be subjects of social justice, but we surely cannot imagine them as contracting parties – they do not have the minds or the existence required to enable *us* imperfect creatures to imagine them as impartial moral judges. They may be worthy of our consideration and deserve moral treatment, yet to represent them as contracting parties at the archpoint would already presuppose that conclusion. As a general rule, there is no reason to represent any special group at the archpoint with a possible interest in social justice. If the group's interests are relevant, information to that effect will be available to, and will be treated similarly by, any impartial agent. As another general rule, whether some group should be represented at the archpoint depends not on their possible contribution to the available information or to the discussion itself, but on the psychological effect that their participation would have on the reader. If their presence challenges the imagination, they damage the credibility of the contract device. And human imagination is, unfortunately, highly conservative; we cannot play too many tricks on it. I believe this last rule is satisfied by the following story:

The final position

Let us imagine a group of ordinary people, reasonably well educated and reasonably intelligent. For the sake of argument, we could say that it includes

Wittgenstein, Elizabeth Taylor, the Lubavitcher Rebbe, Gandhi, Marilyn Monroe, Peter Kropotkin, Jack Rawls, Albert Einstein, Morticia Addams and any other odd clone of familiar persons (cf. Nozick 1974: 310).

We assume that they have nothing better to do than discuss justice. To ensure that this is the case, we free them from all other worldly concerns by postulating that they live somewhere in the far future, at a moment when the sun is about to burn up. They are the last humans and, by coincidence, meet on the steps of the Library of Congress. They have made a campfire of the last wood and gathered around it to wait for the inevitable. At times, they get up and pillage the Library's restaurant; at others, they wander through its corridors and read. Having nothing better to do at nights than to look at the fire and discuss the latest, or in fact last, gossip, they go over a whole range of topics: why the sun is dying, what killed the dinosaurs, who killed John F. Kennedy and so on. At some moment they decide to discuss social justice.

Being well educated humans, we may assume that they are equally rational. Having the Library all to themselves, they are equally well informed and presumably have access to all the scientific knowledge about human nature, history and other subjects that mankind has gathered over the last million and odd years. Thus, they satisfy the three information conditions for an impartial contract theory (R6–8).

Next, we can make either of two assumptions: either we let chance determine the course of events, or we help it a little. In the first case, our library fans will, to some extent, behave like an immortal monkey behind a typewriter, bound to type *Hamlet* one day: at some moment, the question of social justice will be posed and debated in the right way. In the second case, some one or other immediately discovers an early twenty-first-century bestseller, *Reading Wissenburg*, and poses the right kind of question. In either case, condition R10 is satisfied and the debate can begin.

The people in the final position will soon find that the pure notion of justice is of no help in their quest; although they accede to the principles of natural justice (P1–3), they feel that this tells them too little to work with. A quick glance at Plato's *Politeia* has taught them that the meaning of justice depends on your point of view. Consequently, they split their task in two: first, they are curious to find out what the right point of view is, and only then will they discuss the principles of social justice themselves. After this they return to the Library to learn more about concrete societies and concrete questions of justice. From time to time – at lunch, or at night round the fire – they compare and discuss their findings and decide upon the following targets for research, as if looking for a reflective equilibrium. Finally, and if my arguments on these points are correct, they discover the conditions of the archpoint and the subjective and objective conditions of social justice. With this, they satisfy C1–3 and R1–5. By the same token, R11–17 will be adopted.

The question then is: do these people satisfy R9? They may have formulated all the requirements of the archpoint of view and they may have all the necessary information for an impartial judgement from that point of view, but are they also capable of doing the right thing? Do they have the·correct motivation? The easy way out is to make sure that they do: we simply suppose that the strain of living under a dying sun has eradicated every trace of individual character in them. They have repressed all their desires and personal memories to keep them from going insane, and they have done so more effectively than Freud could ever dream of: they succeeded in repressing even their subconscious *id*. Nothing now can stop them from being only and merely *curious* about justice.

Fortunately, I do not think that we are obliged to choose this easy way out. For the people in the final position to be motivated as archpointers, it suffices to claim that, as rational beings, they ultimately cannot have any interest in the outcome of the debate. In the circumstances in which these persons find themselves, society is gone, the fighting's over and done. Whatever direct interests in the principles of distributive justice they may have had have now vanished. They have nothing to win, nothing to lose, and no ties to any vested interests. The influence of feelings like resentment, regret, pride, passion and preference are negligible. Being the rational beings they are, the near-perpetual criticism of one another's views in this *herrschaftsfreier* (undominated) discourse will slowly filter out these subconscious predispositions and their possibly adverse effects on impartiality. Finally, their full reasons, whatever they were, either no longer await fulfilment or if they do, their realization will not jeopardize impartiality. Once the archpointers have decided to put themselves to the task of judging justice principles, they know that this may be the last thing they will ever do. For some of them this may mean that their last opportunity to realize a full reason has passed. For others, the justice debate is an excellent opportunity to effectuate full reasons once more. Yet the only lasting influence this can have supports the curiosity motive, for instance by raising the sincerity of the debate and the completeness of the arguments. As with subconscious dispositions, the critique of others will filter out any influence full reasons could have on the form or substance of the principles of social justice.

Admittedly, the people in the final position are still rather eccentrically motivated persons living under exceptional circumstances. Unusual circumstances may be indispensable for a contract situation in which both impartiality and an intention to come to an agreement must be guaranteed, but perhaps it is possible to move a few steps closer to reality and do away with the typical (want of) motivation of the final position. What we need then is to imagine a motivational structure that is conventional enough not to alienate the contracting parties from us, yet one that at the same time does not in any respect *obstruct* pure curiosity. There may be other possibilities, but I believe that at least Aristotle's description of friendship in his *Ethica Nicomachea* will satisfy our desires in this. Aristotle wrote:

> Friendship then, being a necessity of human nature, is a good thing and a
> precious. So we praise those who love their fellow-men. And one notices in

one's travels how everybody feels that everybody else is his friend and brother man. Again, it is pretty clear that those who frame the constitutions of states set more store by this feeling than by justice itself. For their two prime objectives are to expel faction which is inspired by hate, and to produce concord – concord being like friendship. Between friends there is no need of justice, though men can be just and yet lacking in friendly feeling, which some go so far as to think an element in the highest form of justice, which we saw to be equity. (Aristotle 1959: 1155a19–28)

Philadelphia

A group of friends has just spent a weekend at a chalet somewhere in a distant valley of the Italian Alps. It is summer, and on Monday morning the warmth of the sun causes a tremendous avalanche, completely isolating them from civilization. There is no telephone, no electricity, no gas, and very soon the refrigerator decides to take up studies for a career as a black hole in space. After a day or two, a small plane comes over and drops an enormous load of food and medicine, some books, a recent paper, and a message. The Italian authorities, it says, deeply regret any discomfort tourists in the area may experience due to a *piccolo* bit of ice on the roads, promise to rescue them as soon as possible, and apologize for the expected three weeks' delay in the rescue operation because of a strike of government personnel. In the meantime, a plane will fly over every day and drop emergency resources for 50 persons.

Fortunately, the friends are unhurt and healthy, and the Italian interpretation of food aid turns out to be royal, especially since they only number 30. Nevertheless, our friends have to find something to do for the next 21 or more days. They decide to do what they always do: philosophize. They have formed a network of close personal friends ever since they studied philosophy together, and not being members of a lost generation, they were all able to make philosophy their profession. In fact, they came to Italy to celebrate the twenty-fifth anniversary of their friendship, though because of their philosophical zeal they had all filled the hidden compartments of their suitcases with books and pencils and notes – in case they would find an odd moment of spare time.

A first subject for their conversations naturally presents itself: what if no help arrives, what if they were forced to form a lasting society on their own? Naturally, that society would be one of friends, so they decide to call it Philadelphia. They are too old to start a new society, but the subject fascinates them too much to simply dismiss the question. After a while, their attention is drawn to the problem of distributive social justice – and here they encounter the most intriguing problem of imagining envy, self-interest, conflicts of interests, scarcity; in short: the absence of friendship. As Aristotle said, they do not need justice or principles of justice themselves, neither under their actual circumstances nor, they think, in the hypothetical case under review. After all, they are friends: they love and respect one another, they enjoy one another's company, each one of them would give at least some others everything they might need, and for each of them there is at least one other who is even prepared to die for him or her. They can of course imagine the absence of friendship – they have temporarily left a whole world of envy and scarcity – but it is impossible for them to imagine themselves as not being friends, let alone as foes.

In most respects, the reasoning with regard to Philadelphia is the same as that for the final position. Because these philosopher-friends are well educated human beings, we can again assume equal rationality (R8). Next, we may assume that the suitcases contained all the information required to directly satisfy R6. Being friends, our philosophers will not keep any information from one another, and they will consequently also satisfy R7. If my case was supported well enough, the society of friends will reach the same conclusions as I did, that is, they will recognize C1–3, P1–3, R1–5, and R10–17. Finally, they have the right motivation to satisfy R9: they are curious by nature and disinterested, and we may again assume that they are critical enough to filter out the undesirable effects of conscious and subconscious reasons and inclinations. Hence, Philadelphia is a suitable representation of the archpoint.

The reader may have noticed a certain similarity between Philadelphia and the community as communitarians would desire it to be. Our philosopher-friends seem to share a deep consensus about their mutual relations and the basic end of life, philosophizing. The similarity is intentional. It should draw attention to the relation between community and communitarian and minimal justice. If the Philadelphians need a conception of justice at all – if Aristotle was wrong, even angels may need laws – then we have established that they can imagine minimal justice; they are not destined to think of justice purely as communitarian justice. Better still: not only *can* they imagine minimal justice, they will be *forced* to do so and forced to make it the foundation of the conception of communitarian justice they eventually – may – develop. We have assumed that the Philadelphians are rational. It is irrational to expect new generations or less fortunate members of society to share the view of life of the society's founders; it is irrational to expect a system of education and socialization to work that perfectly (if not at times immoral to want it to work that way); it is irrational to think that a system based on friendship cannot at times falter or ultimately totally collapse. Designing an appropriate precautionary system of minimal justice is, then, the sensible thing to do.

A second motive for matching Philadelphia to the communitarian archetype is to emphasize the darker side of political theory and contract theory in particular: its objective of establishing obligations. The issue is not whether we should live together and submit to the terms of a contract, rather than strive for autonomy or for Nietzschean freedom from morality. Nor am I interested in the question why we should abide by the terms of a contract. Both questions have been dealt with both above and (better and more extensively) by others (see e.g. Scanlon 1982: 111). The question is rather one about the possibility that a political theory is vindicated with an appeal to authority: why should *we* accept a contract *they*

– phantoms created by theoreticians – supposedly back? Justified or not, how can a contract be legitimate without visible support? Like politicians in a totalitarian democracy (Talmon 1970: 251), theorists and philosophers tend to monopolize access to the general will to a sometimes dubious degree (Walzer 1981: 383). In a society, legitimacy ultimately depends on access to and participation in an open political debate, and the realization of justice in turn depends on the legitimacy of the conception underlying it (Nagel 1991: 5). Fictitious contracting parties can justify a theory but they cannot give it legitimacy; ultimately, the readers must decide on the credibility of a theory themselves (cf. Rawls 1995: 141).

7

Do we not bleed?

The elements of principles of justice

Justice demands that we treat equals equally and unequals in proportion to their inequality – so we need a measure for (in)equality, a basis of desert or a criterion for eligibility as a recipient of justice. We now have our archpoint; the time has come to apply this device to these questions.

In this and the ensuing two chapters I shall introduce the elements of a measure of social justice separately and systematically, slowly erecting a multi-storey building. The present chapter starts by asking who or what the recipient of minimal justice ought to be. In fact, it deals with three different but inseparable questions: the criteria for recipiency, the criteria for calling someone a recipient of *social* justice in particular, and the criteria for ordering the recipients' claims to social justice. The reason for treating these three questions in one single chapter is that the answer to each of these questions depends on the identification of relevant differences: differences between rocks and humans, between members and strangers, between the fortunate and less fortunate.

Principles of distributive social justice determine who will give what to whom, on what grounds and in what quantities. 'From each according to his capacity, to each according to his needs', is perhaps the best classic example of a measure of justice. However, a formula like this leaves much unspecified: who exactly is 'each', what are needs and capacities, how are they to be measured? The same ambiguity would be present in a fictitious Lockean constitution giving each person an equal share in political power. The formula looks innocent enough until one realizes that in Locke's view servants and women could not count for real persons as they lack autonomy: they are expected to follow the will of their husbands and masters. Clearly, if it is our intention to present sensible and defensible principles of justice, we cannot dodge the issue of the criteria for attributing recipiency (that is the quality of being a potential recipient of justice). Should the concept of social justice be extended to include themes, persons and things like foetuses, future generations or persons, foreign aid, extraterrestrials, crocodiles or garlic?

Though perhaps politically overcorrect, I shall from now on address all creatures or things that can be the subject of (in)justice as *recipients* and not as humans, mammals or animals. Not all recipients deserve the same treatment, though. The variation in their endowments and in the circumstances in which they exist, or, with a somewhat outdated term, the diversity of their *attributes*, makes it necessary to differentiate between degrees of recipiency. The degree of recipiency is an important indicator for the amount of distributable goods a recipient can legitimately claim. Sometimes there is reason to believe that a potential recipient, Cissy Roo, cannot be morally relevant to us, at least not as a recipient of justice – say, because Cissy is dead. Consequently, one cannot make claims on Cissy's behalf. Sometimes there is reason to believe that Cissy *could* be morally relevant but that she *is* not – say, because she is a Martian and there is no way in which we can influence her fate. Again, no legitimate claims can be made. And sometimes Cissy can be morally relevant only to a degree, because we are not responsible for every aspect of Cissy's fate, or because she cannot experience (un)just treatment to the degree that we can. In the latter case, we do not immediately have to think of Cissy as an animal; tickling the foot of a human who has lost all feeling in her limbs may be undignified and psychologically cruel but it need not be unjust. In both last examples, Cissy can make legitimate claims to a piece of the social cake, but only to the degree that she is a morally relevant subject.

After discussing some bad reasons for recipiency, in the following section I discuss three (better) cumulative grounds for attributing recipiency: life, consciousness and agency. I then turn to the most obvious category of grounds for recipiency, responsibility, and confront the intricate question of the differences between moral and causal responsibility. After that, I deal with a special case of this problem, that of membership of a particular society as a reason for deserving preferential treatment by that society's distributive institutions. In the final section, I ask whether possible persons – in particular, members of future generations – can be recipients.

In the next chapter (Chapter 8), I discuss the object of social justice, the things or rights to which the notion of distributive social justice can be applied. It is obvious that certain things cannot (yet) be distributed for plain practical reasons: we still do not have the elixir of eternal youth or the capacity to distribute innate intelligence. It is, on the other hand, not at all clear that there are also moral reasons against distributing specific rights, which would thereby end up in a sphere where the possession, exchange and enjoyment of rights depended on individual choices. It seems that there can always be a good reason in favour of distributing something, overruling any reason against distribution and in favour of, say, the free market. I shall take this observation as my point of departure and argue for a distinction (based upon their relevancy to a person's plan for a full life) between rights that are beyond distribution, rights that are absolute and irreversible, and conditional rights.

Incidentally, I shall also attempt to prevent any confusion that may arise as a consequence of the diversity of the 'things' that could in principle be distributed: goods and benefits and burdens, rights and duties, activities and experiences, freedoms, obligations and so on. To represent all these distributables with one word I have selected the term *rights*. Rights in the formal and universalistic sense I give them will be defined in terms of so-called right-molecules, that is, as the complete and absolute authority to decide whether p or not-p will be the case; p is always the smallest possible domain (in time, space and use of anything) over which someone can exercise this authority.

'Justice is free of change, forever and entirely pure' (John of Salisbury 1990: 135). Humans and circumstances are not. All kinds of contingent circumstances make a difference for the way in which the idea of justice should be implemented. The justice of the distribution of rights over recipients depends at least partially on the value of the distributed rights. Treating recipients in proportion to their (in)equality is impossible without an intersubjective measure of the value or meaning of rights. Technically, such a measure is referred to as an equalisandum: the property that is to be 'equalized' or distributed in proportion to the recipients's (in)equality. In Chapter 9, I shall defend one equalisandum for each of the two categories of distributable rights: option equality as an equalisandum for (rights to) basic needs and envy-containment for (rights to) further wants. This distinction coincides with the one Brian Barry made between goods that are crucial and those that are not crucial to the realization of a plan of life (Barry 1995: 11, 110, 143).

Chapter 10 is of a different order. Here, the conclusions reached in the preceding three chapters will be rephrased in the form of a more systematic list of principles of minimal social justice, a metric.

In a short epilogue I shall address some of the strong and weak points of the conception of social justice defended in this book. Without giving away more than this, I already want to make one claim: one of the strong points of justice as impartiality is its lack of precision, its openness to contingent circumstances, especially political circumstances. It has been claimed, notably by Michael Oakeshott, that in particular the social sciences either emerged in answer to the *petit bourgeois*'s demand for etiquette books, books telling them how to conform to the lifestyle with which the elite grew up; or that they evolved out of a similar desire to control the unknown by means of handbook knowledge (Minogue 1975: 127). It seems to me that at least the last motive is relevant to the theory of social justice. There are good reasons to strive for a reduction of questions of justice to technical questions, questions at the level of handbooks. One of these is undoubtedly the political need for our modern and relatively young democracies to mobilize support and preserve their legitimacy. Yet desirable as it may seem to have a supremely precise and complete meter, a meter sensitive enough to calculate each and every one's fair share under all imaginable circumstances down to the last penny – despite all this, the quest for such a final word on justice is bound to fail. There is no such meter, nor can there be one. Judgements on justice can be neither very precise nor near to definite; exercising justice is an art rather than a technique.

Four bad and three good reasons for attributing recipiency

A theory of distributive social justice cannot be complete or even adequate if it does not specify who the subjects of distribution, the recipients, will be. A liberally loose specification like 'all humans in society' or 'our fellow citizens' is too imprecise: it is too insensitive to relevant differences between fellow members of society, too insensitive to relevant similarities with non-members or non-humans and too dependent on an undisclosed definition of a thing called society. Designating 'all humans in society' as recipients could have been a tolerable way to avoid a debate on recipiency, were it not for the long list of candidate-recipients proposed by animal rights theorists, environmentalists, internationalists and, indeed, by liberal theorists of justice themselves.

Consider the human foetus in relation to 'us', a group that consists of already recognized recipients – no foetuses included, of course. If a foetus were to be recognized as a recipient of justice, as someone whom we should treat as an equal (at least in some respects), then it should be true that there is no relevant difference between it and us. As a consequence, we can begin to ask if (read: doubt that) there is a relevant difference between a foetus and a future person or future generation, or between future persons and fictitious persons, or between helpless babies and equally helpless farm stock or endangered species, or between humans and (supposedly extremely intelligent) extraterrestrials. If we deny recipiency to the foetus, then, on the other hand, it must be true that it differs from us in at least one relevant respect, say, consciousness. In that case someone might argue for further restrictions on recipiency. Why not also exclude fictitious persons, future persons and generations, animals – or the comatose?

By questioning the naturalness of the borders of the reference group of recipiency, we also put our own moral relevancy in question. Any attempt to illuminate why anyone deserves to be considered as a recipient of justice – as someone who can deserve something, be it more or less or as much as others – any such attempt must answer the following question: by virtue of what aspects, what attributes, can someone or something be morally relevant?

Why do we bother about the borders of recipiency? Why do theorists of justice persist in their attempts to bring animals, the unborn, future generations and foreign aid under the heading of social justice? One explanation would be causal or instrumental. The explanation is not, or not only, in the context of discovery, *pace* for instance Keith Tester's speculations on the reasons why animal rights, and in general the rights of the weak, would interest the strong: because this would acknowledge one's own strength and strengthen one's self-image, and because we are involved in a civilization process that involves the fight against human beastliness (Tester 1991: 149, 177–8, 196 ff.). *Ad hominem* arguments like these, even if true, do not invalidate sound substantive arguments. A butcher who claims that red meat is healthy may be right 'even though' he is a butcher. For the truth of an argument it is irrelevant who voices it.

Hence, we must first of all address the issue of recipiency in terms of genuine arguments rather than instrumental explanations. Before turning to possibly good reasons, I want to discuss, very briefly, three bad reasons for recipiency. They are, it should be noted, not bad reasons in themselves – they are all relevant in political contexts, and some of them are important for moral questions. They just happen to fit badly in the context of social justice. We have already encountered two such bad reasons: ego-boosting and civilization. Neither one tells us why, for example, animals should be considered as recipients of social justice and not as objects of kindness, compassion or the art of cooking. A third bad reason for recipiency, intrinsic value, deserves more attention. I shall approach it from an unconventional side, that of environmentalism, as the most far-reaching consequences of accepting intrinsic value as a reason for recipiency concern nature and, in particular, animals.

In environmental ethics and green political theory, the controversy over anthropocentrism and biocentrism is one of the most widely discussed topics (cf. Wissenburg 1998). The two are fundamentally opposed views on the relation between man and nature. In an anthropocentric perspective, man is the measure of all things; the value of nature is determined by its utility, value or importance for humanity. Biocentrism, as the word says, puts life at the centre of consideration. It is the egalitarian variant of ecologism, measuring the value of all single acts, beings and things by their impact on all other life. One of the main arguments in favour of biocentrism has been the intrinsic value of life, a notion that seems to be incompatible with anthropocentrism. The concept of intrinsic value has been designed to describe some of our basic moral intuitions: it would explain why we sometimes hesitate to do something X, even though we can think of no good reason to stop us, and even if there are good reasons to do X. A classic example is the Last Person Argument. Imagine yourself somehow being the last intelligent being in the whole universe. You are about to die and you have two options: to push a red button and blow up the whole planet and all the plants that still live on it at the moment of your death, or to push a green button and simply fade away. No-one, the story goes, would push the red button, and since pushing it would harm no-one, we should admit that we believe in intrinsic worth.[42]

The problem with intrinsic value is not so much that 'proofs' like the above are often highly imperfect, nor that intrinsic value may simply be a fable, a specific culture's prejudice or a last resort for the perplexed (Wissenburg 1998). The problem is that the whole concept serves little practical purpose. Without additional criteria that cannot themselves refer to the 'intrinsic' status of the object in question, intrinsic value can only help us distinguish between good and indifferent (having or not having intrinsic value), not between degrees of goodness or degrees of deviation from indifference. Nor will the idea of intrinsic value necessarily help us to determine whether an act is good or bad. If torture is intrinsically bad, it does not follow that any subject of torture is a recipient of justice or – in this case – injustice. The relation works the other way around: in order to be sensibly applicable, the idea of torture *presupposes* the existence of (victims or) recipients. The most serious difficulty with intrinsic value, however, is that we have no a priori reason to assume that whatever we seem to value intrinsically, here and now, would also be valued intrinsically from an impartial point of view. Hence, we decide what *actually* has value, and we may decide differently under different circumstances. Belief in intrinsic value is thereby reduced to a specific type of anthropocentrism (cf. Wissenburg 1993).

As seen from the archpoint, intrinsic value could perhaps have been a good reason to qualify things or beings as morally relevant, had it been practicable. As it stands, the best intrinsic value can do for us, if we believe in it at all, is indicate whether or not some particle of the universe could possibly qualify as a recipient – for intrinsic value is in itself not enough to qualify. Perhaps the *Mona Lisa* has intrinsic value, but that seems to be insufficient reason to give a picture the same rights as a citizen, or to deny the same rights to a picture produced with the latest software. The question now rising is whether an alternative account of recipiency is possible, an account that concentrates on the attributes of things rather than on the things themselves.

Such an account will have to be based on what may be called *reciprocal recognition*: if I am a recipient of justice by virtue of my having certain attributes and/or lacking others, and if you have and/or lack the same attributes, you should also be recognized as a recipient. This is simply a complex version of the prime directive in justice, the demand that equals be treated equally, or an extension of the famous Golden Rule: do as you would be done by.

Reciprocal recognition presupposes a point of reference, a primary recipient with whom we can compare the claims (made on behalf) of others to that status. We can, for instance, choose man as the basis on which to assess whether other members of the world of flora and fauna are morally relevant; or we can choose citizens as the basis for the assessment of claims to recipiency made by strangers and those living in Third World countries, and so forth. In the first case we can be accused of anthropocentrism, in the sense that we measure everything by standards derived from the interests of humans, and in the second we can be suspected of chauvinism. Evidently, reciprocal recognition is biased in favour of its point of reference, but this methodological bias does not need to have morally unacceptable consequences if we use what has been described as the method of prior-principle critique (Sen 1980: 197), that is the evaluation of one principle in the light of another, higher principle. In our case, impartiality can serve as the higher principle, and the corpus of arguments for the attribution of recipiency to specific groups as the principles under examination. In this approach, all arguments will be treated equally – those in favour of the adult human citizen as well as those for the unknown soldier of the future or the average cabbage on the field. While focusing on the consistency between these potentially biased arguments and impartiality, the need to argue for, for example, either human/animal differentiation (the existence of a '*prima facie* difference') or human/animal continuism ('diverging but not basically different'; cf. Benton 1993: 17) disappears.

One respect in which an analysis based on this method can still be said to be biased is that of its origin. The probably finite, possibly incomplete and maybe suspiciously selective list of arguments for recipiency is, after all, of our modern human making. Yet the fact that any analysis of moral relevancy is more or less destined to be incomplete and inconclusive, the fact that – as Robert Nozick expressed it – moral theory is underdetermined (Nozick 1974: 45–7), does not make that which it *can* positively sustain false. If z_1 is a requirement for recipiency, the discovery of another requirement z_2 will not alter anything in the status of z_1. Anthropocentric and partial to existing knowledge as the idea of reciprocal recognition may be, one can at least say to its advantage that it warrants a certain *basic* kind of morality and moral action: it poses an important and indispensable limit on arbitrariness by demanding that we do not deny the moral relevancy of others if, in similar circumstances, we would legitimately claim the status of recipient for ourselves.

Finally, if we are to think of recipients in terms of attributes rather than intrinsic value, we shall have to confront dilemmas of a distasteful kind: we shall have to explain – to give an extreme example – why a mentally and physically handicapped comatose human is either 'still' more of a recipient than an animal, or, alternatively, how an animal can be the equal of a human.[43] This is the moment to introduce a new character whom we shall encounter regularly in the coming sections, a hard case – Evelyn Hardcase, as a matter of fact. Evelyn suffers from a mysterious disease which at first made Evelyn completely lame – unable to move even the eyes. Some time ago, Evelyn recovered physically but at the same time became completely mentally handicapped: there was no trace of a self, of self-consciousness, self-control, intelligence or intuition left in the body. In a third phase, which lasted until yesterday, Evelyn was both physically and mentally completely handicapped. Finally, today, Hardcase fell into an irreversible coma. We do not know if Evelyn is still handicapped – the body just does not move and the life-signs are extremely low. Evelyn can go on existing like this for the next fifty years or five minutes.

Let me begin my investigation of better grounds for recipiency with the intuitively attractive supposition that the *harm rule* must obtain. The harm rule demands that for X to be a recipient, some act(s) or state(s) must in some comprehensible[44] way *benefit* or *harm* X. I shall use words like harm, pain, benefit, pleasure, advantage and disadvantage as innocent terms, everyday words that are not in any way indicative of any prejudice on my part for or against hedonism or utilitarianism. They simply mean what they mean in ordinary conversations: that something happens that we feel hurts or pleases us. Note that I do not claim that something cannot be good or bad if it is good or bad for no-one in particular; my far more modest claim is that it cannot be just or unjust if no-one is affected.

Unless the harm rule obtains, it seems that X cannot be a relevant subject of moral consideration, a 'someone' who can be treated immorally or, justice being a component of morality, (un)justly. Consider, once more, the *Mona Lisa*. If we prick it, it will not bleed; nor will it in other experiments show any reaction remotely resembling the experience of pleasure or pain. There is no point in saying that the *Mona Lisa* can benefit or suffer, or that it receives more or less than it deserves. It simply makes no sense to call the *Mona Lisa* a recipient. It can of course make sense to say that a distributor has *spent* too little money on the *Mona Lisa* – but a proposition like that does not entail the recognition of the *Mona Lisa* as a recipient. What it means is merely that the *Mona Lisa* is a resource for undefined recipients and that the distributor has not done enough on their behalf.

Harm and benefit come in many shapes and not all are equally important. First, the good and bad things of life differ quantitatively. As a rule, losing your sight is worse than missing the bus, and finding a companion for life is more beneficial than finding a penny. Secondly and more importantly, forms of harm and benefit can be distinguished qualitatively. It makes a difference, a relevant difference, if the subject of harm is alive or not, if it possesses (self-)consciousness or not and if it has the capacity to be an autonomous agent.

Life as an attribute of a potential recipient[45] is a necessary condition for recipiency, not a sufficient condition (cf. Steiner 1994: 258). This means that without the attribute of life, a creature cannot be harmed or benefited. It also means that a creature cannot be harmed *merely* by taking its life, or benefited *merely* by giving it life. If the classification of an event as harmful or beneficial is a matter of the individual experience of the recipient of life and death, it depends on whether the recipient's life was or will be worthwhile in his or her own eyes. A person suffering from an incurable and very painful cancer may well judge life to be intolerable and death beneficial. If, at the other extreme, there is an objective standard that determines that life is by definition beneficial and death by definition harmful, then the words harm and benefit lose all relevance for concrete human beings: the harm done by taking someone's life is no longer harm to a person but only to some abstract principle. It is harm in a purely metaphorical sense, a harm to no-one. A meaningful evaluation of harm and benefit must somehow take account of individual experience and must regard the presence or absence of life as insufficient evidence of recipiency.

Note that, by making life a necessary condition for recipiency, we can confidently throw out fictitious persons like Sherlock Holmes and Tolstoy's Natasha in *War and Peace*. Lacking life, they cannot be recipients except, figuratively speaking, in their own worlds where their fictitious equals can harm them – and where their author can, somewhat more metaphorically, kill them or, as in the case of Tolstoy and Natasha, kill their character. Likewise, we can discard the interests of past generations. Whereas future persons and extraterrestrials can be harmed or treated unjustly, past generations or persons *have* (sometimes) been treated unjustly. Clearly, this gives them *in abstracto* an interest in justice, and their descendants a real interest in compensation (in so far as that would work out to their advantage). The latter may deserve a larger part of the social cake because of the disadvantages of descending from victims of injustice. Arguments like this have been used in defence of the claims of native peoples or, somewhat more questionably, in favour of affirmative action programmes. The point to note is that it is the descendants who can be harmed or benefited and the descendants who therefore matter; past injustice cannot be rectified, dead victims of injustice cannot be compensated. And, by implication, nor can the living descendants of past spongers be blamed and punished for their ancestors' sins. Future persons are another matter; unlike fictitious persons, they may one day actually live and become recipients. I shall discuss their status later; for now, let us consider them to be ordinary people.

If pleasure and pain are to mean anything to anyone, what is required besides life is consciousness, or more precisely, self-consciousness. Pain (or pleasure) must have a place in order to be experienced, and that place must be a self if it is to be morally relevant. Thus, X's pain over the bad treatment that Y gets makes X rather than Y a recipient; whether Y is also a recipient depends not on X's feelings about him or her, but strictly on the existence of feelings on Y's side.

Time is a complicating factor in this context. I may be under narcosis now, yet the sedation and the operation the doctor is currently performing on me can be said to be beneficial even though I am currently living without self-consciousness (or so we assume). Had I not been under narcosis, I would have experienced a lot more discomfort than I do now, and when I awake in a few hours I shall be able to enjoy the benefits of the operation. Hence, the capacities for pleasure and pain seem to go on existing even while the self is temporarily absent.

On the other hand, it is impossible to prove that a recipient can still be harmed if he or she falls into an irreversible complete coma. Evelyn Hardcase, for instance, can be either of two things. Either Evelyn is aware of pleasure and pain but unable to show it, or Evelyn's self can be said to be permanently absent – the body is alive, but no more than that. We, observing Hardcase, just do not and cannot know which of these cases is true, although we do know that both can be true. Let us suppose the latter: let us say that Evelyn is permanently absent. This is still not enough to allow us to do anything we like with the vacated body. If the occupant of a house leaves her house for a walk or forever, she does not thereby give anyone a licence to burn it down. By the same token, no-one can claim possession of Evelyn's body until we have determined who can legitimately do so. Justice may even require that we keep on treating Evelyn as a pro forma recipient and, for instance, respect whatever wishes Evelyn expressed before being hit by this mysterious disease. Besides, in real life it is hardly ever possible to be 100 per cent certain that a person's self-consciousness has permanently left the still living body.

Once we accept potential rather than actual self-consciousness as a criterion for recipiency, we find that the numbers and kinds of possible recipients of justice are enormous and quite diverse. You and I could be recipients, but so could future persons, Martians, animals and foetuses. (I shall discuss the issue of 'potential' recipiency at more length in the last section.) We will also discover that (potential) self-consciousness exists in degrees, as far as we know: a fish or a dog seems to be more aware of itself than bacteria and less than Evelyn Hardcase might or could be. It is probably impossible to determine exactly how self-conscious a creature can be, yet the concept itself is extremely relevant. Being unprepared to consider what a parrot would say if it could talk, I must leave this question for what it momentarily is: unanswered. Some readers will recognize a familiar argument for animal rights in the argument for self-consciousness as a ground for recipiency: Peter Singer's. Singer, a utilitarian, argued straightforwardly that what ultimately mattered about humans was their interest in (the utility derived from) avoiding pain and experiencing pleasure. Animals, he claimed, have the same interest; it follows that they deserve to be treated as our equals (P. Singer 1979: 48 ff.). My conception of recipiency is, however, not based on self-consciousness and the capacity to experience pleasure and pain alone, nor do I argue for *equal* rights for animals. As we shall see in a moment, the capacity to be an autonomous agent allows us to make a qualitative difference between humans and animals as recipients. Nevertheless, both arguments for animal recipiency can be criticized for the same reason: they would neglect the fact that the relation between man and animal is asymmetrical. Animals are incapable of entering a contract, keeping a promise, returning a favour and so forth. There is, in other words, no reciprocity in the relation between animals and humans, and there would therefore be no sense in giving animals an equal status.

It is true that animals differ markedly from humans, and it is true that the difference is a morally relevant difference. As said before, I shall take account of this difference in a moment. However, the asymmetry argument goes beyond insistence on a gradual difference between animal and human. It asserts that the relations between recipients of justice must needs be symmetrical, reciprocal. But this version of reciprocity cannot be taken as it stands. If we demand reciprocal relations rather than reciprocal recognition (as argued for at the beginning of this section), then we would not only exclude animals but also Evelyn Hardcase and many others. We would exclude children, especially the newborn, as they are about as helpless and unsupportive as animals. Any demand for a reciprocal repayment in the future for the favours that we bestow on them now (such as citizenship, food, shelter, protection) comes down to pure extortion and violates reciprocity: newborn children are in no position to choose, let alone agree. We would also exclude the dying: we can do anything to them we want. They can never get back at us. In fact, it seems that if we require reciprocity for recipients, the concept of justice can only be relevant in so far as we cannot get away with any atrocity we happen to feel in the mood for. Which does not appear to be an intuitively attractive conclusion.

Earlier, I argued that recipiency presupposes a 'someone' who can experience pleasure and pain. In this view, the argument for reciprocal relations adds nothing to our understanding of recipiency, at least nothing that we did not already know. If we try to revise the argument in order to deal with the objections raised against it, we cannot avoid admitting that the interests of children and other 'unequals' are morally relevant despite the asymmetry in our relations with them; that the reason for the relevancy of this similarity between them and us lies in their capacity to experience harm and benefit, that is in their self-consciousness; and that their interests are theirs and not someone else's, in other words, that they are subjects like us and not objects like the *Mona Lisa*. With that, we are thrown back at a more modest conception of reciprocity: recognition of relevant similarities.

Animals, then, are similar enough to humans to count as recipients. Yet they are not our equals. The relevant differences between humans and animals may not be as fundamental as a proponent of reciprocal relations would like them to be; they are nevertheless important enough to prevent animals from being the kind of first-class recipients that humans are. There is one difference between us and them that can neither be denied as a fact, nor underrated as a moral reality: they do not seem to be autonomous agents.

Freedom of mind (autonomy) and freedom of action (agency) find expression in plans of life. The capacity for developing and executing plans of life is not something that comes with a certain degree of self-consciousness. It is a further condition for recipiency in its own right. Conceptually speaking, self-consciousness is neither a necessary nor a sufficient condition for the development of plans of life. One can be conscious of oneself without doing anything, without even feeling the need to decide not to do anything. Moreover, it only takes a memory to devise and stick to a plan. Either consciousness is not required, or our computers are not what we think they are.

The second claim, that the capacity for having life-plans is a condition of recipiency in itself, can be defended intuitively as well as analytically. Intuitively speaking, there is a difference between our evaluations of the harm done by killing an unwilling chicken and the harm done by murdering a young human being. The immorality of the latter seems to be of a different quality than the first. A possible reason for this bias against poultry is that we do not expect a chicken to have a long and meaningful, let alone a planned and remembered, life (for an argument to the contrary, see DeGrazia 1996). Hence, and apart from the cruelty of killing itself, killing a chicken seems little else than hastening its natural death, whereas the murder of a human being entails the annihilation not only of that single individual before his natural time, but also the destruction of his future and the future selves to which he is already emotionally attached.

However, the argument from intuition is inconclusive. We will probably judge more moderately if we know that our murder victim suffered from a painful and fatal disease, and that he expressly desired death more than anything else. In this case, death was part of the dead person's plan of life, and our judgement about this fact is influenced by this fact. Apparently then, there is more to the moral relevancy of the capacity for having a plan of life than its mere existence.

Another argument, one that is not based on intuition, throws a better light on this matter. The capacity for having a plan of life can only justify the attribution of (a special kind of) recipiency if there is (a special kind of) harm done in obstructing it or benefit in advancing it. This in turn means that self-consciousness is required: there is no pain without someone suffering. We can imagine a plan of life without self-consciousness, but we cannot think of it as morally relevant without that quality. It also means that we must ask ourselves what it is that makes the capacity for having a plan of life so special. I have already given away part of the answer: we value a plan of life because it expresses the two typically human attributes of autonomy and agency. In Chapter 4 I offered a defence of the worth of agency and autonomy. There is no need to repeat the arguments here. It is because of the special value we attach to agency and autonomy that each of us finds himself or herself to be morally relevant. Reciprocity then demands that if I am a recipient of justice by virtue of an attribute z, you should also be recognized as a recipient if yours is the same attribute. As a consequence we are obliged to attribute recipiency to other humans but not to animals.

Unlike self-consciousness, autonomy and agency do not qualify someone as a recipient *to the degree* that he or she has these attributes. One qualifies when having the capacity for both, and is disqualified when lacking them. We cannot measure these qualities by their performance. Stoics, fatalists, monks and Buddhists will appear to be less autonomous and less agents than an average New York businessman, but this depends on the observer's different assessment of the possibility of human freedom and action. It thus depends on the reasons, possibly basic reasons, that different people have for believing themselves to be autonomous agents and for how to be or act autonomously – and as we saw in Part II of this book, there is no impartial and objective moral standard for the evaluation of basic reasons.

Further, I do not believe that we can measure autonomy and agency by the degree to which these capacities *exist* either – thereby putting Evelyn Hardcase in the same category as ourselves during the early stages of Evelyn's illness and in that of future persons and animals in later phases. The only supporting argument I can think of is inconclusive and perhaps question-begging; on this point moral theory is likely to remain underdetermined. An animal may deserve the title of recipient less than a human being even if neither one is an autonomous agent, due to a difference in their genetic make-up. The animal never had it in its genes to be a self-conscious self-determining actor, the human did. As a consequence, Evelyn should still be considered a potentially autonomous agent and the animal should not. While in coma, this potential is destined to keep on being potential, but it is still there – probably.

Causal and moral responsibility

Whether a person or animal can be a recipient of justice depends partly on whether (s)he or it can be harmed or benefited, but it also depends on what *we* do. The distributors have to be in a position to influence the existence of a recipient if she or he or it is actually to count as a recipient. A living, self-conscious Martian who happens to be an autonomous agent can be a recipient of justice – but not one of *our* justice, not as long as we do not live on Mars. Moreover, influence itself is not enough for recipiency; causal responsibility is not the same as moral responsibility. (I shall assume, in what follows, an understanding of responsibility that is both conventional and essentially Aristotelian: to be causally responsible one must (a) be able to influence or change something in the world, so that responsibility does not end when one refrains from doing something; (b) know that one can influence or change something; and (c) be able to know how the chains of causality work, more or less, so that one cannot be responsible for completely unpredictable consequences.)

Our inquiry into the moral relevancy of responsibility, to which this section is devoted, will lead us to recognize that a distributor's moral responsibility for the welfare of prospective recipients is necessary to qualify them as recipients and, consequently, to serve as a ground for desert. This again will lead us to investigate a quite different but equally important question concerning responsibility: is a recipient's responsibility for his own welfare a ground of desert? On the latter issue, our conclusion will be an unsatisfactory and provisional 'yes, but . . .'. However, before we temporarily concentrate on grounds of desert, let us first discuss the theme of recipiency and ask what it is that distributors influence.

We influence the future by turning left instead of right, meeting another partner and in due course causing other people to exist, and we influence present lives when driving people down – but giving a million pounds or life everlasting to a genuine stoic will hardly influence her feelings or peace of mind. We can cause circumstances to change and persons (not) to exist, yet do not thereby necessarily change anyone's feelings, such as those of being treated unjustly or unfairly. But then again, not everyone is a stoic.

Now we should distinguish two issues: the influence that a distributor has on people's *feelings* of being treated (un)justly, and the distributor's influence on their *shares*, their means, goods, properties or rights. Ideally, the two come down to the same thing. Justice as impartiality is predicated on the existence of a society of reasonable persons. We, or the archpointers, are assumed to see things from the archpoint, looking only at what a reasonable distribution scheme would be. The conditions of the archpoint force us to consider feelings of support or disapproval only in so far as they are based on the reasonable desires and expectations of reasonable persons. Hence, archpointers judge the justice of distribution schemes on the basis of a universal measure for the *meaning* that allocated rights have to normal people, the equalisandum (see Chapter 9). Ideally, then, influence can be defined both in terms of shares as causing a recipient's amount of equalisandum to change, and in terms of feelings as causing a recipient's feelings about his or her amount of equalisandum to change.

Yet as this is not an ideal world, so I shall stick to the first of these definitions only. In the case of the stoic described above, no amount of earthly goods could influence her feelings, though perhaps there are rights to other things that might influence her. In some other cases, however, the allotment of rights and the feelings about allotted rights cannot be harmonized by an adequate definition of the equalisandum or by a better understanding of the recipient's feelings. A spoiled child can get as much as it asks, even more than any fair share could ever be, and still be unsatisfied. Alternatively, one of the greatest worries of children is to discover one day that their parents are becoming senile and are starting to behave like spoiled children. In cases like these, where the only logic in feelings is pathological, it is practically impossible to influence feelings in any predictable way. They can only be treated justly on an as-if basis: as if the recipients were rational persons.

Defining influence as causing a recipient's amount of equalisandum to change still leaves us with our initial problems: what do we mean by 'causing', and is any cause a good cause – does the simple fact that we as distributors influence, for instance, present and future species of animals create a moral responsibility on our part, and does this make them recipients?

To start with the first question: if we want to make sense of notions like accountability, shame, agency, education, morality and in particular justice, we need an account of responsibility in terms of causality. In principle, the problem can be solved quite simply by following custom, that is by considering every being that is capable of premeditation to be causally responsible for everything it knowingly caused. To deal with deliberate ignorance and uncertainties in calculations, it is reasonable to add that one is also responsible for the risks one takes and for consequences that could have been known. But in this apparently innocent description of causal responsibility, three elements prevent it from being understood as an all-or-nothing concept. One is never 'simply' responsible or not responsible.

Responsibility is often shared. Consider just one grisly realistic example: as a representative of the government, you personally see to it that Mrs A, a Hutu refugee, is put on a plane back to Ruanda. Based on the ambassador's reports, your superiors decided that she would no longer be in danger in Ruanda and that she can therefore be sent back. The next day, your embassy reports that Mrs A is murdered by Tutsi terrorists. Of course, her killers are responsible for her death, but who is responsible for endangering her life in the first place? You, your superiors, the ambassador? Or perhaps your country's parliament which, after all, created or condoned the structures that allowed all this to happen? In our conception of causal responsibility, all those involved in Mrs A's repatriation and in everything that caused it were partly responsible, but it is extremely difficult to assess exactly who was responsible for what part.

The problem of shared responsibility obviously also complicates the evaluation of moral responsibility and the prevention of further disasters. If we blame the organization, we may appear to be clearing the individuals; if we blame the individuals, it looks as if the structure of the organization needs no change; and if we blame both, we may induce divide-and-rule policies with the disadvantages of both other strategies (cf. Bovens 1990a: 89 ff., 123 ff.).

Fortunately, shared causal responsibility and the complications of responsibility in complex organizations are not directly relevant to the issue of recipiency. To be a recipient of justice, it suffices that one's share of the equalisandum can be changed by a distributor, no matter who that distributor is. (The latter point will be discussed briefly at the end of this section.) But these are not all the complications involved in apportioning responsibility.[46]

Chance, of course, is another well-known source of complication. Consider a few simple dilemmas:

(1) If you know that there is a 10 per cent chance that your doing x to Y causes harm to Z, are you responsible for Z's misfortune?

(2) Are you responsible if there is a 1 per cent chance that your doing x to Y will cause Y to harm Z?

(3) Are you responsible for causing x by doing something y that may lead to x if you know there is a chance of x happening anyway, without knowing how high that chance is?

(4) Are you responsible for causing a, which may cause b, which may in turn cause c and so on down to Ω, endless generations from now – all with either known or unknown probabilities?

Or, for a more complex example:

(5) One's responsibility for a distributive action with a 90 per cent chance of being 100 per cent effective may well be judged to differ from that for an action with 100 per cent effectivity for 90 per cent of the recipients.

And then, can responsibilities be ranked at all – are you more responsible in case (1) than in case (3), for instance?

In one respect, chance is irrelevant to the issue of moral responsibility. In general, we do not hold X responsible for what others Y, whom X has affected, do, on the assumption that (and in so far as) these others Y are themselves capable of responsibility – that is, if and to the degree that Y's behaviours are not fully determined by X. In 1991–2, for instance, a television commercial showed fictive pictures of nice couples like Mr and Mrs Amin (parents of Idi) and Mr and Mrs Hitler (parents of Adolf), followed by the text 'if only they had used Jiffy condoms'. The condom makers had a point: the Hitlers and Amins were causally responsible for the existence of their children. Still, no-one holds the Amins and Hitlers morally responsible for what their children did; they – the parents – simply could not foresee let alone help it.

In so far as we fully determine someone else's character or behaviour, moral responsibility cannot be passed on. Suppose that it is a uniformly known law of nature that anyone who was beaten by his or her parents during childhood will, with either 100 per cent or 50 per cent certainty, one day beat up at least one person without any reason at all. For the sake of simplicity, we shall assume that the parents are perfectly autonomous agents, that is their actions are not caused by some outside source. In either case, the moral responsibility is the parents', not the child's. The first case is simple enough: the parents carry full responsibility. In the latter case, however, the complications involved in causal responsibility turn up again. They have taken a risk and are now obliged to explain why they thought it worthwhile or necessary to take that risk.

Yet in cases where chance complicates the apportioning of moral responsibility, it turns out to be irrelevant to the question of recipiency. We can think of the example of child beating again, or better still, a more complicated case involving shared responsibility such as the effect of the temporary occupation of Somalia by several UN member states on justice and peace in the country. What matters for the attribution of recipiency is not the relative degree of moral responsibility that invaders and supporters and opponents of the occupation carry – but the fact that the people of Somalia actually became recipients, perhaps of some nations and perhaps, through (non-)membership of the United Nations Organization, of each and every nation of the world.

Ignorance, subjective lack of available knowledge of one's actions or their consequences, is a third factor that complicates issues of moral, though not of causal, responsibility. To distinguish ignorance from chance, consider the following case. You are a general practitioner and one of your patients has a heart attack. On the basis of recent research it is known that any patient suffering from a heart attack has a 40 to 50 per cent chance of not surviving the next hour; it is as yet unclear what factors make it certain or more likely that a patient will survive. This is chance: absence of precise knowledge, of knowledge with 100 per cent certainty. Now suppose that two of your patients have a heart attack at the same time. You cannot be at two places at the same time, so whom shall you attend to? One of the two is a heavy smoker, with a 50 per cent chance of getting a second and probably fatal heart attack within a week; the other has no known dangerous weaknesses. If you do not have access to this information (for example because the smoker hides it from you), you will act in ignorance involuntarily; if you do know these facts, however, you can cause yourself to act in ignorance. Ignorance causes one to act – perhaps – differently than one would have done knowing more. It does not, however, change one's role as a cause nor, necessarily, one's causal responsibility. Voluntary ignorance in fact adds one more chain of the course of events to one's responsibility.

Sometimes voluntary ignorance is unavoidable, in which case the consequences of acting in ignorance may be (and provided that the act is not intrinsically bad, as I suppose to be the case for the sake of argument, are) excusable. Consider all you could know about the effects of eating a particular sandwich. By the time you have calculated all the certain, probable and possible consequences for yourself and all others, you will have been dead for aeons. Or consider the relation between America and Europe before 1492. In ignorance of one another's existence, the Europeans could not be responsible for the fate of the Americans – and vice versa.

At other times, voluntary ignorance is premeditated, that is one causes oneself to be ignorant where this could have been avoided. Premeditated ignorance can make an enormous difference for moral responsibility. It need not: if the information you deprive yourself of is irrelevant but, human as you are, might tempt you into acting immorally – say, in the case of the doctor above, if the information concerns the criminal records of both patients – acting in ignorance can be a virtue. Yet it can also be a vice. We do not go about catching other people to hang them on hooks through their cheeks, swing them around for a while and be photographed with them, except perhaps in certain houses of ill repute. A principal reason for not doing this is because we know that it may seriously hurt a human being. Some of us do such things to fish, though, and do not bother to find out if their bizarre reactions to being pierced and hung and swung about are not perhaps more than simple reflexes. Assuming that the question can be answered at all, no amount of action or inaction taken to remain ignorant diminishes the fisher's moral responsibility.

Now where do all these complications take us? First, to the rather straightforward conclusion that the least bit of moral responsibility on the part of X for the wellbeing of Y suffices to qualify a living, self-conscious and autonomous agent Y as a recipient in relation to X. Secondly, we observe that these complications frustrate attempts to answer a few other questions that relate to distributive justice:

(1) Should a distributor, who is only in part morally responsible for a recipient's amount of equalisandum, take full responsibility for the recipient's fate? For example: should the German government or the West German taxpayer cover the costs of the environmental problems in East Germany, given the fact that the greater part of these problems dates back to before the unification in 1991? (I assume for the purposes of this example that no other potential caretakers exist.)

(2) If there is more than one distributor for the same recipient or set of recipients, which one should take first responsibility? For example: in a country with local, regional and national governments, social security could be a task of each of the three or of a combination of them – or, alternatively, they could each try to put the responsibility in the hands of the other levels.

(3) Does a recipient's (absence of) moral responsibility make a relevant difference for his or her claims to the equalisandum?

The first two questions are a bit out of place in this chapter. They pertain to a question that cannot be fully answered until we reach Chapter 10, namely that of the designation of the distributor – but I shall nevertheless spend a few words on them here.

Moral responsibility is either taken seriously, down to the last consequence of the last act, or we might as well forget about it. Imagine that you walk past a pond where a child is drowning. No-one else is around, there is no way of getting help, and you can swim. In a way, this makes you the distributor of the little child's life. By not doing anything, you will kill her. Even though you have not caused her to be in these circumstances, you are now morally responsible for her life. By the same token, even if a distributor is only partly responsible for X's current situation, his influence on X's share in the social product makes him morally responsible for X's wellbeing. All this is, of course, under the condition that X can legitimately claim the distributor's help. If the girl in the pond turns out to be merely a pretender who can swim like a fish, her cry for help requires no action.

The second problem, that of shared responsibility for the distribution of the equalisanda, is essentially a question of priority and not of responsibility; it will be dealt with in Chapter 10. Suffice it to say here that, by the same logic as before, all potential distributors are responsible. If one of them ducks his or her responsibilities, the others take over, willy-nilly (cf. P. Singer 1985: 252–3).

The last question, about responsibility as a basis of desert, is the most complicated of all. A positive answer will immediately raise two further questions, namely how to determine the degree of responsibility (a question that I have so far carefully avoided) and how to weigh responsibility relative to other grounds of desert (a question that cannot possibly be answered until we know what these other grounds are). And the answer must unquestionably be positive: moral responsibility really makes a relevant difference. If we were to set it aside as irrelevant, we would not take agency and autonomy seriously, nor, as a consequence, the existence of reasons for acting, nor the recipients' full reasons – which would imply a severe violation of impartiality.

In one respect, moral responsibility is relevant because we apportion praise, blame and other things that can be expressed in terms of the equalisanda, on the basis of responsibility. This is the view of justice that we inherited from Antiquity (cf. in particular Aristotle 1959: 1135^{b}9 ff.). In the light of justice as impartiality, it is quite understandable that responsibility is seen as a basis of desert: it is consistent with the demand that reasons for action be taken seriously. Of course, there is little an impartial distributor can do with moral responsibility except recognize that *something* should be done with it. To the degree that reasons for acting are moral rather than empirical, and given the absence of a criterion for the worth of such basic reasons, all a distributor can say is that full reasons should be respected. But we will save this question for later. There is another, more urgent problem to be dealt with first.

Paradoxically, in a second respect we apportion units of the equalisanda on the basis of *absence* of responsibility, and this in exactly opposite ways: in a sense, good luck is often punished and bad luck rewarded. Or so it seems: the more you earn, the higher the taxes; the less you earn, the higher the subsidies. Arguments for distribution on this basis invariably refer to the fact that a person's misfortune came about 'through no fault of his own', or that her fortune was 'not of her own making'.

In antique times and in pre-modern Christian thought, (bad) luck without responsibility was not seen as a matter of justice at all; it was thought of in terms of *caritas* and divine judgements. In modern liberal theories of social justice, however, somehow luck and bad luck have become the substance of social justice.[47] This might seem to be a minor historical detail, adding up to little more than a new name for the same old rose, but it is more: the inclusion of fortune and misfortune as grounds for distributive justice indicates a paradigmatic change in the way we think about responsibility.

Enlarging the scope of social justice to include compensation for bad luck (*caritas*) and good fortune means, essentially, that the responsibility for the wellbeing of recipients has been assigned to society *regardless* of the reason for changes in the recipients' fortune. There no longer is a direct link between causal responsibility for the creation of an 'unnatural' or unjust state of affairs, and moral responsibility for its readjustment or recompensation. In classical terms, fortune and misfortune are no longer seen as rewards or punishments from God or the gods on the one hand, and as invitations for man to show mercy and admiration on the other – they are now simply cases of repairable and undeserved good or bad luck. Nor has the link between justice and reciprocity of relations survived. Justice is no longer directly associated with an obligation to restore an equilibrium between services rendered and rewards due, as was the case in the classical (Aristotelian) conceptions of retributive and distributive justice.

In a word, justice has been bureaucratized: to make a legitimate claim to justice, it now suffices to show that a change or lack of change in the amounts of a recipient's equalisanda does not harmonize with a society's criteria for such changes. Thus, to elucidate the paradox detected above, responsibility is now seen as a ground for desert in so far as the criteria for social justice demand that one deserved a change in one's amounts of equalisanda, whereas any change in absence of responsibility is judged to be an undeserved change that therefore ought to be compensated or repaired.

It will be clear, then, that there are at least two views on (absence of) responsibility as a ground for desert. In the first and classical sense, responsibility does, and absence of (causal) responsibility for good and bad luck does not, qualify a recipient as deserving treatment according to the principles of distributive justice. In the second view, that of modern liberal theories of justice, both grounds are considered good enough – but never on their own. The absence or presence of responsibility, *together with* the evaluation of changes in wellbeing as fortunate or unfortunate, determines if and to what degree society should compensate changes in wellbeing.

Once more, the difference may seem to be one only in name; either we call all society-based acts of redistribution distributive justice, or we call a specific class of redistributive actions acts of mercy. I could be perfectly happy with either option, if it were not for two things. First, there is good reason to believe that the classical view can violate impartiality. To see good and bad luck as judgements of the gods certainly presupposes an objective (divine) and substantial criterion for desert – a non-impartial view of the good, in other words.

Of course, one can also think of (mis)fortune as calling for corrective redistribution without invoking the idea of divine judgement. But at this point a second objection can be raised, to the effect that such an act of corrective redistribution no longer differs in any relevant respect from an act of distributive justice. There

141

is no difference in the *way* mercy and justice are applied. In either case, whatever it is that is distributed ought to be distributed justly: equally to equals and in proportion to the inequality of unequals. Thus, an act of mercy should follow the same principles as an act of justice. Further, there is no difference in the *amounts* distributed under the guise of mercy or justice. Nothing has been said so far about the total amount of rights or goods that ought to be distributed in cases of mercy and justice respectively. Intuitively, an act of mercy is limited only by what distributors or contributors are willing to give, whereas the upper and lower limits of the amounts assigned in an act of distributive justice are defined by the available new stock (e.g. this year's GNP). But our intuitions in this are misleading.

What happens when (mis)fortune strikes, say, Harry Stottle's wallet? Either money moves from him to Cissy, or to him from Cissy, or it falls from the skies, or it disappears into nothingness. In all these cases, the change not only influences Harry Stottle but everyone else as well: relative to Harry Stottle (and sometimes Cissy), everyone's share in the social stock changes. Moreover, not only Harry Stottle's (mis)fortune was undeserved – but so are, obviously, all these other relative changes. If we want to judge whether any corrective redistribution is called for, we shall consequently have to look at the complete sum of undeserved advantages and disadvantages. In short, there are definite upper and lower limits to the amounts that can be redistributed in an act of mercy, and these limits are not determined by good will; they are identical to the limits for acts of distributive justice.

With this, we have answered one part of the question that we set out to answer, that is how to determine the exact degree of (a recipient's) relevant responsibility or absence of responsibility. We have seen that the latter part is simply irrelevant. The absence of responsibility is no reason against *nor in favour of* the distribution resulting from (mis)fortune, nor one for or against a corrective redistribution (such as an act of mercy), nor one for any exact share in the redistributable stock. If we are looking for criteria for *caritas*, we have to look elsewhere, that is, we have to look for grounds for desert other than (absence of) responsibility.

This still leaves us with the problem of measuring responsibility. Unfortunately, there can be no measurement of responsibility, at least not an impartial measurement. As we saw before, there are three complicating factors, chance, ignorance and shared responsibility, which prevented us from determining exactly how responsible a distributor is for the wellbeing of a recipient – had it been necessary to determine this. The same trinity prevents us from measuring a recipient's responsibility for his own welfare.

Determining each person's contribution in a case of shared responsibility is a technical problem, but one of a complexity that can hardly be underestimated. We would have to map all events and actions connecting each person to an ultimate consequence – but the chain of causes leading to such a simple consequence as the author typing the next word is already far beyond the capacities of anyone to describe. What is more, any rule or system apportioning personal responsibility in a collective enterprise presupposes the impossible, namely that all external influences can be sifted out: chance, ignorance and duress of all sorts (ranging from physical coercion to subtle meddling with the unconscious and to educational factors).

The problems with ignorance and chance are moral rather than technical. To determine when ignorance is excusable we need a conception of 'reasonable' ignorance, allowing us to weigh the costs and benefits of gathering or neglecting information. It is clear that this implies that we need a more substantial theory of the good than weak rationality alone: a criterion for ignorance demands that the moral meaning of consequences, the value of the good and bad things in life, can be measured and scaled. But as we cannot assume the existence of an objective theory of the good without violating impartiality, we cannot impartially assess ignorance.

The same problem hampers any measurement of chance: we need a theory of 'reasonable' risks, and there can be no such theory that does not somehow favour some views of the good life over others, or that favours some full reasons more than others. Analogous to the principle of reasonable ignorance, it would need to be based on a theory about the worth of consequences. Moreover, a principle of reasonable risks would be based on a theory about the proper attitude towards risks, describing whether or not to take a chance when the odds are ten to one, or what to do when the chances are unknown but the consequences predictable. And again, such a theory cannot be impartial. Consider, for instance, Rawls's preference for the maximin rule for choice under uncertainty, which 'tells us to rank alternatives by their worst possible outcomes: we are to adopt the alternative the worst outcome of which is superior to the worst outcome of the others' (Rawls 1971: 152). Clearly, the maximin rule can conflict with full reasons like courage or self-sacrifice for the sake of others, or simply with the desire to live dangerously.[48]

The conclusion that we must draw from the examination of these obstacles is highly ambiguous. Responsibility is a ground for desert, but it cannot be measured impartially. It must be given weight when distributing, but any specific weight given to it is arbitrary and will quite probably constitute a violation of impartiality. Whatever weight the principles of minimal justice can give to responsibility seems bound to be purely formal. In Chapter 9 I shall try to determine to what rights the concept of distributive justice applies, and on that occasion further develop the idea of a purely formal acknowledgement of responsibility. For now, I must leave the issue as it stands.

Society and exploitation

So far, I have argued that a recipient of justice is a living, conscious, autonomous agent for whose wellbeing at least one distributor is morally responsible. My next goal is to find out if each recipient of justice is also a recipient of social justice. The answer will, on the whole, be negative. It all depends, of course, on how one defines society. As a rule, mainstream theorists of justice circumvent this problem by simply assuming the existence of a self-sufficient society. Strangers and foreign countries come into the picture later, if possible one by one – perhaps due to an idealized and rather controversial interpretation of American history. Rawls, for instance, opens his book with the implicit assumption of the existence of a society (Rawls 1971: 3; Rawls 1993b: 43 ff.; cf. Paden 1997b), and only after a very long time incidentally touches on justice between nations – nation apparently being a synonym for society (Rawls 1971: 378). Similar observations can be made about Nozick and Ackerman (Ackerman 1980: 72, 89): they all frame recipiency in such a way that the question of distinguishing *on morally relevant grounds* between members of and strangers to society can hardly be problematical. The difference seems to be there already, as a matter of fact – which it is not. It is an illusion to think that we are born with the freedom to choose to sign protection contracts or to think that any society is self-sufficient (Beitz 1979: 143 ff.) or entitled to the resources that would make it self-sufficient (*ibid.*: 136 ff.) – and it has been some time since colonists discovered really uninhabited lands.

Many of the descriptions or definitions of society that do exist are almost as unsatisfactory as the habit of not defining it at all. First, society is not a co-operative venture for mutual benifit – society is both more, since an exchange of money for tomatoes may be mutually beneficial but is insufficient to build a society, and less, since it can exist on the basis of mass exploitation. Nor can societies any longer be defined on the basis of a shared culture (if ever they could). The borders between cultures, languages, customs, and so forth are or have become too diffuse. The related communitarian conception of society as a thing that is constantly reproduced in the course of a life by unconscious social bonds, by the company of and intercourse with all those with whom we learn to share a common understanding or culture, is even worse. It is already predicated on an understanding of society or culture, one that is justified on the basis of a matter-of-fact (subconscious) consensus only; it can tell us that, but not why members are more morally relevant than strangers. Fourthly, an Aristotelian understanding of society as a perfectly self-sustainable system of relations (Aristotle 1981: 1326^{b}2) has become outdated. The requirements for self-sufficiency depend on the level of luxury or frugality that we – the 'international society' rather than isolated states – desire and believe possible to sustain, and as several environmental problems have taught us, that may only be compatible with a global society. Next, societies cannot be defined with an appeal to a subjectively felt sense of responsibility for or relation to other creatures (compare the concentric circles theory of responsibility in Wenz 1988: 316). In a conception like this, the extent of society is defined by individual fancy or accidents; it fails to give any morally sound reason for distinguishing between insiders and outsiders. Finally, a definition of society as that which is in actual fact a political unity, recognized by others as such and recognizing others as such, is perhaps the worst possible justification for a distinction between members and strangers. Not only does it derive an *ought* from an *is*, not only is the *is* an arbitrary product of pure historical coincidence (cf. e.g. Beitz 1979: 79, 122) – but it is most of all a fiction. None of us are subjects of only one sovereign set of shared institutions: we are part of local, departmental, national, regional and international political units, each with their own conditionally recognized sphere of operation – from the citizens of Basel, who elect their own Roman Catholic bishop, through states, defence organizations, European and other Unions, up to courts of international justice.

If we want to define society in a way that allows us to explain why membership would make a relevant difference, a first mistake that we need to avoid is that of thinking of society merely in terms of the attributes of individuals. An adequate understanding of social justice as *social* starts with the observation that recipiency has nothing to do with the qualities I may happen to share with you – life, sense, responsibility, and so forth. What we really want to know is how a special type of *relationship* between persons can give rise to special questions of justice.

A relationship cannot give rise to questions of justice if there is nothing we can do about it. There is no society between two dead people. The relation or the structure of the relation must be potentially open to change by one of the parties involved. I call only these relations social. In addition, relations need to be changeable in a special way: they must be exploitable or open to the avoidance of exploitation. The notion of exploitation to which I refer here is derived from (Philippe van Parijs's reformulation of) John Roemer's interpretation of exploitation as X-exploitation: a person is X-exploited (X-exploits) if she could be better off (worse off) if X were equalized (cf. Van Parijs 1992: 157 ff.; Roemer 1996). The relation a confessing Catholic has with his or her confessor is, ideally, inexploitable: neither the confessing nor the forgiving parties can be made worse or better off than canon law allows.[49] Finally, society is in essence more than an exploitable social relation: it is a particular structure, an ordered system, of such relations. I already remarked that a society is more than an accidental encounter between me and my grocer. What we usually understand to be a society is a whole set of interconnected persons and relations, an association that does not end with the entry or departure of one or more persons. One special and, for matters of justice at least, highly relevant trait of this system is the fact that, as a structure, it shapes and influences (other) social relations and, consequently, the wellbeing of individuals.

Understood in this sense, as the structure of exploitable social relationships, society is a ground for recipiency in the same way that life, consciousness, agency or moral responsibility is: membership of society is a trait that makes recipients out of creatures, whether they like it or not. Yet the significance of membership is also fundamentally different: it does not create or differentiate recipients as such, but rather adds to and fragments the influence a distributor has on their wellbeing. Note, finally, that recipients can be embedded in more than one structure, more than one society: a local community or a city as well as a province, state, federation and the world community (cf. Beitz 1979: 145). I shall discuss the consequences of this complication – it raises the question, again, of determining which distributor will have the first responsibility for the wellbeing of recipients – at more length in Chapter 10.

Being there

Can possible persons be real recipients? So far I have assumed that they can, but the arguments concerning agency, responsibility and membership would not in any way lose their strength if possible persons – or possible animals, for that matter – were excluded. There is some reason to consider the exclusion of future generations: it sounds quixotic to speak of the agency of, responsibility for and society of, creatures that *do not even exist*. With this intuitive argument against justice between generations in mind, I shall first look at some reasons that point in the other direction: care and impartiality with regard to generations. We shall find these to be insufficient. Next, I shall examine whether perhaps future individuals rather than future generations can be recipients of present-day justice. Again, our conclusion will be negative. Neither possible generations nor possible persons can be recipients; consequently, there is no place for them in the principles of justice – at least, not as subjects. (For a way around this formal objection, see Wissenburg 1998.)

The case for justice between generations is often very poorly sustained. A surprising illustration of this thesis is John Rawls's treatment of the subject – surprising, as Rawls is not exactly known for inaccuracy. Despite its failings, Rawls's ideas have made a deep impact on virtually every debate on future generations in political science and theory, economics, environmental sciences and so forth; it is for this reason only that I discuss it in more detail than it deserves. (For alternative theories, see Wissenburg 1998).

In Rawls's theory, the contracting parties are expected to be mutually disinterested. They neither care for nor detest the wellbeing of others. As a consequence – as one of the consequences – each person's interests carry the same weight. A major exception[50] to this rule concerns their relation to future generations, or more precisely to their direct descendants – for which it turns out that the people in the original position *do* care. That is, it is *assumed* 'that a generation cares for its immediate descendants, as fathers say care for their sons' (Rawls 1971: 288). The contracting parties must be seen as representatives of family lines, not knowing to which generation they belong, or otherwise 'there is no reason for them to agree to undertake any saving whatever' (Rawls 1971: 292). To protect the interests of future generations, Rawls argues, the people in the original position will want the principles of justice to be constrained by a just savings principle (Rawls 1971: 284 ff.).

But why assume that we, or people in the original position or archpointers, should care for future generations? One reason Rawls mentions is that 'men have a natural duty to uphold and to further just institutions and for this the improve-ment of civilization up to a certain level is required' (Rawls 1971: 293). Else-where he defends this duty as inspired by 'the desire to obtain similar liberties for the next generation' and by the duty to represent the interests of others by choosing for them in the way we believe they would choose themselves (Rawls 1971: 208–9). But this seems to be tautological, for the *fact* that our present choices will influence future generations is in itself no reason to *care* for what happens to them, unless it is already *presupposed* that we care. Rawls's second argument is that 'persons in different generations have duties and obligations to one another just as contemporaries do. The present generation . . . is bound by the principles that would be chosen in the original position to define justice between persons at different moments of time' (Rawls 1971: 293). The argument seems to derive its force from an analogy: if, as Rawls argues one section later, we must be impartial towards the different periods in our life instead of opting for, for example, instant satisfaction of present desires at the cost of later benefits, then we should also be impartial between one generation and the next instead of . . . and so forth. The best I can make of it is that the latter choice is itself inspired by the fact that the contracting parties do not know to which generation they belong, yet know that they care for future generations. Which again presupposes the conclusion. Apart from this, it is an argument that might convince people in the original position but not archpointers. It is none of the archpointers' business to determine that one way of looking at the distribution of welfare over a life is better than another – to suppose the opposite would come down to a negation of neutrality with regard to full reasons.

What Rawls shows when arguing for the just savings principle is that if (1) we have obligations to future generations, then (2) it is reasonable to suppose that the people in the original position have the right attitude of care for the interests of future generations. As a consequence of this attitude, (3) the contracting parties choose a particular principle for the treatment of future generations, and (4) we as inhabitants of the real world are, by implication, obliged to follow this just savings principle. In other words, Rawls succeeds in arguing for a particular principle, but – other objections (Paden 1997a) aside – he fails to show why it would be rational to care about our descendants' fate in the first place, and why we should care for future generations in general rather than for our own flesh and blood in particular.

Absence of proof is, however, not the same as a refutation. First, it may be true that we should care about our own descendants and, consequently, about future generations. Secondly, it may be true that we should care about future genera-tions regardless of any attachment to our own descendants. To positively exclude future generations from the class of recipients of social justice, we must refute both theses, as I shall try to do now.

The first argument seems to be Rawls's. I already quoted him as saying 'that a generation cares for its immediate descendants, *as fathers say care for their sons*' (Rawls 1971: 288; my italics). It is reasonable, both in Rawls's original position and from the archpoint of view, to demand that any consideration for future individuals be distributed impartially on the basis of reciprocal recognition. The fact that one child has a caring parent is not a relevant difference between one child and another. A particular child deserves its (caring) parents no more than the parents deserve the child, and no more than other children deserve not to have those caring parents. Moreover, the archpoint of view prescribes that one should be impartial towards certain reasons for action rather than towards the carriers of those reasons; in this respect, a special attachment to some rather than all future individuals cannot be justified.

Now the conclusion of this Rawlsian argument may be sound, but the premise is not. That is to say, it is *not* necessarily rational to want to have children, nor therefore to care for them (as long as they are possible persons), nor to care for future generations in general. In the Rawlsian frame, one can point to the obviously negative if not disastrous effects that being a woman, becoming a mother or being expected to become one can have on life-plans in most societies. Having a more than 50 per cent chance at birth of turning out to be female, the people in the original position would have to be rather hesitant – to say the least – about calling procreation rational. Seen from the archpoint of view, procreation is an issue regarding which one should be impartial. It is always possible that someone disapproves of procreation and that this feeling of abhorrence goes so deep as to be a full reason. For this person at least, it is rational *not* to have children.

Hence there is no sound reason either in favour of or against procreation, and no reason to believe that care for one's offspring is in itself a good reason to consider future generations as part of our present society. Of course, *if* one has children and is responsible for their welfare, it is by implication reasonable to care about the children of others – but that is a very bad reason for principally including future children in the measurement. Unlike others for whom we may care because of their vulnerability and our influence on their wellbeing, this is a responsibility that need not arise.

Having rejected the first reason for the inclusion of future generations, let us now consider the second argument: that we should care about future generations, regardless of any attachment to our own descendants. In the absence of a Rawlsian defence, this conviction could perhaps be supported by an assumption to which Brian Barry occasionally referred, to wit, that no-one deserves to be born in this generation or time (e.g. Barry 1993: 224). From this assumption it nevertheless does not follow that those who come after us can legitimately claim a share in our possessions. In fact, they cannot, as I am about to show. The reason for this is that *generations* cannot be hurt; only individuals can be recipients, and possible individuals are not individual enough to be morally relevant or relevant to distributive justice in particular.

What marks an individual? In his *Reasons and Persons* (1984), Derek Parfit convincingly argued against both physical and psychological identity over time: each of our parts, including our plans, aspirations and mentality, can in principle change or be changed without causing a distinctly new personality to exist. He also rejected a conception of the self as distinct from the things I so far called attributes, like a flagpole in comparison to the flags on it. There is nothing to individuate a self without attributes. Instead, he suggested that the distinctive feature of personality (individuality) is a so-called relation-R, a sense of continuity with regard to previous selves, previous memories of one's self. Hence someone who has been brainwashed by her psychotherapist or the KGB and has begun a totally new life with new aspirations, new knowledge and new feelings, yet still remembers her former self, is the same individual as the former self she remembers. If, however, the memory of this past self is a result of the brainwashing itself (to replace the memory of a 'real' former self), she is no longer the same individual she was before. Similarly, the product of one particular sperm and one particular ovum will be a different person if it is born at a different point in time because its memories and life will differ from the beginning; the result of eugenics applied to a foetus creates a different person than the foetus could have been; and obviously different sperm and ova also produce a different person. Accepting R-connectedness as the basis of individuality creates immense problems for any theory of distributive justice, even more than explanations in terms of psychological or physical continuity over time. As each and every little action that could take place differently may cause different people to exist, the question rises whether we benefit those individuals whom we cause to exist and harm those whose existence we prevent, or vice versa. If we take the difference between persons seriously, the (dis)advantages of one's existence cannot be compared to those of one's non-existence, let alone with those of others's (non-)existence.

Part of the problem can be evaded, Parfit suggested, by making absolute rather than relative comparisons: counting each individual and his or her wellbeing for one and measuring it by an independent standard (Parfit 1984: 358 ff.). Thus, once an individual exists, there is no need to compare the incomparable, that is the life of a once-merely-possible-now-real person with either his non-existence or alternative (once possible, now impossible) persons. The trouble lies in causing their existence as such: is it good or bad to be born – or neither?

Derek Parfit's theory rests on the assumption that propositions like 'I wish I had never been born' make sense. But can we say beforehand that a life will (not) be worth living? Even if we could know the level of technology, the history, and so forth, of that future society, this seems contentious. Imagine the next generation inheriting from us *only* stone and wooden objects and the skill to make them; we and all the gadgets and materials with which we lived suddenly evaporated. Is the life of this future generation not worth living – a kind of life lived before by countless generations? Wellbeing depends, first and foremost, on how the individual living a life feels about life, and only in second place on how others tell her to feel about it in comparison to, say, the glorious past.

Nevertheless, let us assume that there is a certain basic level of welfare below which life is not worth living and at which wishes to be 'unborn' start to make sense. Alternative policies involving the creation of different persons can – according to Parfit – be judged in terms of justice. This idea, however, invokes

149

another, less explicit and less convincing, assumption, namely that future individuals have something like a *right* to a basic level of welfare and to the avoidance of a life below that level – put another way, a right to a decent life or no life at all.

Judgements on the quality of life are difficult, regardless of whether they are retrospective or prospective. They require an unambiguous point of reference as well as answers to the old disputes on what man's basic needs really are, and to what degree an individual's judgement about his own welfare should be trusted or respected.

If we suppose that the first problem can be solved (as it should be in any sound theory of justice), we still have a more fundamental problem to deal with: the right to a decent life or no life at all is meaningless and (or rather: because) impractical. Only in retrospect can we say if a life or part of it was worth living, and only during the short season of Welfare State security might one have ventured to predict futures in terms of welfare over a life. Life is too hazardous for an individual to calculate life-long welfare levels in advance with any degree of certainty.

In this context welfare does not merely refer to *material* wellbeing. It is equally hazardous to predict whether the life of Evelyn Hardcase will be worth living – in Evelyn's own eyes, as we are nothing but agents calculating and deciding in Evelyn's place. Even in a world that hates the disabled, the coloured, the second sex, members of these groups may learn to surprise us and enjoy life. By the same token, no natural or social inequality is sufficient reason to believe that it makes life not worth living – or that it makes life extra worthwhile. (Past generations tried to benefit us by industrializing, but our harvest from the past also entails an ecological crisis which, according to some, more than offsets the benefits of progress.) Only under very special circumstances can we be nearly, but only *nearly*, certain about the value of life – for instance, if we know that a newborn baby has only six months to live and that it will suffer from a horribly painful disease during each of those 180 days and nights.

Now suppose (a) contrary to what we assumed in the last two paragraphs, that welfare over a life *is* predictable or at least predictable enough to know whether or not the borders between a worthy and an unworthy live will be crossed. Suppose furthermore (b) that having children or not having them may cause other people's welfare, for instance that of their parents, to change and fall below or rise above the basic level. For my purposes, it suffices to assume finally (c) that the existence or non-existence of at least one individual Z will cause at least one other person's welfare to cross the border between a life worth living and one that is not.

If (a) is the case, the only choice parents X and Y have regarding the life of their child Z would be one between having or not having that particular child. Yet by assumption (c) the possible consequences of this choice must already be accounted for in their own parents' (i.e. the parents of X and Y) decision made under assumption (a) to give birth to them (i.e. X and Y), as well as in the decisions of other parents to create the contemporaries of X, Y, or Z. Thus, by (a), X and Y do not have a choice and, by repetition of the argument, neither did their parents, grandparents, contemporaries, and so forth. If the choice for one predictable life is predetermined, all are, and if all choices are fixed, none are really choices.

Thus, if we accept both (a) and (c), there is no choice and there is no 'right' to a decent life or no life at all. To save Parfit's thesis we must either reject (a) and accept a deadlock because of the uncertainty of real life, or reject (c), which can only be done if we are fully certain that (b) is untrue – which is absurd. As Parfit's thesis cannot be saved, we must conclude that the right to a decent life or no life at all resembles the right to be loved, honoured and cherished. It is at best a promise to try, at worst a lie. This leaves us with the conclusion that, as far as questions of justice are concerned, it *does not* make sense to talk of future recipients wishing never to have lived, not until their lives have actually been lived, and it *does not* make sense to talk of future individuals as current recipients of justice. It *does* make sense in terms of an already ongoing life (euthanasia and sometimes abortion), as there is an existing individual to which the concept of recipiency can refer, someone for whose opinion we can ask, or about whose ideas we can make an educated guess – unlike a possible person, who merely *might one day* be an individual.

This conclusion may come as a bit of an unpleasant surprise. Intuitively speaking, the welfare of future generations matters. Imagine a world in which the starting positions in life determine later success and imagine a parent who has the means to save money, wants children, subsequently has children, but prior to their birth decides not to save for their future. Or suppose that we – as a society – know that there will be a next generation and yet deplete an important part of the earth's resources. Or all of them. How can we maintain that these practices are unfair towards the children of the future if future generations cannot be recipients of present-day justice?

There are two answers to this question. Both are, I think, good enough to convince even the still unconvinced proponent of justice between generations that the whole issue of whether or not future individuals can or cannot be considered recipients is, in fact, of little consequence.

First, in the real world a generation does not simply emerge at the moment a prior generation ceases to exist; generations live side by side and are as such responsible for one another's fate (cf. Wissenburg 1998). As a consequence, there is a continuous transfer of institutions and rights between coming and going, rather than present and future, generations. This takes care of one part of Rawls's arguments for justice between generations, namely our 'duty to uphold and to further just institutions' (Rawls 1971: 293).

Secondly, principles of justice can protect the interests of future generations in an indirect way, making justice between generations an uneconomic, redundant, concept fit for an encounter with Ockham's razor. In the following chapter I shall argue that using rights in a way that depletes resources is not simply bad luck for those who come after us; it also constitutes improper – unjust – use of rights and resources, depriving existing persons from future benefits. Natural resources are not up for grabs. From an impartial point of view, few things are ours to distribute, own *and* destroy; most things we merely borrow for a while. Hence the operation of principles of justice will be constrained by a duty not to leave the world worse that we found it on entry – whenever possible.

Let me close this chapter with a brief summary of the criteria for recipiency. We have found that, to be a recipient of social justice, it takes:

(1) existence;
(2) life;
(3) potential consciousness;
(4) autonomy and agency;
(5) membership of society, that is a structure of exploitable social relations; and, on the side of the distributor,
(6) moral responsibility for the wellbeing of the recipient.

These criteria are not all equally easy to apply. Consciousness, as we saw, differs with the species. We were able to avoid a whole class of complications by distinguishing between class-A recipients (specifically humans) and others, but animals remain nevertheless positioned on an unspecified scale of increasing moral relevancy. The conditions 5 and 6, membership of society and moral responsibility on the side of the distributor, make it possible that a recipient of social justice has to deal with, or be dealt with by, more than one distributor.

The fuzziness of the concept of recipiency puts up two problems. No priority rules have yet been given, for determining the relative weight of the interests of class-A and class-B recipients (humans and animals) or that of members and strangers, nor for attributing the prime responsibility for just distribution. I shall, of course, try to solve these questions in the following three chapters.

Moreover, as a private person we may feel that our family or friends deserve priority over others (members as well as strangers), but as an archpointer it remains to be seen whether this kind of priority can stand the test of impartiality. I do not consider this to be a problem of social justice, but more one of justice as a personal virtue, and will therefore ignore it in this book. However, if pressed for an answer, I would say that there is an analogy between the circle of friends and the greater sphere of society. Both are essentially structures of exploitable relations, systems in which we operate and through which we influence the wellbeing of others in a special way; both therefore give rise to special obligations and responsibilities.

8

The distribution of rights

I have been assured by a very knowing *American* of my Acquaintance in *London*, that a young healthy Child, well nursed is, at a Year old, a most delicious, nourishing and wholesome Food, whether *Stewed*, *Roasted*, *Baked*, or *Boiled*; and I make no doubt that it will equally serve in a *Fricasie*, or *Ragoust*.

Jonathan Swift, 'A Modest Proposal' (Swift 1959: 260)

Owning – the stringent view

Distribution is a matter of at least one distributor, at least one recipient and of course at least one object of a certain value – young healthy Irish children, for instance. In this chapter I shall look at the last category, that of the objects to which the concept of distributive justice ought to be applied. Rights and other things are distributed in various social contexts – the family, classes at school or in universities, neighbourhoods, communities, nations, continents, unions, churches, clubs, and so forth. For reasons of simplicity I shall talk about distribution only in the context of society, without attention for the possible relevancy of my conclusions in other social contexts.

My discussion of this issue is inspired by two almost classic problems in the social justice debate: self-ownership and original acquisition. The first problem was detected by, among others, Rawls's critics. Since neither a new-born child nor its parents 'own' the child's natural endowments nor 'deserve' them, should these endowments not be considered as resources for a society – and should not society then decide on the development and use of its citizens' endowments? One does not even have to think of the nourishing qualities with which children are reputedly endowed to understand that the consequences of a dictatorship of society can be deplorable: imagine a society coercing its members to serve as slaves in the interest of the state for a period of one to five years. On the other hand, we often find it reasonable that governments keep people from using some of their endowments at the costs of others (their driving skills, for instance, in favour of safety) or that it forces them to use their capacities differently (for instance by forcing a good doctor to work in a poor rather than a rich neighbourhood).

The second issue, that of original acquisition, was raised by Nozick's critics after the publication of his *Anarchy, State and Utopia* (1974). His whole theory is predicated on the inviolability of natural rights but, like his source of inspiration, John Locke, Nozick never took the trouble to account for the existence of natural rights. Once we reject the natural rights assumption and with it seemingly all moral rights or claims before the creation of political institutions, it becomes quite difficult to see how any form of original acquisition could be justified – or any subsequent transfer of goods. On the other hand, if there is such a thing as justifiable original acquisition, notions like (re)distribution and distributive justice might well lose their meaning. No transfer of any good would be just without the explicit consent of the rightful present and next owners. Hence the term 'distribution' would be a mere metaphor for a set of just transfers, just only in terms of commutative justice.

Now suppose that (1) distribution is about the assignment of ownership of goods expressed as rights (I shall introduce a more precise interpretation in terms of moral rights in the next section). Let us (2) furthermore think of ownership in moral rather than legal terms and begin with the following provisional definition of ownership: owning something is defined as *being morally privileged* to control its fate (deciding on use, forms and terms of use, destruction, conservation, and so forth), in distinction to possessing or using something. I call this the *stringent conception* of ownership.[51] It is then (3) clear that the two debates to which I referred a moment ago embody two diametrically opposed stands on distribution. One is a radical interpretation of Rawls, according to which everything not specifically and totally attributable to an individual is a possible object of distribution owned by the society; the other is a radical interpretation of Nozick as claiming that by definition nothing can ever be distributed, as only individuals own things. In between these two positions lies every imaginable set of distributable and tradeable goods.

A theory of distributive justice would be incomplete if it did not take a position on either side of this dispute or somewhere in between. I shall present and defend my own position by questioning, in this section, the stringent conception of ownership that underlies the controversies about original ownership and public versus private ownership. The gist of my argument will be that such a stringent notion of ownership is incompatible with impartiality, as impartiality requires that claims to (most) goods are permanently open to moral scrutiny. In the next section I introduce a rather formal concept of rights to represent all that could possibly be distributed. This concept enables me, in the third section, to deal with the problems of my provisional stringent conception of ownership. I shall formulate a more flexible understanding there, one that results in, among other things, an important distinction between conditional and unconditional rights. Following this, I shall take a look at a second distinction, that between commutative and distributive justice, between rights that can but should not be distributed, and rights that both can and should be distributed. In the final section a third and final distinction will be made between two kinds of distributable rights, quite simply labelled as Basic Needs and Further Wants.

In the radical Rawlsian view, natural resources and undeserved individual endowments are assets for society, simply by virtue of the fact that there is no-one other than society to possess them. It has been noted that this is a *non sequitur*: the two premises according to which (1) there are only individuals plus an entity known as society and (2) no individual has an original right to either his own possibly socially useful endowments or to the previously unpossessed resources she finds around, do not support the conclusion that (3) society alone has an original right of acquisition, transfer and distribution (cf. Sandel 1982: 77). The claims of individuals to their endowments are as legitimate or illegitimate as those of society, because neither party deserved them. Any claim to non-human (that is, all other) resources is hampered by both this problem and the deeper problem of justifying real original acquisition – looting nature – as such.

The radical Nozickean doctrine, it seems, provides a clear solution to the problem of the original acquisition of natural resources and, metaphorically speaking, the acquisition of personal endowments. It unambiguously ascribes original ownership rights to one category of claimants, individuals, at the exclusion of all others, and it gives a reason for this: natural rights. Incidentally, it also protects the liberty of individuals against assaults from the side of the collective. However, on closer look the solution turns out to be far from perfect. There is more than one possible theory of original acquisition, and the reasons for choosing either of these are insufficient. Consider the following four idealized positions on the issue of original acquisition. I do not pretend that they exhaust the list of possibilities, but they will suffice to illustrate the point that theories of original acquisition are underdetermined as far as proving the morality of ownership is concerned. Rights cannot be rights unless every reasonable person should recognize them, and these theories of original acquisition fail to give the necessary reasons for recognition. For perspectives like that of a social contract theory or Nozick's theory of voluntary associations, this comes down to saying that once a society is established, all prior rights or things called rights, whether they already existed or not and regardless of their former validity, have been voided; they have to be acknowledged 'once more'.

According to a first theory, which one occasionally encounters in classrooms, issues of original acquisition and just transfer should be solved by reference to the law and jurisprudence: justice would consist in getting and giving what the law prescribes. However, positive law only determines whether possession is legal, and legal and moral justice only occasionally sleep in the same bed. Being concerned with the distribution of rights over a group, the law is subject to judgements based on principles of social justice; the law offers no justifications, but requires justification itself (cf. Brehmer 1980: 21 ff.).

A second solution in terms of natural law would run as follows. Suppose that an object *P* was unpossessed until now. A person or group *X* takes it (a) either

155

because X badly needs it to survive or, on a less stringent interpretation, (b) because X just likes it. There is no conflict with others, either now or in the future, as X leaves enough objects similar to and as good as P for others to take. We could think of P as a breath of fresh air, for instance, something X badly needs to survive. The theory of natural law would call this act of original acquisition legitimate: nature does not prohibit it in any way. We do not take any risks in adhering to this theory: if nature does not prohibit something, one is obviously free to do it. Still, that does not make it right: *ought* may imply *can* but *can* does not imply *ought*.

This difficulty poses a threat not only to the credibility of the extended natural law thesis (version b) which ultimately boils down to the Marquis de Sade's creed that anything goes that can be done. Suppose that we reduce the doctrine to alternative (a), thus justifying original acquisition exclusively in cases where vital needs are at stake. In this version, anything goes that can be done and saves a life. Clearly, this will not be enough to solve the problem of ownership once and for all, for as soon as scarcity strikes the principle allows (murder and) any involuntary transfer that saves a life. Nor will it work if we also demand that conditions of affluence obtain. Consider a Nozickean (Nozick 1974: 176) dilemma. The first human takes the first breath of air, the second a second, the nth an nth, and by that time the air is out. Person n obviously did not leave enough air for $n+1$, ergo her act of acquisition was illegitimate; $n-2$ did not leave enough for $n-1$ and n, which makes his original acquisition illegitimate; and so forth down to the first human. Of course, the first person's first breath of air only becomes illegitimate at the moment $n+1$ enters the world, and until that time there is nothing rotten in the world, but this nevertheless means that ownership rights cannot be attributed definitely. There may always come an $n+1$. Moreover, natural law does not give any rule for original acquisition and further transfers other than the law of the jungle – without any deeper justification.

A third conceivable scheme, not too much different from natural law, relies on the natural rights of man to vindicate original acquisition. In this view, one is *entitled* to something by – for instance – one's natural right to survival, rather than merely *permitted* by natural law to procure it.[52] Apart from inheriting some of the problems of the natural law approach, the idea of natural rights puts up a new problem: that of finding a criterion to distinguish between the entitled and the rightless. Again, the deeper problem will be to explain how an *is* can be turned into an *ought*, how a natural desire or need, for food or water or shelter, can be transubstantiated into something like natural desert. Which takes us back to the archpoint: no matter from what source natural rights stem, the law is on earth, to paraphrase the Talmud again (Walzer 1988: 29). In absence of an authoritative source of morality, even, or particularly, a divine decree specifying natural rights requires validation and affirmation from a point of view that we can all trust – the archpoint. Without this approval there is no reason why the principles of social justice should respect private property and property rights.

Finally, we could consider strong determinism as a solution. In this view, the whole question of justice and just possession never arises. If X takes something from nature and reserves it for herself, she does so because she has no option. Even if there 'are' other options in the eyes of God or in the light of eternity, X herself is a predestined or determined creature and not in any way an autonomous agent. And without choices, questions about the morality of choices are quite beside the point.

This solution will only work for what is called strong determinism. Any type of determinism allowing subjects the least bit of freedom of choice (so-called weak determinism) must choose sides. On the one side, it can be a morality-sensitive determinism, allowing that some choices are called morally better than others (cf. e.g. Inwood 1985: 72, 81; Sharples 1986: 268 ff.). In that case we would be back where we began: looking for a justification for ownership. On the other side, it could be a determinism that rejects the possibility of assessing the morality of choices and instead explains choices in terms of, for example, chance. The latter approach shares with strong determinism the disadvantages of, first, not taking the subjective experience of freedom seriously, and, secondly and more importantly, not answering the question directly. Both the strong and the chance variants of determinism can still account for the theory and practice of ownership and justice, but this account will be only a metaphor of justice as seen from the archpoint of view. Instead of justifying it, both determinisms will *explain* ideas about justified original acquisition and ownership in terms of power, power relations, human psychology and motivations. Yet in the end, such an analysis comes down to the same thing as the archpoint: it amounts to an explanation of how it comes about that we should believe in the ideas behind an institution like property. In this respect, then, the difference between determinism and morality is metaphysical but not political.

I have tried to show with these examples that any theory about the morality of ownership is underdetermined if it does not give arguments to persuade us into believing in it; entitlements cannot be taken for granted (*pace* Steiner 1994). As argued in Part II of this book, the only way in which we can be reasonably persuaded is by means of the archpoint. The question then arises what the opinion of archpointers would be on the justifiability of original acquisition and of ownership as provisionally defined above.

We can treat both questions under the same heading, that of legitimate ownership. Morally assessing the effect of a transfer is not fundamentally different from assessing that of original acquisition. The question in a case of original acquisition, as we saw, was why a reasonable impartial person should approve of X's owning P. That very same question must be asked in cases of transfer of ownership. Suppose that Harry legitimately owns P, and voluntarily transfers it to Cissy. Being the legitimate owner, Harry is absolutely free to make that transfer. From a natural rights view, this would imply that Cissy now is the legitimate owner of P. But is this also plausible from an impartial point of view? Let us change the example: suppose that the German government voluntarily gives me all its army personnel and equipment, or that it sells all government agencies to Kuwait. Is it still plausible that I or Kuwait are now the *morally legitimate* owners of former German property?

I shall argue that the first thing archpointers would want to do is revise our provisional and very stringent definition of ownership as sovereignty. Remember that we thought of ownership in terms of justified possession. The two most prominent characteristics of possession are, first, the exclusion of others from controlling the fate of whatever it is that one possesses, which includes using the thing – unless, until and in so far as not proclaimed otherwise by the current possessor; and secondly the subjection of the possessed to the possessor. If both can be justified for at least one possessable item, the idea of ownership as absolute sovereignty is itself justified. Conveniently, this turns out to be true, in particular, as I shall argue in the following sections, for the basic determinants of personality.

So far, so good. But the rigid definition of ownership neatly divides the world into two theoretical classes: the class of legitimately ownable things, and that of not legitimately ownable things. All we know about this latter class is that these goods cannot be owned in the strict sense of the word, which does not imply that they should not be used. Imagine that you and I are starving, and in front of us lies a loaf of bread. We do not own it – it belongs to a rich and well-fed woman who will not give it to us – and we cannot buy it, because we also happen to be poor. We are alone and will remain alone (with this loaf) for at least the next two weeks. Should we let it rot, or should we eat it – are we allowed to, morally? The point that I shall be making is that there exists a grey zone between absolutely legitimate and absolutely illegitimate possession, one that forces us to take a more lenient view on ownership and redefine this concept.

We only have to concentrate on the first aspect of ownership to discover this grey zone: are there any good, that is impartial, reasons to allow anyone to decide exclusively whether anyone else will be granted or denied the use of something, call it a gadget? To begin with a relatively simple case of original acquisition, assume that only Harry Stottle is *able* to give others access to the gadget. Without Harry, the gadget would be inaccessible if not non-existent – as is the case with, for instance, original thoughts, ideas and capacities, but not with their physical reflection. As no-one else *can* possess gadgets like this one, Harry is evidently its exclusive possessor. It is equally evident that if Harry's gadget can save millions of lives, we may see reasons to force him into giving others access to it, which means that we would be denying him the right to own it. But unfortunately we cannot: Harry has threatened to destroy the gadget, or kill himself, or he simply refuses to co-operate, or perhaps it is physically impossible to force Harry to co-operate.

In a case like this we may believe that Harry's behaviour is repugnant and unjust, but there can be no question about his right to possess the gadget. There is nothing we can do to change the fact that he possesses it, and we can neither deny him the right to own his gadget nor give him that right. It is not a question of feasible rights, or practicable rights, or non-formal rights – Harry's possession of it is simply a matter of fact.

The picture changes when we assume that Harry can be forced to co-operate. This time, possession is no longer a mere matter of fact. We *can* do something about Harry's control over the gadget: we can acknowledge it, thereby establishing Harry's ownership rights, or deny him ownership. Why should his autonomy, or whatever else is hurt in the process of compelling him, weigh more than the lives – and autonomy – of millions? Framed in this way, there is hardly any space for doubt as to the intuitive morality of 'repossessing' Harry's gadget and assigning ownership to a more trustworthy institution. Whether Harry should be compensated for his loss or honoured for his work is another question, and one that we need not go into here; what is important is the discovery that Harry's ownership rights are not indisputable.

Next, consider a third and a fourth case. In the third case, Harry possesses a unique gadget that could enable exactly one other, already happy person named non-Harry to feel, for a fraction of a second, the smallest possible amount of extra happiness. In the fourth case, Harry is no longer unique in possessing a millions-of-lives-saving gadget; there are a few other people who possess equivalent gadgets. In both cases, Harry's co-operation can be enforced.

In the third case, we will be indifferent or almost indifferent between Harry's (and our) options of giving access to the gadget and withholding access. From a utilitarian point of view, for instance, simply asking Harry to co-operate may be discomforting enough to compensate for the gains of co-operation. From a non-aggregative consequentialist point of view, the effects access for non-Harry will have on Harry and non-Harry cannot be balanced against one another – they are not the same person. If Harry himself would feel the least bit of hesitation about non-Harry's access to the gadget, that would be enough for us to conclude that access is not all good. From a deontological point of view, Harry's choice is not a matter of principle. There is no duty to make non-Harry happy or happier, though joy may be a side-effect of the fulfilment of duty; consequently, happiness itself is not an argument either for Harry or, if Harry disregarded his duty, for us. There could be a duty not to keep gadgets to ourselves, but a duty like that could only be a duty if it concurred with a categorical imperative, which does not seem to be the case here.

The fourth example is more complicated. Obviously, if someone else offers her gadget in Harry's place, there is no direct need to force Harry to co-operate, but there still is no clarity about his right to own a gadget and deny others access to it. If no-one else wants to co-operate, we may have a new dilemma, that of choosing who should be pressured or even tortured first – but at least we now know that all gadget-possessors are in the same situation as Harry was in the second example.

In all these cases an archpointer, not judging as we did on the basis of intuition only, would need more information than the examples gave. The archpoint demands that we postpone our judgement on full reasons, not on others. As a consequence, archpointers should know whether any full reasons are involved. They would want to know why Harry made his gadget and wants to own it, and why any non-Harry wants to use it. With that information, they would be able to assess whether assigning ownership to Harry or society is reconcilable with impartiality. Clearly, this is still not enough to settle the issue of ownership once and for all. Yet there is nothing more archpointers, as archpointers, could say.

Adding still more information would change little; the archpointers would simply become more like us. Suppose that we add a few facts. If it is known that the millions whom Harry could save have no lust for life, in fact suffer intolerably and fiercely dislike life, and Harry's gadget would not change that, then the archpointers' moral judgements on the cases presented might be influenced. Hence, they would need information about the particular society's current morality or (in absence of consensus) moralities, information that will not increase the value of the archpointers' judgement. In so far as no full reasons are violated, an archpointer can add nothing to the public debate on the morality of ownership, as she can only have a different, not a better, view on issues involving other than full reasons. As we saw in Part II, there is no yardstick for the better point of view.

Our four examples, however, give enough information to draw one general conclusion: we have found that, in any individual case and given the moral context of a society, there may always be a more weighty reason against X's ownership than there is in favour of it. Even if exclusive possession of the gadget is of vital importance to X (he may die without it, his personality may cease to exist, or he may lose all joy in life), who has full reasons sustaining his claims to ownership, others could attach the same value to X's not excluding them. Preferring one person's full reasons over those of others is unfair, as we should treat equals equally and the claimants are equal in an extremely relevant respect – yet clearly a decision must be made. Any decision in such cases will necessarily be unfair towards someone, as someone's full reasons and life-plans will be frustrated. There may be a less and a more fair solution, and none will perfectly satisfy everyone, but whatever the solution turns out to be, it clearly cannot be one that gives any weight to claims, reasons and arguments, and at the same time builds on a conception of ownership as absolute sovereignty. As long as there are rival claimants, possession is a source of conflict and ownership rights remain open to debate. We must therefore reconsider our definition of ownership.

What it is to have a right[53]

Our discussion of the provisional definition of ownership given above led us to the conclusion that ownership, the moral privilege or right to possess something, must be (re)affirmed by a reference group, society, under the constraints posed by justice as impartiality. We also found that not all ownership rights have to be unconditional rights, rights with which no-one may interfere: there was a case for believing that at times an ownership right will be a right to use rather than (absolutely) possess a thing, and to use it only in particular ways, places, periods, or circumstances.

Before I turn to the ensuing question of distinguishing and justifying conditional and unconditional rights, I want to reflect a moment on a more technical question: how should we conceive of rights? After all, social justice is concerned not only with the distribution of property; principles also allocate non-material liberties and duties, benefits and costs, goods and bads. Can all these different things be put under the same heading of 'rights'? In this section, I shall introduce a conception of rights very similar to Hillel Steiner's (Steiner 1994) that allows us to do so, that is, that enables us to talk about 'that which is distributed' with this one single term, rights. The account I give of this conception is, I admit, not perfect – on occasion it is even fairly superficial. However, my first aim is to present a conception of rights that works for us, not one that fits in perfectly with the ideas about rights that are normal in deontic logic. I shall discuss the links between my conception of rights and the conventions in deontic logic at the end of this section. Readers who, on the other hand, find this section still too technical can simply skip it. I shall provide a quite untechnical summary at the beginning of the next section.[54]

In everyday speech, one has a right to something (a book, a house), a right to do something (freedom of press, opinion and speech, the right to vote), or a right to be something (happiness, freedom, survival). One has such rights if and only if one has the authority to decide whether or not to exercise, enjoy, profess, utilize, or whatever, the right in question. If the authority is lacking, the term 'right' is used in the very different sense of a right (in the first sense) that is limited by external obstacles, or by internal inhibitions like a sense of duty or morality. In either case we are, for the sake of this argument, talking about rights in a metaphorical sense only.

A bit more formally, a right in the simple non-metaphorical sense is the undivided authority to decide (this phrase will be explained shortly), or the full control over, whether or not a specific X will be used in a specific way Y to a specific purpose Z. Against this background, I define:

X as a set $\{x_1, x_2, \ldots x_n\}$ of objects;
Y as the set $\{y_1, y_2, \ldots y_m\}$ of means; and
Z as the set $\{z_1, z_2, \ldots z_l\}$ of ends.

Note that I do *not* assume that X, Y and Z are disjoint. A book can function as a means or as an object.

The basic material out of which rights are made will be called – for want of a better word – right-molecules or *r-molecules*.[55] They define a person's physical and moral freedom, at one particular moment and place, to autonomously determine whether one particular object shall be used in one particular way to one particular purpose. More formally, an r-molecule is:

(1)   an element (x_a, y_a, z_a) from the set $X \times Y \times Z$;
(2)   at one particular moment in time and on one particular place (t, p).

I shall make two assumptions regarding r-molecules:

(1)   condition $\mathfrak{C}$, the condition of absence of instrumental obstruction: it is not true that it is physically impossible to influence (x_a, y_a, z_a). The absence of instrumental obstruction is what distinguishes a genuine right from a formal right (I assume, for the sake of argument, that there are no other conditions inhibiting the exercise of rights);[56]
(2)   an r-molecule is something over which one and only one person i has sole and exclusive control, that is i *sees to it that* (cf. Lindahl 1977: 28) one of the two possible worlds will exist: the one in which i sees to it that (x_a, y_a, z_a) is the case at (t, p), or the one in i sees to it that (x_a, y_a, z_a) is not the case at (t, p).

In summary, an r-molecule is a quintuple denoted as i: $\mathfrak{C}$ (x_a, y_a, z_a, t, p), or, shorter, as $i^\star(x_a, y_a, z_a)$, or, still shorter, simply as a, b, c, and so forth.

An example of an r-molecule would be $i^\star(x_b, y_b, z_b)$, in which x_b stands for this book, y_b for burning it page by page and z_b for the purpose of expressing outrage. $You^\star(x_b, y_c, z_b)$ means that you can throw it out of the nearest window as well and $you^\star(x_b, y_c, z_c)$ means that you can also do that to express confusion. All this of course at the appropriate time and place only.

It is impossible to count and catalogue all possible r-molecules; there is too much time in eternity and too much space in infinity. Moreover, the exercise of authority over r-molecules can cause other r-molecules to exist. Research activities, for instance, can lead to the discovery of new possibilities for action and to the invention of new machines or techniques – all of which comes down to the unexpected creation of new r-molecules. Luckily there is often no need to be too precise. In practice, we assign complexes of r-molecules and call these complexes 'rights'. They can be (nearly) all-purpose rights, for instance a right to read one particular book for (nearly) any purpose; or (nearly) all-object rights, such as a right to save a life at (nearly) any cost; or (nearly) all-means rights, such as a right to use a book in (nearly) any way to teach a class. A right can also be a complex of such complexes. My freedom of expression, for instance, would be the Marcel Wissenburg-version of the following human right for European citizens:

EU citizen: $\mathfrak{C}$ $(x_{1-n}, y_{1-m}, z_{1-p}, life, European\ Union)$

in which x_{1-n} stands for all the capacities required to think and communicate, y_{1-m} for all the means needed to communicate and z_{1-p} for the purpose of expressing any public or private opinion.

In everyday life, we often take it for granted or do not bother to check that complexes like these can be imprecise and incomplete, that is that my right to make tea, for example, may interfere with or be limited by other rights. I am perfectly free to drink tea, or bathe in it, or colour my ceiling with it, or offer it to a guest, or do anything with it that I want to, as long as I do not use it to drown someone, which would interfere with other, higher rights. Even if we would want to assign complete complexes of right-molecules, we would not be able to do so. It may be possible to give a complete listing of all the things one can do with a knife, but it is space- and time-consuming to describe with perfect precision when and where one can do all those things, as time and space, the conditions (t, p), can be divided infinitely.

Although I also define a right as a set of r-molecules, I nevertheless prefer to use the term 'right' in a more specific sense. I assume the existence of precise 'moments' and 'places'. For reasons of simplicity, I shall mainly speak of rights as rights to *have* something, x_a-rights. As such have-rights are sets of r-molecules, they can also be expressed as rights to *do* some things y_{1-n} or as rights *to be* some things z_{1-m}. Thus, I do not want to suggest that one cannot have rights to free speech or to happiness (in so far as compatible with condition $\mathfrak{C}$); it is simply more efficient to pretend that only one variant of rights exists.

There are several types of rights.[57] Remember that an r-molecule was defined as $i^\star(x_a, y_a, z_a)$ and denoted simply as a, b, c, and so forth. Rights are complexes of r-molecules. A *basic right* r_a is defined as a right over one single r-molecule a:

(1) r_a is the authority to decide that a and the authority to decide that $\neg a$; or

(2) r_a means that *it shall be the case* that i *sees to it* that a, or that i *sees to it* that $\neg a$.[58]

A basic *duty*, to describe just one other possible type of right, is a limited basic right, limited by taking away the element of choice. A basic duty d_a is the authority to decide that a, a basic duty $d_{\neg a}$ is the authority to decide that $\neg a$. Basic duties give one an authority to do something rather than to choose to do it.

A *complex right* is a set of one or more basic rights and/or basic duties, e.g. (r_a, r_b). Incidentally, the addition of more basic rights does not mean that one's choice of alternatives grows to the same extent. Suppose that:

a is $i^\star(x_1, y_1, z_1)$;
b is $i^\star(x_1, y_2, z_1)$;
c is $i^\star(x_3, y_4, z_5)$;
d is $i^\star(x_1, y_4, z_5)$.

A complex right (r_a, r_c) gives one four options, four possible worlds: (a, c), $(\neg a, c)$, $(a, \neg c)$ and $(\neg a, \neg c)$. The complex right (r_b, r_c) also gives four alternatives, but (r_a, r_b) only gives three: $(a, \neg b)$, $(\neg a, b)$ and $(\neg a, \neg b)$. In English, this means that one cannot have one's pudding and eat it.

Some complex rights, like the complex (r_a, r_d) in our example above, consist of basic rights with at least one common denominator, a shared x, y or z. A complex right is a *perfect right* $\mathfrak{R}x_a$, $\mathfrak{R}y_a$ or $\mathfrak{R}z_a$ if it contains all possible basic rights with regard to an x_a, y_a, or z_a. Suppose that (r_a, r_d) is the complex right to use a particular fruit knife either to stab in self-defence or to cut an apple with. If these were all the things one could do with that fruit knife, it would be a perfect right of the $\Re x_a$-type. Rights in the real world are always imperfect or *conditional* rights, in other words, perfect rights with a long list of exceptions.

By analogy, we can see a complex duty as a combination of two or more basic duties and a perfect duty as a universally valid complex duty. In ordinary language, the last would be expressed like this: 'whatever you use to whatever purpose, see to it that you use it only in this the right way'. The third version of Kant's categorical imperative, demanding that one should always act in such a way that mankind and each human are never merely means but also ends (Kant 1974: BA66), is a beautiful example of a perfect duty with two common denominators. Note, however, that complex duties are merely a special case of complex rights.

By definition, an r-molecule cannot be at two places at the same time or at two moments on the same place. This allows us, in theory and at the end of time, to neatly divide the universe in r-molecules and, as no two persons can be attributed with the same r-molecule or right, to assign all rights once and for all. Steiner (1994: 80) calls this property of formal rights compossibility. In practice, of course, things are different (cf. Steiner 1994: 201). Real-world rights are in general defined as if they were perfect rights with implicit exceptions, exceptions that are given by the legal and jurisprudential context and by what is physically possible. It is often impossible to describe and assign conditional rights with the same degree of precision that the theory allows us to imagine.

I shall assume that the archpointers take a mean position between these extremes: their principles of social justice should assign complex rights with perfect precision – but they can only assign those rights that are already known to be in existence. In other words, I assume that the archpointers are capable of determining exactly who is allowed to use the word processor I am currently using, and when and where, provided the parameters of the problem do not change. Archpointers cannot definitely decide on my wordprocessor if a new claimant can fall from the skies, and they cannot assign rights to cars running on grass as long as these have not been invented.

The theoretical precision of this conception of rights has a second practical disadvantage. The complex rights that social justice distributes can, as we saw above, include liberties as well as duties, the good and the bad things in life, the profitable, the useless and the disadvantageous. The model can represent all these things in a simple way. Yet there is one kind of duty that it cannot represent this simply: the complementary duty others (can) have to respect or even protect the rights of individual i. As an r-molecule can only be assigned once, it cannot be the subject of one individual's right and of another individual's duty. A complementary duty would have to be expressed in terms of its implications: if I have, in practice, a duty to respect your freedom of speech, I have, in our model, a (complex) duty to see to it that certain things (r-molecules) that would physically obstruct your complex right to free speech do not happen.

This brings me to the last subject of this section: the fit between this model and the existing convention in deontic logic on the proper description of rights. We have already implicitly dealt with one difference in modes of expression: whereas my complex rights are defined in terms of an individual and certain objects, rights as understood by a leading deontic logician, Kanger, are relational: they describe the relation an individual has to another individual regarding objects (e.g. Kanger and Kanger 1966: 86). As I just said, we *can* take account of relations, of the complements of one individual's complex rights in the rights bundles of others. We do not *need* to, though: there is no reason why we should not think of a right as a general principle assigning some kind of authority to an individual *i*, as a *consequence* of which *i* has this authority with regard to all or some other persons.

A more important difference between the conception of rights presented here and current conventions in deontic logic concerns the notion of *simple rights* as first described by Kanger (Kanger and Kanger 1966). In Kanger's taxonomy the following four types of simple rights exist:

(1)   a *claim*: X has versus Y a claim that $S(X, Y)$ means that: it shall be that Y causes $S(X, Y)$; or, in Lindahl's terms: Y shall see to it that F.

(2)   a *freedom*: X has versus Y a freedom that $S(X, Y)$ means that: not: it shall be that X causes that not-$S(X, Y)$; in Lindahl's terms: it is not the case that X shall see to it that not F.

(3)   a *power*: X has versus Y a power that $S(X, Y)$ means that: not: it shall be that not: X causes that $S(X, Y)$; in Lindahl's terms: X may see to it that F.

(4)   an *immunity*: X has versus Y an immunity that $S(X, Y)$ means that: it shall be that not: Y causes that not-$S(X, Y)$; in Lindahl's terms: it is not the case that Y may see to it that not F.

The expressions $S(X, Y)$ or F in these descriptions refer to imaginable states of affairs between the right-holders X and Y (cf. Kanger and Kanger 1966: 87–8; Lindahl 1977: 43). Consistent combinations of these four simple rights and their counterparts (the counter-claim of X versus Y that not $S(X, Y)$, and so forth) are called atomic types of right (Kanger and Kanger 1966: 92).

The model of *r*-molecules and basic and complex rights which I described in this section is perfectly compatible with Kanger's – if we disregard condition ℭ for a moment, a condition that limits the application of the notion of a right to possible instead of imaginable worlds. The (x_a, y_a, z_a, t, p)-part of an *r*-molecule describes a state of affairs. As the absence of a relational aspect in *r*-molecules is unproblematical (see above), we can therefore simply 'translate' $i^*(x_a, y_a, z_a, t, p)$ as $S(i, j)$ according to Kanger's vocabulary, or as (i, j, F) according to Lindahl's. I defined a basic right r_a as meaning that it shall be the case that i sees to it that a or that i sees to it that $\neg a$. In Lindahl's vocabulary, this would be expressed as Shall Do(i, F) or Shall Do($i, \neg F$). Hence, like freedom, power, immunity, their counterparts and the atomic rights which can all be described in terms of implications (i.e. special cases) of a claim (Shall Do(i, F) – cf. Lindahl 1977: 52 ff.), basic rights can be translated into simple rights. Conversely, simple and atomic rights can, as we saw, be expressed in terms of r-molecules. The reason why I discussed rights in terms of basic rights and duties rather than in those of simple and atomic rights is that, for practical purposes, the everyday notions of (basic) rights and duties are sufficient to illustrate the possible range and force of complex rights.

Ownership – the rights version

In the preceding section I introduced an interpretation of the term 'right' that would allow us to understand all distributable goods including both duties and rights-in-the-usual-sense-of-the-word with this one word. I defined a *basic right* as having permission to perform so-called r-molecules, an r-molecule being one person's using one object in one particular way to one particular end at one particular time and place. A basic right is composed of two duties: the (basic) duty to do a and the (basic) duty to do not-a; we are permitted to choose. The r-molecules are, in a way, the basic stuff out of which the universe of rights as we know it is composed. A *complex right* is any combination of basic duties. My permission to cross this particular street at this particular moment, the light being green, in order to pursue my walk is a basic right; our common permission to cross it for whatever purpose provided the light is green is a complex right – and (what's in a name) so is our common duty *not* to cross when the light is red. To all this I added condition $\mathfrak{C}$, the assumption that it must actually be *possible* to use an object in one particular way to one particular end. Condition $\mathfrak{C}$ precludes, merely for the sake of simplicity, the attribution of imaginary rights, say, rights to determine the colour of the sky or the volume of a one-dimensional line. This formal conception of rights furnishes us with a new means to define ownership: to own a thing is to have a complex right to it. It does not provide us with any answers to the problem of justifying and assigning ownership, though. Can ownership, unconditional or not, be justified at all? In particular, can the aspects of subjection and exclusion, which are inherent to ownership, be justified? Are there things beyond rights – things that cannot legitimately be owned, or to which the (affirmation of) rights is irrelevant?

In this section, I shall distinguish four separate spheres of rights: the spheres of conditional and unconditional ownership, that of unassignable rights and, the sphere to which I turn first, that of what lies beyond the reach of rights. The distinctions made here will be merely formal; a specification of the various categories of rights will follow in subsequent sections.

There are things that cannot be distributed or legitimately owned except in a purely symbolic way: triangular cubes and square circles, gnomes and goblins, unicorns and the perpetuum mobile. Of course, one might try to distribute rights to such things, but the rights would be empty. They are totally irrelevant to the issue of social justice, and were fortunately already excluded with the help of condition ℭ in the previous section. However, I want to draw attention for a moment to one thing that, despite the fact that it stands beyond possession and ownership rights, is relevant to social justice: the self, or more precisely its vital parts, full reasons.

We can choose between two extreme positions with regard to self-ownership: either the self including body and mind owns itself, or it does not. If it does, as in Nozick's theory, a basis has been established for claims to the fruits of one's labour, as mixing one's labour with an object like an apple tree or the hardware of a computer would imply that one mixes the self with the world. In a manner of speaking. If the self does not own itself, it is free for grabs. Society would have the same rights to it as the self itself, or perhaps even more as society in a way mixes its labour with particular selves, offering it education, opportunities and co-operation. In mixing itself with a self, society then becomes that self – and might, the theory goes, claim it for its own purposes. In practice this could mean that society has a right either to force an individual to become the excellent doctor he could be even though he himself would rather become a mediocre tennis player – or that it has the right to tax an individual for the contributions to society she could have made by becoming a diplomat, but does not because she decided to become a rugby coach.

The position I shall choose is dictated, on the one hand, by the conception of the self defended in previous chapters, and on the other by the grammar of our new conception of rights. I shall split up the Nozickean self of body, mind and thoughts in (1) a core self, the vital parts of the self to which the notion of subjective neutrality referred, (2) the natural endowments (abilities and capacities) of the self, in so far as these are essential to a full plan of life, a life in accordance with one's full reasons, and (3) other endowments. The first category is beyond rights – it does not fit in with the grammar of rights; to the second category a self has inalienable rights, and to the third its rights are conditional, though in practice still inviolable. I shall discuss them in this order.

A body, a mind or a person can be possessed and perhaps even owned – it is imaginable, though untrue, that someone's full reasons are best served by a life in slavery, that she assents to enslave herself and that slavery is justifiable. The relevant aspects of the self, however, are beyond possession.

The idea of self-possession or self-ownership would make sense in a context of natural rights, as with Nozick, and in general in the context of theories where the self is a physical rather than analytical entity (cf. Cohen 1986: 110). In the context of our grammar of rights, however, it is nothing short of mysticism to talk about self-ownership or about the self as 'owned'. From the point of view of a distributor, the self is something that drops from the sky right through her hands. It cannot be snatched and possessed like a house or a shoe, it cannot be owned in the sense of a right to do y_a with something x_a for the purpose of z_a, it can only snatch and possess itself. Any attempt to take and redistribute a 'self' requires that the self (the R-related memories or, specifically, a person's full reasons) is separated from the physical body in which it exists, and the result is its annihilation. Moreover, to allow changes in the initial distribution of selves would be to violate the very first demand that we posed on theories of distributive justice: that they do not opt for supply-side solutions.

Of course, one might suggest that annihilating a self is one thing – the only thing next to not annihilating it – that an outside force can do with it, for which reason it could be the subject of a right. Yet to (have a right to) destroy this analytical entity, one has to (have a right to) destroy the physical entity housing it; one cannot destroy the elves without destroying the books and minds within which they exist. Hence it is impossible to create an *independent* right to a self. The existence of such a right contradicts condition $\mathfrak{E}$ – it would be like giving a blind man the right to look in a mirror.

The relevant aspects of the self, full reasons, are beyond rights; things other than the self are *not*. To some of these things inalienable or unconditional rights exist, due to the fact that the conditions of the archpoint dictate equal respect for every imaginable set of full reasons, and hence imply the existence of a basic freedom of consciousness for each creature capable of developing full reasons. To the extent that a person's natural endowments are necessary conditions for her life in accordance with her full reasons, to that same extent one has an inalienable right to these endowments.

By natural endowments I mean all the physical and mental abilities that go with being a particular individual: one's own innate endowments as well as endowments that only develop later in life (for instance an ability to grow a beard or bear children). The concept excludes the abilities of collectives (the ability of some couples to procreate), abilities acquired with help from others (for instance better sight due to spectacles), and all endowments an individual could have had but does not actually have. Thus, the ability to see is not one of a blind woman's endowments, whereas the exceptional abilities of an *idiot savant* or a mutant are (their) natural endowments.

Note that I am not saying anything on the source of innate endowments – that is, on the difficult problem of whether distribution of natural endowments by means of genetic engineering can be allowed. Supposing for a moment that genetic engineering is not an intrinsically bad thing – the question is unresolved – it is still, in terms of its consequences, not an issue of distributive justice. Genetic engineering is not simply a matter of allotting abilities and opportunities to selves, but – at times, and the demarcation line is vague – also one of causing different people to exist. Making, to use a euphemism, adaptions in an embryo so that it will not have a freestanding ear lobe changes hardly anything (in most societies), but changing the sex of an embryo will make a fundamental difference: the child will have different hormones, different abilities, a different status and different chances, different experiences, different memories, different plans of life, different reasons and, all in all, a different life. It will be a totally new child, a different self. The same will be true if the embryo were to be adapted to our ideal of health – giving it limbs if it has none, curing its diseases before they even develop, ensuring that it will later produce the right hormones in the right amounts, and so forth. Nevertheless, genetic engineering and beliefs about the desirability and distribution of disabilities or spectacular capacities are undeniably ethical issues, issues of great importance and increasing practical relevance – but they are not a matter of distributive justice.

A moment ago, I introduced the terms 'inalienable' and 'unconditional' without any explanation. I shall explain them now. By unconditional I mean that there can be no better reason against the existing distribution of these rights to the natural assets that are essential to the full life (that is against the way nature distributed them), no reason forceful enough to trump their importance to the possessor of these rights. A right is inalienable if, even though it is *actually* possible to, say, enslave people and hence 'alienate' their rights, it is morally forbidden to do so – for instance because those rights are unconditional.

The reasons for attaching the adjectives inalienable or unconditional to rights to vital natural endowments are twofold. First, and this accounts for their not being 'beyond' rights: rights to natural endowments are not beyond judgement. Natural endowments can be grabbed and used: people can be enslaved, they and their abilities can be means and not ends. Secondly, to account for their inalienability: having or discovering natural endowments creates, helps to create, and helps to live according to, full reasons. Finding out where one's strengths lie often helps to choose a course in life, to develop the dispositions required for that life, and to discover the reasons that ultimately rule one's life and choice of a plan of life. If rights to natural endowment were conditional, it would in principle be permitted to take them away or to manipulate them. Indirectly, this opens up the way for judgements on full reasons, which would be a breach of subjective neutrality.

To illustrate the impact of unconditional ownership of natural endowments, imagine three cases. In the first, Cissy Roo's full plan of life, her full reasons, can only be satisfied if she leads a physically active life, for instance as a sports woman or as a doctor or a priest, on call for 24 hours a day. In this case, she has an inalienable right to her kidneys, without which she would be unable to live her full life: each alternative and essentially equivalent way of life requires two healthy kidneys.

In a second case, imagine that her kidney could save a life including certain full reasons, but that giving it would destroy Cissy's prospects on a full life. The kidney is and remains Cissy's unconditionally. Observe that this does not imply that we *prefer* one set of full reasons (Cissy's) over anyone else's. It is simply because we cannot choose between both sets that we should not even think of choosing between both lives (contrary to what a utilitarian might do).

The bad news is in the third case. If there is a chance that Cissy could be a good priest with one kidney only, her right to the second kidney is theoretically conditional. As this is a general principle and not one for Cissy only, the consequences could be most bizarre: one can envisage a society in which a government of body snatchers forces its subjects to adapt their lives and bodies every time it thinks that brains and limbs and organs are required elsewhere. However, the practical consequences of this criterion in terms of alienability are far less worrying. The dictatorship of the body snatchers, the enforced redistribution of natural assets, implies the enslavement of people in the interest of other people's plans of a full life, which violates impartiality. Body snatching may not prevent full lives from being lived, but it certainly hinders them arbitrarily to the equally arbitrary benefit of others. To defend the redistribution of your capacities to Harry, the distributor would have to assert that Harry's plan of life is better than yours, and that the distributor's judgement on plans of life and full reasons is better than yours. (The argument does not work the other way around: a 'decision' not to redistribute natural assets does not imply that Harry's plan of a full life is less valuable than Cissy's. Impartiality makes it impossible to choose between the two, and it is for *that* reason that natural assets cannot legitimately be reallocated. The distributor cannot be held responsible for the initial distribution of talents and imperfections.) Hence *any* right to *any* natural asset is inviolable and we can, for all practical purposes, consider any right to natural assets as unconditional.

Although this section only discusses the formal distinctions between the various spheres of rights and absence of rights, it might help the imagination to have some examples of unconditional rights. One is the – general – right to life: no individual, in particular no individual attempting to fulfil a full plan of life, can do without this natural endowment. As a consequence, governments cannot legitimately distribute and redistribute rights to life. A second example of an inalienable right is the right to the capacity to influence the polity and to excel in this capacity: it may be required to protect one's chances on living a full life. However, not every individual needs or wants this protection; it depends on the individual's set of full reasons. The same is true for other inalienable rights like those to further the full life of others, to one's intelligence, to good looks, to a misshaped nose, to pain, to one's digestion and other bodily functions.

Turning now to conditional ownership, the first thing to observe is that the word 'conditional' implies that a claim is being made, that arguments to sustain this claim are possible and demanded, that claims can be contested, and that counter-claims can be made for which these same things are true. A conditional right to own X exists in so far as and so long as, reasons against it do not overrule those in favour of it. What makes them conditional is the fact that no matter how scarce or abundant they are, claims to them *can* be compared, evaluated and ordered. Respecting full reasons demands that we at least do not obstruct their execution, where and whenever possible. This gives every recipient a *prima facie* right to whatever furthers his or her full life – though the rights of others often put limits on the degree to which valid claims can become genuine rights, even if they satisfy condition ℭ. Moreover, even in absence of competing claims, a claim need not become a right. That only one candidate appeals for an available scholarship is not enough reason to give it; we also need a positive reason for recognizing the candidate's claim. Hence it depends on the strength of arguments whether we should agree to a particular distribution of conditional rights and accede to an instance of ownership, transfer or expropriation.

I shall not bother the reader with more examples. By definition, conditional rights cover everything that is part of the three other spheres, that is everything that is not beyond rights, an inalienable right or unownable. Within these boundaries, conditional rights exist to everything that is either one's own or someone else's natural endowment but not indispensable for the full life,[59] to everything that is not a natural endowment but conducive to someone's full life and to everything that is simply pleasant, without any relation to full lives.

Finally, we reach the realm of the untouchable. Unlike the sphere of unpossessable things, this sphere consists of things that can be possessed but to which rights are unassignable. The distinguishing characteristic of this sphere is that it contains a particular type of right that can but should not be given: the right to destroy objects of conditional rights. Alternatively, and according to the grammar of complex rights, one could say that conditional rights are complex rights, complexes of on the one hand simple rights to an object and, on the other, of a set of simple duties dictating things one should not do with the object. In these terms, the sphere of the untouchable consists of such duties alone.

There are things we just should not destroy unless using them is unavoidable and there is no other way to use them but by destroying them. Even then, we ought to try to replace them by the best possible substitute. As a matter of fact, we should not destroy *anything* that could be owned by anyone else, anything that is not absolutely but only conditionally ours: the resources making up the whole of non-human nature, other people's capacities and the artefacts created by mankind, including political and social institutions. (For an application of this idea to environmental questions, see Wissenburg 1998.)

The reasons for this have little to do with the intrinsic value of things or with future generations – but everything with the six or more generations of actually existing individuals around us. Conditional ownership depends on arguments, on reasons of which the soundness may change over time or depending on the information we have. Today, my word processor is of almost vital importance to me, but tomorrow I may no longer need it and it may become indispensable for my neighbour at the university. At this moment, my government could decide that it ought to pay a part of Zimbabwe's national debt, but within minutes it may learn that Chad has been flooded and needs the money more, forcing the government to revise its earlier decision – as long, of course, as it has not actually been effectuated.

Others may turn out to have better claims on goods than I have – they merely have not yet made those claims, have not been able to do so, or have not been heard. They may even be unaware of their own good reasons, as it takes time to develop or discover (full) reasons. In this context then, the first-come or finders-keepers principle is not a warrant for justice – my claim may be prior in time without being prior in terms of urgency or necessity. As far as the morality of individuals and distributors is concerned, the best thing to do is to follow a safe-bet principle: avoid doing anything you would not want to be a universal practice.

Of course, theory is often an unpractical thing. Following a general duty not to destroy the objects of conditional rights unless unavoidable means starving or thirsting or freezing to death – whichever comes first. The best and most practical way of saving at least the spirit of this duty is to demand that an object should not be destroyed unless unavoidable, that if it must be destroyed it should be replaced by an identical object, that if this is impossible an equivalent object should be made available, and that if the last is also impossible, a proper compensation should be provided. This duty, which is expected to protect the interests of other recipients, also protects those of future generations in a roundabout way. Its effect will be that we leave the world no worse than we found it on entry – in so far as that is humanly possible.

Conditional ownership

We now have some idea of the kind of goods that are distributable. Excluding unconditional rights for a moment (as societies should recognize rather than distribute these), the category of distributable goods is identical to that of the objects of conditional rights. Our next question is whether all that is distributable should in fact be distributed and judged in terms of distributive justice, or if there is also room for the free exchange of rights and hence for commutative justice. To use Brian Barry's terms: can there be a sphere of goods, the distribution of which is 'discretionary' or 'irrelevant to social justice' (Barry 1995: 11)? Or in plain and simple political terms: should the state be the omnipresent all-powerful judge of all its citizens' acts, or can individuals and organizations operate in a free market – and if so, to what extent? Selling books or giving marks to students can be seen as matters of both commutative and distributive justice. The distinction between the two is, as explained in Part II, first of all a matter of a vertical or horizontal perspective: a transfer can be assessed as an act of distribution if it is public (from the whole of a group to separate members) and as an exchange if it is a private affair between formally equal persons. In the case of just distribution, the value of the distributed goods equals the value a person has deserved, whereas a just exchange is one of things of equal value.

Thus, paying one's only employee can be judged as distributively just or unjust in terms of the division of the product of a co-operative venture and as commutatively just or unjust in terms of the balance between the employee's labour and the employer's financial reward. If labour itself were the basis of desert, both perspectives would lead to the same assessment of the employee's just income, and the difference between the two approaches would be trivial. The allotment of incomes over a society can, by the same token, be analyzed as the distribution of the social product, or as the sum of all exchanges between individuals.

By convention, liberal theorists of social justice make a distinction between commutative and distributive justice on the basis of 'ultimate' ownership. In the grammar of complex rights this means that a right is the subject of principles of distributive justice if each transfer of it requires the approval of society, and that it is subjected to principles of commutative justice if only the parties to the exchange need to approve. If society ultimately owns something, transfers are called distributive, whereas if individuals or organized groups within society (including, incidentally, state agencies) are the ultimate owners, transfers are seen as exchanges. Which perspective we choose thus depends on the conditions we, as archpointers, attach to the rights that we – initially – distribute.

Even under a system of mostly conditional rights, either distributive or commutative justice and public or private ownership must somehow ultimately take precedence over the other, or either one must have its own sovereign sphere of goods to rule over. The reason for this is that the claims we can make in terms of distributive justice and those in terms of commutative justice tend to clash, and without some priority or demarcation rule such conflicts of interest cannot be resolved. Consider a randomly chosen individual's vocation. Jill sincerely wants to be a doctor, but it is the state and not the university that assigns the right to study medicine, and the state does so on the basis of distributive rather than commutative considerations: its criteria are society's demand for doctors and the costs of their education, instead of the willingness of students and universities to enter into a contract. Consider another person's inheritance. Jack's mother died, and left him nothing but an antique and quite valuable silver teapot, which she inherited from her grandmother, who in turn had inherited it (and so forth). Jack would never even think of selling it; all the worth it has for him is purely emotional. Its commercial value would not play any role until after Jack's own death, when his barbaric children will want to sell it. Yet six months after his mother's death, the state knocks at his door and, in the name of equality of opportunity, demands that he pays taxes over his inheritance – thus forcing him to sell the teapot. Or consider, finally, a collective good. The inhabitants of a small village somewhere in Scotland decide that the main road through their village, which has been ruined by their own traffic as well as by outsiders, needs to be reconstructed. They pay for this with their own and borrowed money, making serious debts and afterwards start taxing outsiders for the use of the road. Again, the state interferes in the name of equality of opportunity and freedom of movement and whatever other reasons, prohibiting what it calls 'this kind of robbery'.

Why is it that the arguments for distribution and those for exchange clash? First, because both types of principles are often to someone's disadvantage. Distribution, as every defender of pure capitalism can affirm, limits the freedom and opportunities of possible sellers, whereas exchange, according to another once popular creed, leads to the extortion of those whose bargaining power is weakest. Obviously, the opposite is also true: distribution can be to the advantage of the weakest and exchange to the advantage of the seller.

A second and less self-interested reason is that both systems offer opportunities for (im)morality: private ownership creates numerous forms of individual responsibility, distribution creates similar forms of collective responsibility, both to be exercised in good or bad faith. Hence, a choice for one system or the other implies choosing for a particular view of man and responsibility.

Last, but in fact prior to the other reasons, the two systems can conflict with one another simply because they can apply different standards to situations. In a distributive scheme, an individual's share in worldly goods and freedoms is determined by an independent standard for desert; in exchanges, it is based on a standard of (not desert but) desire.

Still, there are situations in which distribution and exchange are theoretically compatible, due to the fact that some goods are to some extent interchangeable. Food can be distributed without taking away anyone's freedom to prefer certain types of food or anyone's freedom to exchange rice for food-stamps – in the ideal situation in which there is no real scarcity of any kind of food. Likewise, we can imagine a situation in which food in general is freely exchangeable, with the exception of one scarce good (say, caviar), to which each member of the population is given an equal purchasing right. For distribution and exchange to be fully compatible here, we must also allow anyone who chooses not to buy caviar to have the freedom to sell her right to interested others, and we must assume that everyone will end up with the exact amount of caviar he or she desires after all exchanges have taken place. The problem with these theoretical cases is, however, that they presuppose a world without scarcity or, were that condition satisfied, one without strife, as scarcity is not a necessary condition for disagreement about claims to rights.

The choice, then, for a collective or private system of ownership or a 'mixed constitution' is not simply a matter of convention, unlike the difference between commutative and distributive justice. It is a choice that involves an evaluation of one class of moral arguments (those for private or collective ownership respectively) as being better than those for the other system. Ultimately, it is a choice between the rights of the individual who claims the ownership of all he or she creates or appropriates, and society which claims that there are no rights to appropriation unless acclaimed by society and no rights to the monopolization of the fruits of one's labour if – as it claims to be – society itself is ultimately responsible for creating those fruits.

So how would archpointers deal with this question? At first sight it seems that the question could never even arise: complex rights are assigned unambiguously to one particular individual. Transferring a right is 'grammatically' impossible; the only thing that comes close to it is a situation in which one individual's complex right ceases and another's begins. Nevertheless, even archpointers can choose between a free market and collectivism: they can decide *not* to assign certain complex rights. When and where they do so, the question of a distributively just transfer ceases to exist; it has then been moved to another realm, that of private transactions (gifts, theft, inheritance) and commutative justice. The question that does not disappear is that concerning original acquisition. The archpointers still have to decide whether to allow individuals to exercise authority over aspects of the world without being controlled by society, archpointers or principles of social justice. Do the archpointers have a reason to do so?

Note, first of all, that this discussion of rights has as yet not resulted in a bias in favour of either an all-powerful state or that other extreme, libertarian capitalism. Conditional rights are universally contestable: it does not matter who has the conditional right to, for instance, this book or to the nomination of cabinet members – the right remains conditional upon the existence of good reasons. If there is no (longer a) good reason for giving Harry a welfare benefit, he should not (or no longer) receive one; and if there is no good reason for an act of original acquisition, there is no right to whatever was acquired.

Recent debates on original acquisition have resulted in a stalemate. To summarize the course of events, it began with Locke's classical liberal theory of original acquisition (Locke 1924), later adapted and defended by libertarians like Nozick and Steiner. Nozick argued that an individual, having created an object (having 'mixed his labour with a substance', as Locke might say, and leaving enough and as good), is thereby free to decide what to do with it – sell it, destroy it, give it away, or whatever. (Note that in Locke's own theory mixing one's labour is neither a sufficient nor a necessary condition for justifiable original acquisition.) Then came the social liberals, for the last quarter of a century primarily represented by Rawls, who argued that no-one deserves the abilities (natural endowments) that allow her or him to create certain objects or to perform certain practices. By default of other legitimate authorities, then, the ultimate decision on transfer and possession is society's. Finally, some sharp minds noticed that lack of good reasons on the side of individuals does not amount to a positive proof of the legitimacy of society's claim on the individuals' products. To make it a sound argument, one would have to suppose that everything 'on' an individual – natural endowments, social training, products – is ultimately the product of society and/or of social co-operation.

However, such a move would not be very convincing. The conclusion would still not follow from the premises: we have, as yet, no reason to assume that 'we made it' implies that 'we own it' – that is, that creation justifies ownership. The same argument applies, *mutatis mutandis*, to Nozick's justification of private ownership. Moreover, the argument reifies society: 'caused by society' may also mean 'caused, to varying degrees, by a limited number of other autonomous individuals' (parents, teachers and preachers). A parallel argument applies to the case of libertarianism, where the individual is more or less reified, as if she were fully autonomous and as if nothing on her had been caused by any outside force. Finally, whereas Nozickian libertarians disregard the claims others, as causers of the causer, may have on the product that an individual caused to exist, social liberalism basically denies human autonomy.

The way I offer out of this dilemma is only a partial solution. It affirms the justifiability – in principle – of private ownership but still presupposes that 'mixing one's labour' is a necessary condition for ownership. Its point of departure is William Galston's conviction that, though neither the individual nor society may have deserved the natural endowments of individuals, the way an individual directs the development of his talents should be considered a private achievement (Galston 1991: 131). Society or individuals in society influence me but they do not *make* me; they merely create the favourable circumstances in which, or the duress under which, I develop and employ my talents. My natural endowments, my talents and genetic make-up, do not necessarily make me either. Given a minimum level of intelligence and self-consciousness, I am capable of choosing whether I shall develop, use or ignore certain talents – and which. I build my own character, I am ultimately responsible for what I do with my assets; my vote in the process of production and acquisition of the fruits of my labour is decisive. Society or my causers in society cannot claim credit for the use I make of my talents, nor demand anything in exchange for facilitating my activities – not unless I voluntarily and in advance agreed to their help, and not unless they are also prepared to compensate me for the loss of my dreams when it turns out that society could live with, but does not want, more painters, poets and artists. Otherwise, society's claims to my products amounts to nothing short of an attempt at extortion. It follows that I can lay a valid claim to part of my products; it does not follow that society or others cannot also claim some of it – in so far as they actively co-operated with me, rather than forced me into something. The employer can claim her share in what I make using her tools rather than my hands only, but society cannot claim its share in the extra profits I make after it forced me to become an unhappy physician instead of a happy artist. However, the valid claims of other persons or co-operations are of the same kind as mine: they derive their force from personal and voluntary decisions to develop and use some talents rather than others. Either way, archpointers have a good reason to allow private ownership, that is, to give individuals uncontrolled authority over the rights they legitimately acquire.

Then again, what does not follow is that an individual should not agree to give up or (in the language of complex rights, metaphorically speaking) hand over his rights to society – under circumstances and given good reasons. And there can in fact be good reasons for overruling the reasons in favour of private ownership. Without as yet claiming that they are better and stronger, there can be reasons against private ownership. If society has a moral obligation to distribute, say, financial support for the elderly, it also has an obligation to acquire the necessary means whenever possible, and its citizens have an obligation to make these means available. Reasons of this kind can be better and can therefore overrule justified claims to private ownership. The point of reference for judgements on the strength of arguments is, as always, the archpoint. What matters about rights from that point of view is their meaning for, their impact on, the realization of individual plans of life.

Earlier, I made a distinction between two kinds of life-plans: plans for a full and for a complete life. The first consists of full reasons only, the second concerns all aspects of a life and includes specific ways of realizing the plan for a full life. As to the first, an archpointer wants to be impartial with regard to full reasons, but she will give precedence to (the protection of) full reasons (the full life) over other, more disputable reasons (the complete life). Hence, she will judge that an individual should give up any 'privatized' right if the individual in question cannot use that right to live a full life, and if it is essential to the fulfilment of someone else's plan of a full life. I shall assume for now that this is the complete verdict an archpointer would give (the issue is pursued further in the next chapter). It may, however, be possible to go further and demand that a right that is essential to Cissy's full life should also be given up if the present owner, Harry, needs it less – that is, even if Harry could use the right for his own full life. In this case Cissy's reasons are still stronger than Harry's. Of course, if my (indivisible) food is equally indispensable for both your and my prospects of a full life, there is no reason for me to give it up. Finally, it may be possible that the archpointers go so far as to judge that Harry should give up any right merely because Cissy needs it more (not: cannot do without it) for her full life than Harry for his.

With regard to the second type of life-plan, an archpointer cannot judge on the value of different (plans for) complete lives. All she can say is that plans for a full life take precedence and that, for this reason, the opportunities to live a full life should be safeguarded. Hence, she will decide that Cissy should give up non-essential conditional rights (that is rights that do not bear any relation to her full life) if political necessity so requires, that is, if the redistribution of those rights is a necessary condition for the survival of the social structure that allows full lives to be lived. Again, I shall not suppose, but can imagine, that the archpointers take a more radical stand: they might decide to apply this principle to rights that do influence Cissy's prospects of a full life but are not indispensable.

Thus, to summarize this section: there is some reason to exclude certain rights from distribution and to recognize the institution of private property. Yet property is not sacred; property rights can be overruled. By way of an illustration: I should accept taxation (add some of my rights to the social stock), first, for the relief of famine unless that would cost me my own life; and I should accept it, secondly, if it was used to raise unemployment benefits to a level allowing the deaf to buy a stereo TV-set instead of mono, if that were the only way to prevent a civil war and if the arguments of the deaf were consistent with the principles of natural justice and the demands of impartiality – which they probably are not. (I shall explain this last condition in Chapter 10.)

In closing, I want to draw attention to three points. I may have established that the interests of distributive justice can overrule private rights, but that does not entail a decision on the form of the institutions that are to distribute rights, let alone a decision in favour of a bureaucratic state, or for any state, for that matter. One can still imagine a perfectly libertarian stateless society that lives up to the principles just described, by mobilizing its members on a voluntary basis every time one of its members is in need.

I also should repeat that this scheme, like many others, presupposes that making (mixing one's labour) implies owning. It is a very strange and unsatisfactory axiom, one that involves something like the transubstantiation of a self (or its

177

endowments) in an object and, as this does not seem to subtract anything from the self, the mysterious multiplication of the self. Another loose end is that the mixing–owning theory cannot account for the symbolic or emotional value we attach to our personal goods (my genealogical notes, Jack's mother's teapot, your marriage portrait), which is often far greater than their market value or the emotional value attached to the products of our labour.[60] However, I cannot think of a less metaphysical alternative to mixing–owning (others are equally obscure), and I do not see it as my task to develop one here. For our present purposes, the importance of this or any theory of legitimate ownership does not lie in the precise way in which it legitimizes private property but in the observation that even if private ownership can be justified there can be impartial reasons in favour of (re)distribution, reasons overruling those for private ownership.

Last, having affirmed the existence of distributable rights, of an object for distributive justice, we should now ask ourselves what the *subject* of justice is: should we apply principles of minimal justice to the intentions of distributors, to the results of their distributing or to the processes by which they distribute? The choice can be narrowed down, first, by observing that we should care more about either procedures or results than about the distributor's intentions. Whatever those intentions may be, they must by definition be directed at distributing justly or at a just distribution; the latter or last defines the standard for the first. Secondly, we can notice that if we care about results, we should not care about *final* results, about end-states, since it seems to be impossible to maintain any distribution of rights. Suppose that a society one day reaches the ideal end-state, the ideal distribution of rights. Now having a right – one right – means having the authority to decide between p and $\neg p$; having more rights means being able to create several distinct possible worlds. The exercise of each and every one of these rights can change the impact of other rights, it can create new ones (research for instance sometimes leads to new inventions), or it can void them. The result is a new distribution of rights, that is, one diverging from the ideal end-state.[61]

The choice, then, comes down to one between what Nozick referred to as procedures and patterns. Now procedures are important for at least two reasons: for one, because we need certainty to 'plan' life and hence need a stable basis on which to build expectations, and for another, because we want to ensure that no matter how recipients get their fair share, they do not get it by violating impartiality or other recipients' rights. Patterns on the other hand are important because we want to ensure that the distribution is not just impartial in the everyday sense of the word as indifference as to who exactly gets a share of rights; all that is the function of a just procedure. We also, or rather, want impartiality with regard to conceptions of the good, that is, we do not want two people to end up with the same quantity of rights but different subjective qualities, or the other way around, unless there is a relevant difference between them – relevant as seen from the impartial point of view. Fortunately, we do not need to assign relative weights to patterns and procedures. We can have them both.

Our point of reference in this is the explanation Rawls gave for his choice for the basic structure of society as subject of social justice: being the composite of the institutions distributing basic rights and duties, the basic structure is the basis of our expectations, permeating almost every aspect of life and influencing our chances at success for our plans of life at the most basic level. It shapes and directs lives, it can favour 'certain starting positions over others' (cf. Rawls 1971: 7) and it therefore precedes any attempt at being just or advancing justice on the side of individuals and non-political institutions. The result of Rawls's choice is a recon- ciliation of pattern and procedure: if the basic structure of society satisfies certain principles of justice, the aim of ensuring socially just patterns is sufficiently met.

Although we cannot use the Rawlsian notion of a society, having chosen earlier (see the end of the previous chapter) for a redefinition of society as the structure of exploitable social relationships, we can still use Rawls's idea of a basic structure. Rawls, after all, specifically referred to institutions as making up the basic structure of society. Institutions, understood as organized, regulated and formalized forms of co-operation with a basis in positive law or in tradition and custom, are extremely basic. Without them, the benefits and burdens of co- operation in other (mostly voluntary) organizations are accidental and uncertain. Every instance of social interaction inside or outside such organizations would be little more than that – an instance, a unique incident without any relation to other incidents except coincidence. Without the chains of institutions, of some kind of 'basic structure' of social relations, the freedom to lead a secure life, let alone a full life, cannot be ensured or enforced.

As Nozick correctly observed when attacking patterned principles of justice, taking the basic structure of society (in our case, the structure of institutionalized exploitable relations) as subject of justice means subjecting procedural justice to the demands of a patterned principle. Still, we should notice that it also means subjecting the pattern to the demands that procedural justice imposes on it: those of being fair and predictable, of offering an impartial and secure basis of expecta- tion. 'Only against the background of a just basic structure . . . can one say that the requisite just procedure exists' (Rawls 1971: 87).

Distribution and the limits of justice

I have just, incidentally, defined two kinds of distributable or redistributable rights: those that should be (re)distributed to allow full lives to be lived and those that could be redistributed to allow complete lives to be lived if political necessity so requires. I shall call them, corresponding to the qualities that make claims in either area valid, respectively the sphere of Rights to Basic Needs and the sphere of Rights to Further Wants. So far, I have merely supposed that the difference between the two was clear; in this section I shall try to underpin this assumption and elucidate the difference.

The simplest approach would be that of describing basic needs, as further wants are simply everything else. Yet this seems to be impossible: basic needs are the things we need to pursue a full life, that is, rights that give us at least an opportunity for unhindered reasonable self-development. The fact that our conceptions of a full life differ seems to imply that our basic needs, as means to individual ends, differ as much as those conceptions do – unlike Rawls's basic needs as described by the objective list of primary social goods with their seemingly interpersonal substitutability and the list's supposed interpersonal validity (Rawls 1982: 172). However, the full life is one in which we can realize our full reasons, in which we have the opportunity to live up to the standards we set on our behaviour (compare Barry's conception of crucial goods, Barry 1995: 11, 84). And the conditions under which, or rights through which, we are free to take responsibility for our own behaviour and actions can, to a large degree, be generalized: we are equals in many relevant respects.

We all have certain physical and mental needs: we need life itself, air to breathe, water to drink, food to eat, a place to sleep, nearly always shelter and clothing, a time and a place to reflect on our actions and whatever cures are available to secure our physical and mental capacity to act.

In order to develop a sense of self in the first place, not to mention plans of life themselves, we also have certain social needs irrespective of the kind of society in which we live. For example, we need means and opportunities to communicate, to inform and to be informed. A full life can, but need not, be lived in splendid isolation. Without a mutual understanding of what is going on, only a recluse could live her life as she wanted, and even she needed a social environment earlier in life to imagine and develop her plan of life. Depending on the circumstances of society, then, we need at least a language and often enough the possibility to read and write. Next to communication, we need some general education, again to enable us to conceive, find or choose a path in life.

Thirdly, we need a social environment and a status in this environment as a psychological point of departure for our individual development and – obviously with the exception of the future recluse – as a place in which to realize our plans later on. Further, we have political needs. We plainly must have the formal freedom to live according to our conception of a full life.[62] We also need to have a voice both in the collection and in the (re)distribution of rights so as to represent our interests in basic needs and further wants.[63] Finally and in order to secure the previous two political needs, we must have a voice in decisions about the structure of exploitable relations, including an exit-option.

Admittedly, there are visions of the full life that are exceptional in that they do not require most of the needs listed above some of the time and some of them all of the time. Apart from some minor rights during childhood, a Buddhist may need nothing more than a place to meditate, and he may well be able to meditate in the middle of a battle. Here, the beauty of the idea of distributing conditional rights to basic needs, rather than distributing basic needs themselves, becomes apparent. On the one hand, a society that does not provide for the basic needs of its members is straightforwardly partial to the plans of those who (can) help themselves and those – like Buddhists – who need no help. In other words, such a society violates impartiality. On the other hand, a society that directly distributes food and beds and housing violates impartiality in the opposite direction. It seems to force those same members who can help themselves or need no help into accepting wasteful, unwelcome and even harmful goods – and into paying taxes, thus punishing their independence. If we distribute rights instead of goods, the problem can solve itself. The distinguishing feature of rights is that they leave us a choice; a conditional right can be the freedom to do or use a thing, within the circumscribed limits and within the limits of physical possibility – it need not be a duty, let alone anyone's fate. One is not forced to use the right to vote, or the right to write, rule, talk, or even the right to breathe; once conferred, one is free to use it – or not.

The sphere of basic necessities consists of all that is due to us, all we deserve by virtue of our status as class-A recipients with the capacity to develop plans for a full life. It differs from the sphere of further wants in two respects. For one, further wants bear no intrinsic relation to the full life nor, consequently, to the distributor's duty to safeguard opportunities for fulfilling plans for a full life. Secondly, the grounds for deserving further wants differ. As to the first point: further wants at best facilitate certain ways of living a full life more than others; their presence or absence does not, however, make a full life possible or impossible. If, say, generosity is part of someone's plan for a full life, wealth can but need not make it easier to be generous – it may also give rise to avarice – but there are other means and other courses in life to the same end. If intellectual excellence is part of it, a career in the academic community is not essential to that aim. Depending on the actual form and condition of society and one's own talents, a career in the world of big enterprise or as a craftsman can at times be more expedient.

Moreover, further wants can be totally unrelated to the full life. A desire for wealth, for a video or for a particular career may be the product of peer pressure, envy, greed, seduction by commercials, lack of self-respect, or any combination of these or other factors. (Think of 'the Joneses syndrome': when the Joneses buy a new car, their neighbours suddenly also want a car, preferably more impressive.)

As to the first difference between basic needs and further wants, the absence of an inherent relation with the full life implies that no-one deserves further wants, at least not in the same sense as one deserves basic needs. This is, nevertheless, no reason not to care about the way in which further wants are distributed, nor one for believing that their distribution is irrelevant to the issue of minimal justice. We should care about something else to which the issue of their (just) distribution is indispensable: the preservation of social order and social co-operation. It is this last trait that, as I hope to show in the next chapter, offers a viable and morally acceptable criterion for the just distribution of further wants.

Let me end this chapter with a very brief listing of its main results. What we have done is, first, distinguish between several classes or types of rights, and secondly, describe the implications of this classification for minimal justice.

The types of rights I distinguished were:

(1)   a *basic duty*, the permission to see to it that *a*;

(2)   a *basic right*, the permission to see to it that *a* or ¬*a*;

(3)   *complex rights* as sets of one or more basic rights and/or duties (from there on we assumed that 'right' and 'complex right' were perfect synonyms);

(4)   a sphere of 'that of what lies *beyond* the reach of rights' – things that cannot possibly be the subject of a right, like a person's full reasons;

(5)   *unassignable rights* relating to things that can be possessed and to which rights can but should not be given, like the right to destroy objects of conditional rights;

(6)   *unconditional* or inalienable *rights* to a person's natural endowments, in so far as these are necessary conditions for a life in accordance with that person's full reasons;

(7)   *conditional rights* to everything not already covered by 4 to 6;

(8)   *distributable rights*, a sub-category of 7, as opposed to rights that are the object of commutative justice;

(9)   *rights to basic needs*, a sub-category of 8, comprising every distributable right that is essential to the pursuit of a full life; and

(10)   *rights to further wants*, the remaining distributable rights.

Minimal justice, as discussed so far, requires:

(1)   that vital aspects of the self are considered to be beyond the realm of ownership rights;

(2)   that an individual's rights to his or her natural assets are recognized as unconditional, inalienable rights;

(3)   that conditional ownership rights cannot include a right to destroy the object of a right unless destruction is unavoidable, in which case the good in question should be replaced or restored, or a proper compensation should be provided – in declining order of preference;

(4)   that conditional rights to basic needs be distributed if morally required; and

(5)   that conditional rights to further wants be distributed if – to put it bluntly – politically necessity so demands.

9

Equalisanda

Wel aen dan, wie van ons had oyt Broots ghebrek, en was te ghelijk bekommert
om de Booter?
(Pray tell me, who of us was ever in need of bread, and at the same time
worried about the butter?)

Franciscus van den Enden (1992: 204; my translation)

Types of equalisanda

In the preceding chapters I argued that minimal justice is concerned with the
protection of the inalienable rights to a recipient's natural endowments and with
the distribution of complex rights to basic needs and further wants. We have also
uncovered several grounds of recipiency. Yet we are not quite ready to give
practical sense to the basic maxim of justice, the demand that equals get an equal
treatment and that unequals are treated in proportion to their inequality. We
cannot treat equals equally:

(a)   as long as the rights that recipients get have only a purely subjective mean-
      ing, a meaning that cannot be communicated given uncertainty about the
      identity or comparability of different persons's feelings;
(b)   as long as the meanings of rights are measured by different and incompatible
      standards; or
(c)   as long as we cannot compare the positions of individuals relative to one
      another.

These three interpretations of equality in terms of (a) interpersonal comparisons,
(b) one-dimensional measurement and (c) intersubjectivity in senses differing
from (a) and (b) offer three possible ways to design equalisanda. In this chapter I
shall be concerned with the quest for an intersubjectively acceptable measure for
(in)equality, an equalisandum.

The search for this measure of inequality is the common denominator of two opposed schools of thought with fundamentally different interpretations of the expression 'equal treatment'. In the first view, usually branded egalitarianism, the presumption is that all recipients are basically equal and consequently deserve to get an equal part of the social stock. However, egalitarians admit that equality is a controversial notion.[64] Rights or goods do not mean the same to people, or do not affect them in the same manner and to the same degree, as humans are undeniably different – by accident, of course (in this view), and not by nature. Other things being equal, a blind, deaf and mute man probably gets less (joy, utility, or whatever) out of a ticket for the Eiffel Tower than the average healthy person; a person with jaded taste will have a different opinion on the digestibility of fast food than the average homeless person. Clearly, an egalitarian cannot measure equality by the number and amount of goods a person holds; instead, some abstract quality is required that allows comparisons between all these different goods and the different values they have for different people. In social justice research, this quality is often referred to as the equalisandum, 'that which is to be equalized'.

Non-egalitarians do not intrinsically care about the quantity of rights that people get relative to one another. For them, equal treatment may very well result in inequality – in fact, in their view distributive justice should often lead to inequality. Aristotle is one of the best known representatives of this school; the theory behind honours, orders and medals illustrates the position best. One could say that non-egalitarians try to take the difference between persons seriously. They acknowledge that individuals differ in their mental and physical make-up, in status and position, in what they do and how they do it, and as a consequence in what they deserve or need. Some, for instance, need more food than others; some deserve a Knighthood and others do not.

Nevertheless, non-egalitarians insist upon some form of equal treatment: there ought to be an equal standard for the desert or need of all, so that the objectively same achievement is rewarded either with the same reward or with intersubjectively equivalent rewards. Note that the latter option in effect (though not in theory) erases the difference with egalitarianism, as moderate egalitarians allow deviations from equality if deserved or needed. A difficult point for non-egalitarians is the determination of the relevancy of the reasons offered for (un)equal treatment. Like egalitarians, they need a universally acceptable measure for individual need or desert – a measure for 'that which is to be proportionally equalized', the equalisandum. There is as yet no need to choose between these interpretations of equal treatment. We shall postpone an answer to this question until the first issue on our agenda, the designation of an impartial equalisandum, has been addressed.

First, let me remove a source of possible confusion. Principles of justice are traditionally classified as being either essentially principles of equality, or essentially principles of need, or essentially principles of desert.[65] In everyday life, these categories suffice to distinguish the kinds of reasons that are thought to be relevant to (un)equal distribution. To be given a share on the basis of need, one has to suffer from something, preferably (I assume, to avoid confusion) something un-deserved – a disease, a defect, a disaster. To get or be denied a share on the basis of desert implies that one has done something admirable or abominable, even if nothing more than (not) being born of noble blood. Further, to receive equal shares of anything implies either that no reasons whatsoever can justify inequality, or that no-one should or can pass judgement on (private) reasons. Consequently, one might expect that these three notions could serve well as equalisanda: the more you need, for instance, the more you should get.

In the realm of theory, however, the distinctions between need, desert and equality are far less clear. A principle like 'the working poor should get a com-pensation equalizing their income to that of the average citizen' can be defended in terms of more than one category: they do not deserve their poverty, yet work hard for their money, and their bad luck should therefore be compensated; they need the money to survive or to reach a tolerable level of welfare; or the basic equality of all humans should be reflected in everyone's wealth and income. In fact, principles that look like need-principles may be desert-principles and vice versa: 'to each according to his contribution' may well refer to a basic psycho-logical need for rewards and 'to each according to his professed preference' could just as well be based on the conviction that we deserve all we desire. Most importantly, the three principles fail to establish clear measures for (un)equal treatment: they do not specify the quality in which recipients are equal or by which their differences in need or desert should be assessed.

The debate on social justice of the last twenty-odd years has resulted in a long list of possible equalisanda, often criticized and dismissed as either needing in-admissible premises or leading to counter-intuitive (inconsistent) results. These equalisanda are basically of three kinds: they are result-oriented, opportunity-based, or means-based. A popular result-oriented equalisandum was and still is individual utility. It is most often used as a basis for the comparison of (changes in) social states: the sum of individual utilities, average utility and other aggregates of individual utility are the fundamental ingredients of utilitarian and welfarist schools in moral philosophy and (especially) economics. These schools have, from the early beginning, been under heavy fire exactly because of the aggregate character of their measuring devices. In its most simple incarnation as a counter-argument to the crudest version of utilitarianism, total utility, the critique insisted that utilitarianism could not distinguish between two societies with the same total utility, in one of which utility was distributed equally, whereas in the other, millions suffered and one person enjoyed all the pleasures life can provide. John Rawls criticized utilitarianism along these same lines as not taking the difference between persons seriously; in his view, the justice of a state of affairs should have some relation to what individuals get, and not to what they get in average or sum. Essentially, as Jan Narveson (Narveson 1973: 73) observed, utilitarianism is more interested in making happy people than in making people happy. In short, utilitarianism was thought to be unable to assess the distributive aspects of social states.

Now, apart from the fact that modern versions of utilitarianism are less vulnerable to this kind of critique,[66] objections to its aggregate character and its supposed inability to deal with the distribution aspects of justice cannot be used against utility as an equalisandum. If someone uses wine to get drunk, it does not mean that one cannot also use it to cook. The fact then that utilitarians use individual utility to compare social states does not prove that it cannot be used to compare individual positions within one social state, that is to assess the distributive rather than aggregate aspects of states of affairs.

Two questions now rise: can utility actually be used that way, and if so, should it? Presupposing that an *intra*subjective measurement of utility is possible in itself (cf. Smart 1986: 32), the first problem is essentially one concerning intersubjective measurement. I discuss this point only to show that it is a problem; I do not intend or need to solve it. Basically, utility is a subjective measure. One can ask an individual to rank and even assign values to her rights or to alternative bundles of rights, but we have no reason to suppose beforehand that Harry's marks will be comparable to Cissy's. Harry and Cissy may both rank their individual rights to drive a car highest, they may both value it with a 10 on a scale of 1 to 10, but that still does not tell us if Harry and Cissy derive the same satisfaction from their respective rights, simply because we do not know how (say) happy a 10-right makes either one of them.

So let us suppose something else as well, namely that there is a certain 'similarity' of utility scales and utility experience (cf. Smart 1986: 33). How would this intersubjectively comparable quality be measurable? One strategy to ensure an intersubjectively correct measurement might be to simply ask Harry and Cissy to value each other's bundles of rights, for instance, asking them how they would feel if they were to trade places. This would at least tell us how strong their feelings are relative to one another. Or so it seems. If Harry values his own life (bundle of rights) with a 6 and Cissy's with an 8, and Cissy's values are directly opposite, all we know is that they seem to prefer to trade places. As an alternative to refining the techniques for comparison, we could consider a second strategy: that of developing an objective rather than intersubjective basis for comparisons, a kind of lie-detector measuring the physical signs of excitement and anxiety. Or, thirdly, we could try to argue that the differences between the characters and emotions of persons are irrelevant from an impartial point of view; what ought to matter is each person's position relative to his minimum and maximum possible utility. There is something to be said for the last: perhaps one cannot make a fundamentally depressed person as happy as a maniac can be even on his worst day (Ackerman 1980: 47), so why take the impossible as a basis for policies?

But let us assume that an adequate interpersonal measurement of utility were possible both in theory and in practice. A more important question is whether we should base principles for the just distribution of rights on the utility that those rights produce for their recipients. The answer is a plain no.

Utility is a universal meter; one can rank religious comfort, political freedom, material possessions, sexual satisfaction and whatnot on this one scale. The implication is that all complex rights are comparable *qua* satisfaction (cf. Sen and Williams 1982: 6). It follows that it can also be used to measure two distinct categories of rights *separately*, as in John Rawls's theory, where two fundamentally different kinds of primary social goods are distributed according to two different principles based on what are in fact two distinct equalisanda: liberties are divided equally in an advanced society, and material goods can be distributed unequally if that is to the advantage of the worst-off. Instead, utility could have been applied to both spheres without blurring the normative distinction between the two. The distinction I made earlier between basic needs and further wants is of the same type: it presumes that the two categories are not interchangeable, that they should not be measured on one scale but should instead be valued for their own reasons. Nevertheless, utility can theoretically measure both.

Yet utility *should* not be the standard for even only one of these categories: being result-oriented, it cannot be an impartial standard. It can measure results only in terms of one conception of the good, that is, the good of enjoying utility in some form. It therefore discriminates against other conceptions. To summarize Bruce Ackerman's argumentation against utility: if shares in the social stock were to be distributed on the basis of utility, one person would be more deserving than another because of the satisfaction they would derive from their shares and *not* because of the (for instance) moral value they attach to their respective courses in life – that is, not on the basis of the standards their conceptions of the good or of a full life prescribe (Ackerman 1980: 46 ff.; cf. Barry 1995: 82). One could argue that these latter standards are in fact measures of individual satisfaction (utility). One can argue with the same force that they have nothing to do with individual experiences, that, for example, individual happiness is of no interest to the full life, but that creating wisdom and beauty, undergoing God's decisions, or learning to live with and assent to one's fate is all that matters. Either way, 'we search in vain for a neutral yardstick for measuring the "real" value of different conceptions of the good' (Ackerman 1980: 48).

With this, we have found a strong argument against all result-oriented equalisanda (satisfaction of wants, needs, preferences, creation of wisdom, experience of divine mercy, and so forth) in general: any measure for the effect of rights-packages can be attacked as being partial to some conception(s) of the good and partial against another or others. Unfortunately, Ackerman's anti-equalisanda argument is so strong that it can also be turned against means- and opportunity-based equalisanda, the application of which of course implies discrimination against result-oriented equalisanda.

Before I try to solve this problem, I nevertheless want to spend a few words on these other two types of equalisanda. In recent years, several means- and opportunity-based equalisanda have been proposed. I cannot discuss them all, nor do I need to. The choice for an equalisandum depends, first and foremost, on the fit between the equalisandum and the theory in which it is to operate. My principal concern in the following sections will therefore be that of showing why archpointers would accept the two equalisanda I propose, option equality for rights to basic needs and envy-containment for rights to further wants. In this context, it is worthwhile to look at a problem that two of the more successful equalisanda encountered.

In his 1980 Tanner Lecture, Amartya Sen argued that one of the main defects of John Rawls's equalisandum, primary social goods, consisted in Rawls's pre-occupation with 'good things' rather than with what a good does or means to people (Sen 1980: 218). With this, Sen reflected a widely shared feeling that Rawls's theory might be insensitive to the special needs and demands of some recipients. It is all very nice to distribute, say, freedom of movement equally, but a lame man is more interested in the actual capability to move than in the formal freedom to do so only. Even though Rawls's principles of justice, in particular the rule demanding genuine equality of opportunity, would probably let this man end up with the means or capabilities that he in fact requires, it seems to be intuitively wrong not to be concerned in the *first* place about capabilities – especially since the whole idea of primary goods is to enable people to live as they may (reasonably) like.

Embracing Rawls's egalitarianism but rejecting his orientation on goods, Sen proposed that justice should be concerned with *equality of basic capabilities*, with 'being able to do certain basic things' (Sen 1980: 218) – a proposal for a means-oriented equalisandum which he refined in later years (see e.g. Sen (1993) and Cohen's (1993) critique of Sen). At about the same time, Ronald Dworkin advocated his own primary-goods alternative to Rawls's: *equality of resources* (Dworkin 1981: 283 ff.; for comments on Dworkin see Schokkaert 1992: 102). Like Sen, Dworkin felt that what mattered to people was being able to pursue one's chosen course in life, rather than having the means to live what a distributor believes to be the right life. Dworkin suggested that instead of using a necessarily controversial list of primary goods, recipients should pool their resources and, being given equal purchasing power, buy or regain the resources they really want at an auction.

Both equalisanda are designed to give people equal starting positions in life; their aim is to alleviate the effects of the undeserved differences in capacities with which we are born. Capability and resources are, however, ambiguous concepts: they refer to means or capacities but also to opportunities, at least if they are to be less formal than Rawls's primary goods – which was clearly Sen's intention (cf. Sen 1993: 33, 44). To have the resources to move requires legs or an alternative to legs, but one also needs something to walk on and one needs the absence of obstacles to walking (like ropes around you or people pointing their guns at you); to be capable to vote one needs to be registered as a voter as much as one needs elections. Yet in these two means–oriented equalisanda the notion of opportunity is virtually absent.

Clearly, opportunity without means is not enough – but neither are means without opportunities. An impartial equalisandum should be a measure of the effect rights have on their recipients' lives, more precisely on their capability (means *plus* opportunity) of leading lives of their choosing. Regardless of the role that we would want to assign to equality in starting positions or to inequality in later life, the standard by which we measure the inequality of recipients should take account of what their rights *can* mean to them, not merely of what they *might* mean.

Equality of options

Ackerman's anti-equalisanda argument actually averts any attempt to arrive at an account for all kinds of equalisandum except one. It excludes equalisanda based on interpersonal comparisons and those based on a one-dimensional measure for the meaning of rights (compare alternatives (a) and (b) in the first paragraph of the previous section). The way is still open for a last type, one that is inter-subjectively acceptable and allows for comparisons of the individuals' positions without falling in the trap that Ackerman set. The Dworkin-like equalisandum that I propose for basic needs, equality of options, satisfies these conditions. It allows an overall equal (equivalent) distribution of fundamental rights by letting the utilitarian measure her welfare in terms of utility, the Rawlsian in terms of primary goods, the substantialist in terms of an overall good, and so forth.

The basis on which we can compare rights to basic needs, the trait these rights have in common, is not that they enable us to make others work for us, or to make things happen for us, nor, conversely, that they give us the potential to do what others want us to do. Rather than as means to dominate or be dominated, rights to basic needs must be understood in terms of the capability to remain independent: undominated and undominating (cf. Spinoza 1951: 295; Terpstra 1990: 332). Their function – in Sen's words, what they do to people, or in Cohen's, what people can do with them – is to allow people to live a full life. Rights to basic needs offer both the means (capabilities, resources) to that aim and the opportunity. Whether and to what degree we use them is our own choice. It is in this sense of a two-dimensional concept, as both the means and the opportunities to live a full life, that I shall use the word 'option'. Basic needs have been defined as the necessary means to a full life, and being the subject of complex rights, they also, by definition, offer genuine opportunities for a full life. It should then come as no surprise that rights to basic needs can be expressed in terms of options, the synthesis of means and opportunities. What may be more surprising and what certainly requires a justification is the decision to choose options as an equalisandum, rather than means or opportunities. Why should option equality be the impartial standard for judgements on the value of individuals' bundles of basic rights?

One reason, a necessary but not sufficient condition, has already been discussed above: if a certain right were to give you all the opportunity in the world to do something, say eat, but not the means, say a mouth, it would be as empty as when it gave you all the means but no opportunities to eat. Either way, the right cannot have more than a formal meaning. To be capable of representing the meaning that rights and goods have or can have for people, an equalisandum should take account of both aspects.

What makes options an *impartial* equalisandum becomes clear when we consider the effect of its application to basic needs. The principal common feature of rights to basic needs is the freedom they give to live the full life we want to live, the freedom to determine our way of (rather than path in) life. Without basic necessities, it would be impossible to be free to realize any set of full reasons; even the notorious Ch'an Buddhist would no longer have a choice. With rights to basic needs on the other hand, we *are* free to use all, part, or none of them in any way we feel to be consistent with our conception of the full life.

Not all basic needs are equally basic for all of us. Clothing, for instance, is obviously more important the colder it gets. Yet basic needs do not have to mean the same to each to be equally important for all. Impartiality demands the postponement of judgement on full reasons and on sets of full reasons, that is, on conceptions of the full life. They all deserve the same respect, but that respect cannot remain purely formal. To express equal respect for, while at the same time avoid prejudice against, any possible plan for a full life, impartiality should extend beyond full reasons to both the means and the opportunities that are – together – indispensable for a full life. Hence, the set of means and opportunities one person necessarily needs for a full life is just as valuable and just as important as any other's.

So much, then, for the intersubjective acceptability of our equalisandum. Anyone accepting the conditions of the archpoint will accept subjective neutrality and, as a further consequence, accept an understanding of a just treatment as an equal treatment with respect to full reasons. It is now also easy to see why equality of options escapes Ackerman's anti-equalisanda argument: it does not require interpersonal comparisons and it leaves everyone's private convictions as to what matters about basic needs – means, opportunity, results – a matter of, precisely, private convictions. Again, it allows the utilitarian to measure her welfare in terms of utility and the substantialist to measure it in terms of an overall good.

Equality of options defines the basic criterion for judging claims to basic needs: any partial or total lack of options on the part of a recipient counts as a good reason. It also defines, at least in principle, the standard for a just distribution of basic necessities: equality. Impartiality with regard to plans, means and opportunities for a full life implies that, first of all, unequal starting positions in life should be regarded as totally undeserved. No plan for a full life being better than any other, each recipient should get an equal chance – means and opportunities – for realizing it. Secondly, inequalities that arise later in life should be seen as *prima facie* unjust, that is, unjust until proven just. As impartiality forbids judgements on full reasons, any condoning of option inequality, inequality that is due to different ideas about the full life or to developments in one's conception of a full life, comes down to condoning violations of subjective neutrality. This accounts for the *prima facie* injustice of inequality of options. There is, however, one factor that might seem to be able to tip the balance in favour of inequality: irresponsibility. The woman who capitalizes her rights – first her further wants, then her basic needs – and wastes what she has capitalized on classic vices, not in the pursuit of a full life but out of a plain and pure lust for pleasure (assuming the two to be mutually exclusive in her case), will seem to have forfeited her rights.[67] Yet when I return to this matter of prodigal daughters in the next chapter, I shall argue that even the most irresponsible recipient deserves the benefit of the doubt, as far as her bare survival as an autonomous agent is concerned.

Option equality is an egalitarian equalisandum: rights to basic needs give means and opportunities to live a full life, and if those means and opportunities are distributed equally, then all's well and just. So much for theory. A conversion of this principle into practice will confront us with a nasty problem: that of measuring options. Measuring the means-aspect of one basic need (e.g. amount of food) will be difficult, but as a rule not more so than determining if a person is still alive, in that it is not technically impossible. Although they can be satisfied to different degrees, most basic needs can be *represented* as either below or above a level of sufficiency, that is, as what methodologists call dummies, zero-one variables. Either one has enough food to survive, reproduce and live a full life, or one is starving; either one has a voice in politics and a place in society or one does not. Measuring opportunities may be equally difficult for similar reasons, and adding all means and opportunities together while still making sense of it is – well, an expert's job. I admit the difficulties and I admit that quantifiability could help us understand the further implications of option equality – but I do not admit the existence of a fundamental problem. In the first place, one does not need to combine all scores on all aspects of option equality to determine whether someone is worse off than another in some respect rather than another; in this sense, an overall equalisandum would be less precise and less sensitive to the effects of moral pluralism than a set of segment measures. Secondly, measures of justice do not have to allow measurement on a microscopical scale to make sense, even political sense. Like beauty, virtue, melancholy and other 'weakly' measurable qualities, the notion of having options to live a meaningful life can be understood without figures that are exact down to the last digit.

Containment of envy

Option equality is not a good equalisandum in the sphere of rights to further wants. Whatever these rights may have in common, it is not that they are crucial (Barry 1995: 84) or essential to the full life, or even contribute to it. Lacking a relation of necessity to the full life, further wants do not offer opportunities or means to that aim, and therefore cannot be evaluated in terms of options. As already remarked at the end of Chapter 8, the archpoint in fact does not enable us to define any equalisandum for rights to further wants *as such* at all. They may be scarce goods but remain 'merely' luxury as compared to basic needs: at the end, or in the end, the criteria for a life worth living can hardly be the merits of our cars and wallpaper, the number of lovers loved and ruined, or that of soccer games seen on TV. Yet from the archpoint of view or from any human point of view, it cannot be irrelevant that further wants mean enough to people to continuously fight about them in each and every social context. Being the object of so much social conflict, they satisfy any condition of social justice they can satisfy.

Then again, what rights to further wants exactly mean to the individuals who have them or desire having them depends not on their full reasons but on two other factors. One is a very broad and very contingent psychological and social context: culture and subculture, profession, persuasion and convictions, status, family, education, friends, peer pressure, one's inclination towards or away from conformism, personal and general economic prospects, and so on. All of these influences shape an individual's preferences, some of them rationally, others in an irrational direction. Outsiders as they are, archpointers will be able to perform some Brandtian cognitive psychotherapy and sift out the irrational desires, leaving them with a small set of tastes, preferences and basic moral motives.

At this point the second factor that gives meaning to rights comes in: the individual's theory of the good, her plan of a complete life. And here also the usefulness of archpointers to the debate on distributive justice in a society ends. We allowed archpointers to have encyclopaedic knowledge of the society or societies on which they judge. We assumed that this knowledge can include every fact there is to know about any person's social ideal, anyone's concrete ideal for his or her personal life, any conception of the good life expounded by ideological, religious, or other segments of society, and, if available, the whole community's (i.e. the communitarian) consensus on the good life. But all this knowledge is in vain, as the archpointers lack one piece of information that would allow them to judge on individual and societal views on the good from a higher point of view, namely which moral view is the right one. The whole point of defining impartiality was, after all, to make archpointers unable to choose sides on the kind of moral issues that we ourselves are unable to decide and (should) believe to be undecidable.

To cut a long story short: an equalisandum measures the strength of reasons for claims on parts of the social product, but the archpoint does not allow judgements on the kinds of reasons that are relevant to further wants – and therefore it cannot compare these goods and rights themselves. There is no impartial equalisandum for further wants as such (cf. Barry 1995: 11, 110, 143).

Nevertheless, the issue of the distribution of rights to further wants does have one aspect that not only requires but also allows an impartial appraisal. As sources of conflict, and notwithstanding the emancipatory influence social conflicts may have, further wants are a potential threat to the fabric of society and thereby to the individual's prospects for a full life; the more intense the conflict, the greater the danger. An almost self-evident example is a civil war of the kind Somalia experienced in recent years. Crops and farmlands were destroyed and harvests stolen, causing on the one hand famine among farmers and other ordinary citizens, but benefiting on the other hand the warlords and their gangs, who ended up having far more food than they basically needed (not to mention other 'luxury' goods). There was, in principle, enough food for everyone to survive, and without war there would have been plenty, so the problem was not a supply-side issue of real scarcity but a matter of extreme unfairness in the distribution. In their fight over – initially – further wants like status, family affairs and relative political autonomy, the warlords literally tore their society to pieces. To use an understatement: they violated the precepts of minimal justice by furthering some full lives at the expense of others.

If we want to protect individuals and their life-prospects against discrimination of at least this most fundamental sort, the distribution of goods and rights in the sphere of further wants must be judged by its impact on social peace and individual security, on the options for leading a full life. The equalisandum I propose in this context is containment of envy – envy, as a *pars pro toto* label, referring to all the possible reasons for discontent and for claims to further wants. It is a purely formal measure of individual discontent over the distribution of rights to further wants, not a substantial criterion interpreting (dis)content as (lack of) opportunity, means, utility or individual desire/satisfaction. Our second equalisandum cannot judge reasons as reasons. It can only measure the strength of feelings and it should measure individual feelings rather than a more abstract quality like total or average (dis)content, as social peace depends more on the distribution than on an aggregate of (dis)content.

How can envy or discontent be measured? One possibility is the well known (non-)envy test, introduced in economics by Hal Varian, in mainstream social justice theory by Ronald Dworkin (Dworkin 1981: 285) and, in the different shape of the exploitation test, in analytical Marxism by, amongst others, John Roemer (cf. Roemer 1996: 317). Dworkin applied the envy test to the distribution of scarce goods (resources) that shipwrecks on a desert island would agree to after a fair auction. If none of them wanted to trade her packet of goods for that of anyone else, the distribution satisfied the envy test; if it did not, it appeared that the resulting distribution of resources was still not totally fair. The envy test has many advantages – for one, it neatly circumvents the problem of interpersonal comparisons – but it also has three disadvantages: it measures opinions on *existing* bundles of rights only, it only measures whether desires and preferences are *equally* satisfied, and it cannot guarantee *full* satisfaction.

As to the first problem: social co-operation is not guaranteed, and envy will not disappear, when no-one wants her neighbour's rights and goods. I may not want to trade places and jobs with my closest colleagues or with anyone, but that does not stop me from envying others for parts of their bundles of rights. In one of the better worlds I can imagine, no-one would desire to have my income, yet I would be a millionaire. Envy or discontent is, in other words, not limited to actually existing distributions. It applies to all feasible and even all imaginable distributions. For that reason a useful envy test will have to take account of at least all feasible (re)distributions of the existing stock, rather than of discontent over the existing allocation only.

The envy test's bias for measuring *equal* satisfaction only is problematic for two reasons. In the first place, we do not want to ensure equality *per se*; unlike options, envy-containment is not an egalitarian equalisandum. We want a certain degree of social peace and hence a scale for envy that registers more than a simple yes or no. It is, for an analysis of envy in itself, totally irrelevant that the best warrant for co-operation in a particular society at a particular point in time is an equal distribution of discontent. Secondly, equality of (dis)content is not the only imaginable way of avoiding the problem of intersubjective measurement. There is still the simple and more accurate alternative of asking people how envious they feel — though, admittedly, the idea is simpler than the implementation.

For the sake of argument, I assume that we only want to know *how* envious people are, and not what rights they are envious of. In the real world we have political institutions and bargaining mechanisms to fill in these not unimportant details. We can then imagine an envy-containment test as a four-stage procedure. At the first stage, recipients are asked to look at the bundles of rights to further wants they and others actually have and at the feasible permutations of these bundles. Subsequently, they are asked to scale their sense of (dis)content on a scale from, say, 0 to 10. They should, thirdly, indicate at what level of discontent they would consider separating from society (in the rational choice idiom: indicate the baseline for co-operation) and at what level of discontent they would start or join an uproar. Finally, the data for a whole society are assessed in the light of the potential for social unrest they may reveal.

Needless to say, this method is sensitive to strategic behaviour, for instance, to lying, cheating and misleading. Recipients can easily exaggerate their discontent or raise their standards, if they suspect greed to produce sweet grapes. However, the same is true of the original envy test.

Finally, the envy test does not guarantee *full* satisfaction. 'If two people, one of whom is a Hindu, have an equal amount of beef, neither envies the other (i.e., neither prefers the other's share to his own) but the Hindu is not satisfied since his share is of no use to him.'[68] This is a deficiency that cannot be repaired, since repairing it requires a supply-side solution, that is, the creation for each individual of bundles of goods or rights that actually *meet* her wants and desires. It just goes to show that there is more to the good society than distributive justice alone.

There is one possible objection to this whole scheme of equalisanda and rights that is too obvious not to discuss: do we really need two equalisanda, or is it possible that envy-containment and option equality are the same thing or that one of them is merely an aspect of the other?[69]

To reduce option equality to envy-containment, it would have to be true that chances of living a full life are, in fact, instances of envy-containment over further wants. Now this would, first of all, mean that supporting full life-plans is

Table 9.1 The distribution of rights

Rights are complex rights made up of r-molecules.			
Can they be owned?	Can they be alienated?	How are they to be distributed?	Using which principles?
unownable: vital aspects of the self	no	no	equal respect
unconditional: (essential) natural assets	no	no	equal protection
untouchable: the right to destroy	no	no	save, replace, restore, or compensate
conditional rights in the strict sense	if morally required	basic needs: option equality	equality
	if politically necessary	further wants: envy-containment	minimize envy

merely instrumental to the ultimate aim of protecting the social structure, which was meant to facilitate full lives in the first place. This cannot be our intention. Secondly and worse, it would imply that giving options to live a full life can never be at odds with containing envy. Fortunately, a counter-example is easy to find: imagine 10 million radical Buddhists realizing their full plans of life in what used to be a consumer society of 15 million people – it is hard to believe that the remaining 5 million will ungrudgingly accommodate themselves to a crashing economy destroying *their* prospects for a full life. The envy test may be met (no non-Buddhist would want to trade places or shares with any Buddhist in so far as further wants are concerned) but there is now no guarantee that the basic needs of all 15 million are still met – say, dignity for the Buddhists, work, bread and dignity for the rest.

To be able to reduce envy-containment to option equality, on the other hand, it must be true that containing envy is one means, possibly among others, of giving people options to live a full life. Thus, as envy-containment is by definition aimed at the protection of the social structure, protecting the social structure would by definition further the realization of full lives. In this view even the most basically unjust society, one wilfully distributing little or no bread but a lot of games, would not be totally unjust. However, there are ways of furthering social peace without impartially furthering full lives – all it takes is the kind of state terrorism that typically attracts the warm attention of Amnesty International.

Apparently, then, there is no reason to suppose that options and envy-containment can be brought under the same heading. They define two different equalisanda for two different realms, each of which determines a distinct aspect of the (in)justice of the basic structure of society. In the next chapter I shall examine the way in which these standards can be applied. I want to close this chapter with a summary, in the form of Table 9.1, of the specification of complex rights which I gave in the last two chapters. The first column divides the possible objects of complex rights into categories of ownership rights (or impossibility of ownership rights), the second indicates when rights can be the object of (re)distribution, the third couples these to equalisanda and the fourth column, alluding to the principles of social justice ruling the distribution and protection of rights, gives a preview of the following chapter.

10

Principles of minimal justice

Principles for options and envy

Up to this point, I have discussed separate issues in the theory of social justice and not principles of justice as such. I have asked to whom justice should be done: who is to be a recipient and why? I have examined what it is that a distributor should distribute, in which connection we distinguished several categories of rights and described a proper subject for the principles of minimal social justice. Lastly, I discussed equalisanda, the bases of comparison for the distribution of rights.

Between the lines, I touched on two other problems: that of the identity of the distributor and that of the grounds of desert (the reasons for getting more or less of the equalisandum). With regard to the first issue, we found little more than that (1) the existence of a diversity of distributors in the real world may complicate the allocation of responsibility for distributive justice and that (2) we were as yet unable to decide whether state and state-like institutions or the free market would be best fit to facilitate distributive social justice. However, I hope to show in this chapter that this is enough information to allow more precise answers.

My conclusions regarding the second issue were more specific but equally unordered. I argued that to count as a recipient of social justice and hence to be deserving, one should necessarily exist, live and be the subject of a distributor's responsibility. Three other qualities make a difference for the degree of recipiency and, consequently, for the degree of deservingness: consciousness, the possibility of autonomy and agency and membership of society. The recipient's responsibility and irresponsibility, I posed, should also be taken into account, as should, finally, the availability of the options and envy-containment equalisanda. What I did not discuss was the effect that these nine elements will have on recipients' shares.

In this chapter I shall link these separate propositions together and construct a complete measure of minimal justice, step by step, working more or less backwards through the preceding chapters. I start with principles for the distribution of options (rights to basic needs) and envy-containment (rights to further wants) as such, that is, without reference to other elements of a scale such as types of recipients, grounds of desert and the shape of the distributor. I do not want to claim that the list of principles with which we shall end up exhausts the list of possibilities, but I do believe that it gives an adequate description of where an understanding of justice as impartiality takes us.

The chapter's (and book's) final section is reserved for a moment of reflection, an appraisal of its achievements and shortcomings – if not to congratulate myself, then at least to be one step ahead of the critics.

Defining a principle for the distribution of options for a full life requires that we take account of the scarcity of rights to basic needs in a specific way. There can obviously be too few options: circumstances like famine, thirst, sickness, political oppression and coercive isolation all obstruct the full life. Scarcity of this sort need not be a primarily distributive problem. If impartiality demands that we show equal respect to all (fellow) recipients because of their capacity for having a plan for a full life when *distributing* rights, it seems that we have a similar and perhaps even greater duty to prove this respect when *producing* rights. Political rights can be created, food and medicines produced, all to and above the level of sufficiency. Distributive justice analysis is, however, not concerned with supply-side solutions; it must start out literally from what is given, that is the stock of rights at a particular point in time. Nor is distributive justice, in so far as it deals with the distribution of options, concerned with abundance. Once the necessary conditions for the realization of an individual's plan for a full life have been satisfied, additional rights become the object of further wants rather than basic needs.

As argued in the previous chapter, rights to the available basic needs ought to be distributed so as to guarantee equality of options. Option equality answers the demand to respect each and every individual's full reasons and plan for a full life without taking sides and without directly or indirectly favouring some reasons and persons over others. Any argument for an unequal distribution of the equalisandum implies that we choose sides, which is by definition unjustified and unjustifiable – in principle. There is one legitimate exception to this rule, and that is *not*, as some readers might expect, a Rawlsian difference principle.

Before I introduce the exception that I intend to allow, let me first explain my reasons for rejecting an unequal distribution of rights to basic needs if that is 'to the greatest benefit of the least advantaged', to copy Rawls's criterion for justifiable inequality (Rawls 1971: 83). Rawls believes that an unequal distribution of certain primary goods can serve as an incentive for those who are directly benefited by the difference principle, which will lead to a growing production of the goods in question, which will in turn via a trickle-down effect leave the worst off better off than equality would have let them be.

Now let us suppose that the same mechanism could work in the case of rights to basic needs. Basically, there are two kinds of incentives to be reckoned with:

investments, or extra resources that are physically or economically necessary to allow growth, and pure incentives, extra resources needed to motivate those now better off to produce more. (The distinction between these two will be dealt with more extensively below.) The latter type of incentive is clearly incompatible with impartiality: the inequality in question is unnecessary, as those profiting from pure incentives *could* also have produced more without an incentive and with another (impartial) attitude. Giving in to demands of this kind comes down to giving in to blackmail. In the case of pure investment incentives there is no blackmail, but we do have another problem. The theory of distributive justice is not concerned with the justification of growth or other supply-side solutions to questions of basic needs. To justify a growth policy (note that inequality may not even be necessary for growth to occur) other political ideals like human dignity, emancipation or positive freedom have to be invoked and those ideals would have to take precedence over the ideal of social justice. I can very well imagine that this is possible and even morally required, at least in the poorest societies, but it would still mean a deviation from justice in the name of a higher ideal, which is a choice that cannot be justified from *within* a theory of distributive justice. If and when a society decides to deviate from justice, all that a principle of justice for rights to basic needs can add is that burdens should not be distributed unequally unless that is really physically unavoidable, because there is no reason why anyone should suffer more than anyone else – other than voluntarily.

Which brings me to the real exception to options equality: unavoidable inequality. Some sources of options are simply indivisible. The one remaining unit of a serum, for example, cannot save the lives of two or more dying patients. Under such circumstances and if no-one freely withdraws his claim, all that can be done is to choose between a violation of equality by denying one person his chance to survive – and the *fiat justitia pereat mundi* option of withholding it from everyone. Unfortunately, the last and easiest solution is also the worst: it apportions no options and allows no full lives to be lived at all. Which leaves us with a necessarily tragic choice for one rather than another life. In situations like these, the best approximation of impartiality is chance: though in the end it indirectly favours one plan of life over another (a violation of subjective neutrality), at least chance avoids the graver sin of *directly* judging persons and reasons.[70]

Bringing all these considerations together, the following principle for the distribution of basic necessities emerges (its formulation is admittedly easier than its implementation):

(1) Rights to basic necessities are to be distributed so as to give recipients equal options for a full life. Unavoidable inequalities should be as small as possible and should be randomly distributed, with an equal chance for all to win or lose.

To illustrate some of the effects of this principle, let me discuss two examples. In the first case, Harry Stottle has been caught stealing the works of Plato from a bookshop and setting fire to them in front of the shop. As he did such things before, he has been sentenced to three months in prison and he has lost his active and passive voting rights for that period. Whether Harry deserved this is a question of retributive justice; whether laws allowing citizens in general to be locked away and to be deprived of political rights are just is, on the other hand, a question of distributive justice. Judged by our first principle, one would have to say that it depends. It depends, in general, on whether convicts still get the basic needs required for a full life – food, medical aid, shelter, and so forth. It depends in particular, first, on whether Harry and his likes still have a voice in politics,[71] that is, whether their political opinions can still be heard outside the prison walls. This is an empirical question, or in other words, it is uncertain. It depends, secondly, on the influence a prison sentence has on one's status and role in society. One could argue that prison sentences, especially when combined with the loss of political rights, are a form of symbolic banishment from society, but again one would have to ask whether the *actual*, empirical result is the same as that of genuine banishment. Finally, and if it turns out that under circumstances (in certain countries) symbolic exile obstructs the full life, it depends on whether we can reasonably maintain that criminals are not class-A recipients.

As a second example, consider the prodigal daughter introduced in the last chapter. She – say, Cissy Roo again – sold or threw away all her rights, including her house, her clothes and the contents of her refrigerator; she spent it all on gorging, gambling and gigolos and now lies in a dark alley recuperating from the effects of very bad wine. Like Harry's condition in the first example, Cissy's fate in terms of basic needs is both presumably the result of plain stupidity or irresponsibility and *prima facie* unjust. Like Harry, Cissy seems to satisfy all the requirements for full, first-class, recipiency. Whether she should be given a second chance in life and whether Harry should temporarily be barred from his options thus depends on the strength of second-thought arguments against their full recipiency. We cannot (or, for the sake of argument, shall not) deny their existence, the facts that they live and that they are conscious, their capacity for agency and autonomy and the fact that there are distributors with a moral responsibility for their fates. The remaining options for exclusion, if we want to exclude them, are that we try to argue that Harry and Cissy cut their ties with society or that their irresponsibility makes them less deserving.

Now assume that Harry1 acted quite responsibly: he knew what he was doing and he knew what the consequences would be. He burnt Plato's books as a protest against impartiality, against a society allowing bad tastes, and he had the welfare of society in mind. He acted, among other things, on full reasons. In some respects this puts his action in the same class as civil disobedience and conscientious objection. Harry2, on the other hand, acted in an uncontrollable fit. Cissy1 let her passions get the better of her; somewhere on the road to ruin she lost sight of what she was doing. Cissy2 knew what she was doing – having a good time. We cannot deny the status of full recipient to Harry2 on grounds of irresponsibility without denying it to Cissy1 as well, but we cannot deny it to Harry2 – what happened to him was pure and undeserved bad luck. Nor can we deny full recipiency on grounds of responsibility to Cissy2 without also denying it to Harry1, but we cannot deny it to Harry1 without judging on full reasons, that is, without violating impartiality. Hence arguments based on responsibility or irresponsibility alone are simply not strong enough to justify the partial or total exclusion of both Harries and Cissies from rights to basic needs.

We are left, then, with the argument that Harry and Cissy themselves cut the ties with society. The fact of the matter is that Harry and Cissy are still both deeply embedded in social relations of all sorts; if anyone has cut these ties, it must have been society itself. Which brings us to the question of the criteria for membership or citizenship: when can a society justifiably admit or expel members? Now, I cannot discuss all possible criteria,[72] but we should note one – politically suspicious – criterion that is of particular relevance to our cases: the structural danger that massive immigration would pose to other recipients' options (cf. Goodin 1992: 11; Woodward 1992: 68). The argument behind this criterion for non-admission is that even though inequalities between those born in the Third World and, say, inhabitants of Monaco are or are thought to be undeserved, Monaco has a right to refuse to admit immigrants from the Third World should there one morning stand 5 million of them at the border, as admitting them would totally ruin Monaco's opportunity to guarantee an acceptable minimum level of welfare even (especially) to its current citizens. It is far-fetched to compare Harry1 to 5 million immigrants, but one might argue that he, unlike Harry2, Cissy1 or Cissy2, poses an in principle similar threat to his society's opportunities to guarantee the options of its members, and that he can consequentially be said to be less deserving of membership and less deserving of the status of first-class recipient. Harry1's action was, after all, intended to destroy or contribute to the destruction of a just and impartial basic structure. Once more, the argument is politically suspect and far-fetched, and it is not one that I myself believe to be sustainable, but it is the only reason I can think of for excluding recipients from rights to basic needs.

I shall let these cases rest at this point; this is a chapter about the construction of principles and not about their application. All I wanted to do was to show that our first principle is a *practical* principle, in that it allows a meaningful debate on and analysis of the distribution of options and basic needs, and that it is a *critical* principle in permitting us to question the morality of existing practices and intuitions.

The case of principles for rights to whatever fulfils a further want is quite different. Here we do not have a good reason for equality – nothing in this sphere is essential to a full life, so whatever distribution rule is chosen, it need not make judgements on or show disrespect for full reasons. The sources of further wants, the reasons behind claims in this sphere, are to some extent coincidental with regard to the person: they derive from an extended plan of life which in its turn, as a specific adaption of a conception of the full life, is given shape by purely external conditions like the structure of society, its culture, one's genetic, physical, cultural and family background and so on. And just as no-one really deserves innate capabilities, no-one deserves the society and the place in it in which one finds oneself. In short: to the extent that they are externally caused, no-one deserves the reasons one may have for one's further wants. Under these conditions every distribution rule based in the content and meaning of further wants themselves, including equality or chance, is arbitrary.

In so far as these reasons are *not* externally caused, one is responsible for their existence and deserves them. Yet even this fact cannot support a – any – distribution rule. It indicates that people partly create their own wants and reasons for wants, not that they do so with the help of an unquestionable objective criterion for the value of wants, a criterion that is acceptable from an archpoint of view. There is no such criterion. It is still possible that specific conditions in a specific society dictate an equal distribution of rights to further wants in the cause of envy-containment, but precisely because this depends on contingent circumstances we cannot pinpoint 'the' best distribution rule for all societies and times.

Nevertheless, we can put some formal limitations on the political freedom of choice regarding distribution rules. For example, the impartial protection of plans for a full life demands that (1) the distribution of rights to further wants should not lead to a social breakdown. For very much the same reason, (2) it should not induce any individual to prefer sabotage or secession from society back to a limited or total state of nature, over staying in.[73] Leaving society altogether (which is not the same as emigrating to another society) certainly diminishes the departing individual's chances of accomplishing her plans of life. By taking her possible contribution to society with her, she probably also reduces the chances of others. Thirdly, hindering plans for a complete life implies hindering at least some full lives, that is, violating the requirement of subjective neutrality. Consequently, a distribution scheme for this sphere must do more than merely prevent self-destructive behaviour; it need not actively *further* the individuals's pursuit of a complete life, but (3) it ought at least not to *hinder* them in this.

It takes no more than a glance to see that these three limitations will in some cases be incompatible. The non-hindrance condition (3) and the prevention of individual exit (2) are compatible only if the first gives way to the second: the minimum a distributor or a distribution system can do to avoid hindrance is to meet as few further wants as possible without making the exit-option more attractive than a life in society. It does not work the other way around: forcing one person to leave a society to whatever benefit of others means denying her rights to further wants *and* basic needs. These two conditions will, in turn, have to give way to the prevention of a social breakdown. As in the case of indivisible basic needs, a choice must be made between lifeboat-ethics (protecting as many persons and interests as well as possible) and sacrificing the meaning of justice to the pure idea of justice. In summary, we find the following principle for the distribution of rights to further wants:

> *(2) Rights to further wants are to be distributed according to rules that minimize envy,*
> *first down to a level preventing the distributing institution from breaking down, after that*

down to a level at which no-one prefers leaving this institution above staying and beyond
that down to a level at which the pursuit of plans for a complete life is minimally
hindered.

In an ideal world of angels and plenty, where envy never occurs, this principle is probably superfluous; it is clearly designed for the non-ideal world in which the conditions of justice obtain. The last part of the principle, nearly demanding the promotion of complete lives, still allows a very large degree of inequality in treatment and in circumstances. It is left up to concrete societies and individuals to determine the degree of inequality they find acceptable. In principle even an egalitarian can live with inequality – as long as there are good reasons for it. Unfortunately, the second principle does not contain a test of reasons. It allows all imaginable sources of envy: racism, sexism and other forms of discrimination that are, to say the least, quite suspect from an impartial point of view, changes in tastes, in needs and in plans of life regardless of personal responsibility, incentive-based arguments and ultimately also pure extortion. Anything goes, it seems, as long as everyone accedes to whatever reasons for (in)equality are advanced. Now perhaps envy and envy-containment should be measured impartially – but should impartiality go so far as to sacrifice the wellbeing of minorities (*qua* strength of conviction) to the whims of majorities?

Impartiality does not imply that all reasons are equal and equally good. It allows tests for the consistency and rationality of convictions. What it lacks is something that a real society may have: either a communitarian view of the good life, or a liberal political system reconciling different views of the good, both allowing the creation of standards for the ultimate moral quality of claims and arguments. (Which, incidentally, should not be taken to mean that communities and liberal societies have such standards by definition, nor that those standards are reliable.)

An archpointer will not find every degree of (in)equality acceptable, nor every reason for maintaining social peace or for preventing secession. Although minimal justice is not concerned with contingent factors like the particular sense of justice of particular individuals and societies or with actual economic growth figures, it does pose some limits on the *kinds* of arguments citizens would be demanded to embrace for the benefit of social peace. A first limit is clearly reached where claims are only supported by, by definition inadmissible, judgements on full reasons: 'You shall not have access to a university, for society is not interested in supporting weaklings that basically want nothing but to be loved by others, which you say is your ultimate aim in life.' This maxim is a special case of a more general precept: respect for recipients should be translated into respect for their claims.

In the eyes and vocabulary of an archpointer, the basic reason for the existence of social institutions is the protection of full life-plans, and the reason for valuing full life-plans lies in the respect that we owe to each possible recipient of justice by virtue of his or her capacities for recipiency. To those who are our equals in this respect, who can account for their actions, ultimately in terms of full reasons, we owe equal respect. And we do not show this by neglecting one person's reasons or accepting another's without any investigation (let alone by doing both). They – reasons and persons – all deserve to be heard and investigated seriously. In this context, the conditions of the archpoint can again be helpful: a distribution rule must be compatible with these conditions or it cannot be called (minimally) just. Again, the conception of minimal justice does not furnish us with methods to corroborate moral arguments about further wants as such. It can only, on formal grounds, refute those arguments that violate its basic demand for equal respect.

One of the conditions of the archpoint, the condition of weak rationality, plays a central role in assessing the acceptability of arguments. It demands that we reject fallacies and accept logically sound arguments, which would be impossible without even considering arguments for or against a distribution rule. It also demands three other things: (1) that arguments should be logically sound; (2) that arguments, in so far as they are based on facts, are confirmed by the facts; and (3) that arguments, in so far as they are based on a moral evaluation of facts, are not inconsistent with or unsupported by the moral theory or theories in terms of which they are defended. Finally, weak rationality suggests a more substantial limit: that one is held responsible for the things, the character traits, abilities, actions and ideas, for which one *is* responsible – no more and no less. If we are to respect recipients for the capacities that make them recipients, we cannot at the same time call those capacities morally irrelevant.

Further criteria for the evaluation of claims to further wants can be found in the principles of natural justice. Distribution rules and arguments for them must be consistent with these principles, that is, every difference in treatment must be based on a relevant difference between recipients.

We can now formulate a third principle, which, as it in fact excludes certain reasons for discontent and certain sources of envy, logically precedes the second principle formulated above:

> *(3) Rules for the distribution of rights to further wants must be compatible with the respect archpointers owe to recipients of justice.*

This principle excludes: distribution rules chosen without consideration of arguments pro or con; rules based on logically fallacious arguments, on arguments inconsistent with the facts they refer to, and on arguments that are inconsistent with or not supported by the moral theories in terms of which they are defended; rules presupposing responsibility for more or less than what one is actually responsible for, rules based on judgements on full reasons; and rules that are incompatible with the principles of natural justice.

To get some impression of the strength of this principle, let us consider some cases of discrimination and threats. Why, to begin with discrimination, would one refuse to give a woman (as a representative of the whole set of possible victims of discrimination) the job of, say, school director? One well-worn argument points to the risks of hiring women: they are presumed to become pregnant or to marry or both, and quit the job. Now there is good reason to assume that if no-one or nothing (like husbands, families, laws and cultures) forces them to, mothers and married women will not quit any more than married men or fathers would (or should). The facts, then, do not support discrimination. Still, the defender of conservative family values would contend, pregnant women will give birth one day and take leave, whereas men do not. But are women responsible for what men do? Under different circumstances, in some modern societies and in recent years, both parents take leave and, incidentally, take further care of their children – ideally in equal amounts. Yet let us suppose that even under these more favourable conditions, women still give up their jobs sooner and more often than men, for no identifiable reason. If one were to use this as an argument against women, one would ultimately be thrown back at one of two arguments: either that women are intrinsically unworthy of any (or this particular) public respons-ibility, or that the consequences of being a woman will keep women from adequately fulfilling their responsibilities. Perhaps such reasons are sound on some view, but not on any that is acceptable to an archpointer: the things a person is born into, like class, caste, society, body, skin colour or the 'intrinsic worth' attached to any of these things are not of his making and cannot therefore be held against him. Or her.

Threats, to move on to another example, are made in terms of what is known in bargaining theory as the non-agreement point, the point at which the benefits of co-operation equal the costs. They appear in different shapes, the most obnox-ious being blackmail, extortion, or, as Robert Nozick called it, unproductive exchange. 'I want you to give me some of your goods or rights, thus creating a state X_1 in which I feel better off than now, at my basic level in X_0 – or else I shall create X_2, which you will generally find to be far less attractive than either X_0 or X_1.' I could be the classic robber demanding your money or your life. I could be a tyrant dealing with religious dissenters or minorities by threatening to exclude them from, say, anything but their barest needs.[74] I could be your best friend making a joke. Or I could be a slave or a victim of crime fighting for my civil rights against you, the establishment or the criminal.

For the moment neglecting the 'or else X_2' part, which is always the heart of a threat, we find a simple basic level negotiation argument. Arguments of this kind seem to violate only the first demand posed by our third principle, that of considering arguments. Without the X_2-part, the legitimacy of threats and of distribution rules brought about by threats depends solely on the quality of the argumentative context: is the threat part of a debate on claims in which further arguments are submitted, and if so, do these other arguments pass the test of admissibility?[75]

It is the X_2-part of a threat that is most disturbing, the part that announces that I shall not give in an inch to any argument however strong – perhaps not even if X_2 is also worse for me than X_0. An attitude like this cannot be justified unless, again, the argumentative context allows it: (1) it must leave no room for the evaluation of arguments and counter-arguments (think of a totalitarian state), or (2) the other party must boycott the discussion or (3) rejects the result. Next to this, (4) at least one of my (suppressed) admissible arguments must unconditionally sustain my claim against any admissible counter-argument.

Related to threats are demands for zero-sum redistributions, for incentives and for investments. I can be brief about the first and last tactics. A zero-sum redistribution transforms a state X_0 into X_1, by which one party gains whatever the other loses. If the demand is disguised as a threat, it should be judged by the same standards as a threat; if it is not, it is a basic level argument and should be judged as such. Investment arguments are, perhaps surprisingly, hardly different. Their general structure is as follows: 'I want you to give me some of your rights, so that I can transform X_0 via X_1 into X_2, in which we will both gain relative to X_0.' (Note that the step from X_0 to X_1 is a zero-sum redistribution.) If the results of an investment harm some other recipients, it is a threat to them and a simple basic level argument for those benefited. If, on the other hand, an investment benefits at least the investors and harms no other recipients, that is, if it is Pareto-optimal, no threat is involved. Unfortunately, there probably is no such thing as a free lunch – or an unpolluting non-competitive enterprise.

Genuine incentive arguments are more complicated. On the surface they look like investment arguments: 'I shall create X_2, in which you as well as others gain relative to X_0 and no-one loses, provided that you give me an incentive creating X_1.' The difference with the investment argument lies in X_2: a state approximating X_1, with the difference that I will not lose relative to X_1. If it is impossible to reach X_2 without going through X_1, an incentive argument can be seen – and judged – as a legitimate investment argument, or rather, investment arguments can be seen as special cases of the incentive argument.

If, on the other hand, it were possible to get to X_2 without passing through X_1, a more interesting difference with investment emerges: the profit I make in X_1 could have been avoided. One might then be tempted to call such an argument for genuine incentives a negative threat: I still get more in X_1 and X_2 than in X_0, but instead of loosing, you will gain. In fact, this is what Cohen thinks about genuine incentives. In his eyes, any call for incentives comes down to extortion, as my gain in X_1 is totally unnecessary and even distracts from the gains of others in X_2 (Cohen 1991; the point is also implicitly made in Boudon 1976: 105). In other words, when incentives are not investments, they may be efficient (as Rawls argues) but they will have little to do with justice and everything with greed. Cohen is right, although only in a pseudo-Rawlsian context where everyone is supposed to desire the maximum advancement of the worst-off and where desert plays no role. From a non-Rawlsian point of view, genuine incentives cannot be condemned offhand. They can, at the very least, not be condemned on the basis of Cohen's critique of Rawls: it is not evident that justice would oblige anyone to *actively* support (economic) growth. Moreover, in a non-Rawlsian view of justice there may be good reasons to reward special efforts, even in advance. The third principle allows us to discuss these reasons.

One last remark regarding the arguments of the discontent: the principles I proposed will not, or will hardly, work if the recipients of justice are irredeemably envious, greedy, or jealous. Ultimately, their actions and desires will not merely obstruct the workings of a just social structure, but simply ruin it. I do not consider this to be a disadvantage of my theory specifically; as a rule, every theory of justice presupposes just citizens.

Principles for the public realm

The basic structure of society does more than withhold or distribute conditional rights in answer to basic needs and further wants; it is concerned with the distribution and protection of *all* rights. If it is to be just, it should protect the legitimate and reasonable expectations of recipients in all respects, that is, with the inclusion of their unconditional, inalienable rights and, beyond rights, their self-ownership. Formulating principles for these categories is simple, as we have already discussed their content in an earlier chapter:

(4) Each person's full reasons are inviolable; no social institution is allowed to distribute or redistribute (rights to) this vital aspect of the self.

(5) Each person has an unconditional right to his or her natural endowments, in so far as these are essential to that person's full life, and an inalienable right to his or her other natural endowments; no social institution is allowed to redistribute or limit rights to either category.

The protection of both identified and as yet unidentified legitimate expectations requires that we put a general limit to the exercise of conditional rights. There are several ways to envision such a limit. In an everyday conception of rights, a conditional right is a freedom to do or use something under particular restrictions: 'You have the right to take bus 50 at 12.05 from Whooping Bus Station to Whooping Shopping Centre, provided you pay the usual fare.' In this view, some things should just not be done with or to the object of the right. In the conception of rights formulated above, a conditional right is a (set of) complex rights, for instance (loosely formulated): 'You have the following set of freedoms: to take or not take bus 50, to take it at Whooping Bus Station and to get off at Whooping Shopping Centre; you do not have the freedom not to pay the usual fare.' In this view, some rights just should not be owned or distributed. Summarizing the conclusions we drew at the end of Chapter 8, we end up with the following principle for 'untouchable' rights:

(6) Conditional rights are to be distributed as rights that are limited by a restraint principle: the object of a conditional right should not be destroyed unless that is unavoidable; if it cannot be used without destroying it, it should be replaced by an identical object; if that is impossible, an equivalent object should be made available; if that is also impossible, a proper compensation should be provided. (Cf. Wissenburg 1998)

In most cases, this principle is easy to apply. Consider once more the right to take the bus. After having arrived at Whooping Shopping Centre, I might fancy blowing up the bus. Yet it is reasonable to suppose that others will want to use a bus, even that bus, for similar trips, and that their reasons for wanting to travel may well be at least as good as mine for blowing it up are. In private terms, then, I should not destroy the bus after use; in distributive terms, I should not be given the right to destroy it after use. Of course, our using the bus destroys it bit-wise; there is a limited number of passengers it can carry and a limited number of miles it can cover before falling apart. As the next passenger's claim can be at least as good as the last one's, the bus has to be replaced by another or, if progress makes buses obsolete, by its modern equivalent. Part of the bus fare is – or should be – put aside for that purpose. The restraint principle stops being applicable, obviously, when (a) a right cannot be used without destroying it and replacement is impossible, or when (b) there will be no more claims to a certain right. There is no reason for the last living being in the universe to replace the last bite of bread it will ever take.

In the real world, the distribution of conditional and unconditional rights is hampered by the fact that circumstances and times are a'changin', which can give rise to the re-examination of a present distribution and ultimately to redistribution. A just social structure is, however, expected to safeguard legitimate and reasonable expectations, a purpose that seems to be at odds with the kinds of principles described so far, principles that allow constant and immense redistributions. On the other hand: imagine a society satisfying these principles. One day the earth shakes. Numerous houses and possessions are destroyed, hundreds of people are hurt or ruined. We can safely assume that they badly need medicine, food, housing and other basic needs. Given an otherwise unchanged social stock (that is, excluding supply-side solutions), how can we not answer these legitimate new needs and wants without repossessing rights from those who suffered less, thereby possibly endangering the stability of the social structure?

In more general terms, the problem we face is that of redistribution as compensation for the (un)deserved (dis)advantages for or changes in plans of life. The aim of compensation can never be to restore a prior situation: bygones are by definition bygones. We can pay unemployment benefits or create new jobs, but we cannot undo the initial bitter experience of being sacked. And still less can we restore situations that never obtained, like being reborn with instead of without sight. Justice cannot undo injustice or misfortune. Compensation is, at best, an attempt to create a *ceteris paribus* approximation of the world in which some accident had not occurred.

Now whether claims to compensation are in themselves legitimate – that is, disregarding for a moment the effects of compensation on stability – depends to a large degree on the role responsibility plays in these claims. The third principle holds recipients accountable for using or abusing opportunities, and, by not attributing responsibility for fate or fortune, it qualifies them for compensation in other cases. Thus, if people willingly and consciously choose to run a risk, the consequences might well be theirs and theirs alone, but if brute bad (or good) luck hits them compensation can be legitimate: we should see it as (mis)fortune that they do not deserve and that we did not deserve to miss.

However, the distinction between choice and fate does not appear to be the whole truth about responsibility and compensation. Consider Cissy Roo, who jumps after a drowning child, saves it, but in doing so breaks a leg. Should she pay for her own crutches? Imagine the driver of bus 50 being drunk and running straight into Whooping Shopping Centre. The driver is injured through a fault of his own; the passengers are also injured, but their fate is not of their own making. Are we to treat the passengers and let the driver bleed to death? Or let us reverse the case: what if we are not dealing with bad but with good luck? Applying the same distinction in the same way, risk-takers can keep whatever they win, but people who gain 'through no good deed of their own' should lose their winnings. Imagine yourself buying two lottery tickets for £1 each (that is, making a risky investment). You keep one of the tickets for yourself and give the other to your best friend. Both tickets turn out to be good for a prize of £50,000 – but only you can legitimately claim the £50,000; your friend loses everything or never even gets to see the money. Choice and fate, then, do not really seem to be – at least – the only intuitively relevant criteria for compensation.

To accommodate our intuitions, we can of course introduce more and more subtle criteria. For instance: there is bad luck in a good cause, as when Cissy broke her leg, and bad luck in a bad cause, as when a burglar gets shot. Another possible distinction is that between taking risks while knowing that compensation awaits you, and doing the same knowing there will or may be no compensation. Or we could try to measure responsibility by the degree of reversible or irreversible indoctrination by parents, teachers, social environment and peers. However, the finer the distinctions, the clearer it becomes that what we are doing is not simply determining the right to compensation by the kind of responsibility involved. We are also and primarily trying to justify or correct our intuitions, by comparing worlds with what we feel to be (mis)fortune to the *ceteris paribus* worlds with compensation. We compare these worlds by their moral quality, by their desirability in terms of our individual conceptions of the good. The reason why some of us will believe that Cissy should get free crutches is that she deserves them as part of a reward for her moral excellence; others will argue that Cissy's choice to save the child was unavoidable in view of her upbringing, so that her accident was *un*deserved and called for compensation; still others will maintain that Cissy is *not* entitled to free crutches (though everyone is free to pay for them for her), because compensation schemes should not in any way invite or discourage the private initiative. To summarize: the way we distinguish and judge (ir)responsibility and (mis)fortune depends on our convictions regarding the good.

The point of minimal justice, justice as impartiality, is to avoid such judgements as much as possible. It offers a minimal conception of the good precisely to escape the never-ending discussion of the good life. Responsibility does play a role in such a conception, but only in a formal sense and only in so far as further wants are concerned.

Compensation is implied by the principle for basic needs, which demands equal options for all, but not because of any form of responsibility or fate. If, through no fault of my own, I am born without a limb or lose one *and* if this makes a difference for my options on a full life, the principle demands that I should be given the options that I would have had with a limb, even if this implies that I will get a larger piece of the basic needs cake. If the same happens to me because of a risk I took, or because of a conscious act of self-mutilation, I should *still* be 'compensated'. Regardless of the way in which I practice or betray my full reasons, no government, no church committee, no judge and no meddlesome neighbour has any business with my conception of a full life as such. If we were to apply standards of responsibility to the distribution or redistribution of basic needs, a fundamental rule of impartiality would be violated: that of postponing judgement on full reasons.

In the sphere of further wants, the role of responsibility can only be formal. However we conceive of fate and fortune, they are not in themselves grounds for desert: neither good nor bad luck are deserved. The only reason for (re)distribution that our principles allow is envy-containment. As for responsibility, we, *as archpointers*, have no means of determining when a risk is acceptable, when foolishness is absolvable, or when effects are excusable. We do not even have the certainty of an indubitable moral theory distinguishing good from bad luck. In short, as archpointers we cannot determine to what degree responsibility should make a difference for someone's share of the distributed rights – but we do know that responsibility can make a difference. The third principle formulated above takes account of responsibility in precisely this formal way: it demands that responsibility be taken seriously, that recipients be asked to account for every self-inflicted change of plans, needs and wants, and for every consequent claim. Whether or not responsible behaviour should be rewarded and irresponsibility punished remains undetermined; being archpointers cannot help us there.

One more thing needs to be said about restrictions on the compensatory distribution of further wants: compensation has effects in two directions. Suppose that, because of a misfortune or because of a recognized right to compensation for the consequences of responsible behaviour, Cissy Roo deserves some kind of compensation. Other totally innocent recipients will then lose part of their, up to that moment established, rights to further wants. As this reduction of the means to lead the life they choose is not their own fault, they would in turn have – paradoxically – a similar right to compensation. Consequently, Cissy loses some of her gains, through no fault of her own, and deserves compensation. And so forth. Even without repetitive compensation, compensation may clearly be counter-productive: it can lead to uncertainty about expectations, to disappointments, and it will ultimately create rather than contain envy. Envy-containment, as directed by our second principle, cannot be successful where the expectations it gives rise to are either deceptively certain or openly uncertain; it only works when it ensures the satisfaction of the expectations it legitimizes, and thus only generates *reasonable* expectations. The same is true for basic necessities: a government that could know that it promises more than it can give provokes unreasonable expectations. In both cases, a basic structure can only be just if its distribution rules are either certain and valid for a long term, or if they are explicitly incidental:

(7) *Distribution rules should not give rise to unreasonable expectations.*

As with other principles, this one will only work (that is, be compatible with other principles) if recipients themselves are tolerant enough not to pose unreasonable (unsatisfiable) demands.

Safeguarding legitimate expectations is not just a matter of the right distribution pattern or procedures, but also and foremost one of the right institutions. We want a really *basic* structure, one able to create and subsequently maintain distributive justice, one serving as a sound basis of expectations on which to build plans of life. Even if it cannot always or in all respects ensure that each person's basic needs are covered or that social peace is secure for all, a just social structure must at least ensure that its principles can be implemented as far as scarcity allows. This puts a certain lower limit to the possible shape of social and political structures – the very *least* we may expect from a society is that it be guarded by a dozing night watchman state, ready to react at the first sign of trouble – but no upper limit. We thus return to the issue of private and collective ownership.

The bias in favour of private ownership, which we gave the benefit of the doubt in Chapter 8, does not necessarily lead to a preference for commutative means (read: a free market structure) to the distributive ends of a social structure. The theory of justice as impartiality is underdetermined in this respect. Its principles limit but do not fully determine the precise *shape* of a society – free market, collectivism, or anything in between. Unlike Rawls's theory, it does not bind us to a market society with a corrective (patterning) state or to a priority of liberty over equality. Collectivism can be as minimally just as private ownership. The precise shape of society is more a matter of political efficiency than of justice: it depends on given empirical conditions and on the values that a society should incorporate next to justice. (Compare in this context Charles Beitz's (1979: 183) important distinction between moral and political structures.) We can very well imagine a libertarian society satisfying all human needs and wants simply on the basis of exchange and, if necessary, benevolence, provided the members of society are the right kind of people. However, in real life humans are not expected to always be honest, benevolent, sensitive or even rational. They would be morally obliged to share some of their rights with others if the basic needs of others are urgent enough or if political necessity so requires, but moral obligations are not the same as moral actions. In itself, a libertarian society or any social system based primarily on exchanges between individual and groups is neither distributively just nor unjust – yet it is plainly not safe or basic enough to warrant justice. In fact, it is not a basic structure at all, not even a safety-net that can be expected to catch the worst problems humans may experience in markets and in voluntary associations. Conversely, private property and property rights, freedom of trade and exchange, freedom of initiative and creativity, and commutative justice can exist but cannot be safeguarded without a distributive basic structure of society delineating and protecting a private sphere. Again, just how broad the domain and range of this private sphere will be is a matter of convention, of politics and of political virtues other than justice. From the point of view of minimal justice, all we can say is that the actual composition of society is never for ever, and that, in so far as anything can be certain, individuals should be able to rely on the safest possible basis of expectations – laws, not humans:

(8) *The basic needs and further wants of recipients should be covered by a just social structure of distributive institutions, at least to the extent necessary for the protection of their options and the containment of envy.*

Principles for recipients

As remarked earlier, recipiency is a fuzzy concept. The principles of minimal justice described so far are all predicated on the existence of virtually identical recipients, human beings who share the same city, province, government and citizenship, and the same membership of the United Nations, the European Union, or other inter-state and international institutions. But not all recipients of social justice are equal. To count as a recipient of social justice, certain criteria of moral relevancy had to be satisfied (see Chapter 7). In the first place, it must be possible to be subjected to (un)just treatment. A recipient must live, he or she must have something of a personal identity, and he or she must at least potentially have enough self-consciousness to experience pleasure and pain, harm and benefit. Sedation, coma or schizophrenia do not disqualify for recipiency; being literally a plant or being the one and only fictitious Natasha Rostov, however, do – as far as we know. Autonomy and agency, or the capacity for making plans of life, are required for full recipiency, though not for recipiency as such: some animals are still in a way recipients of justice. Finally, to be a recipient of social justice one must be a member of a society – a structure of exploitable social relations – and one's fate must be partly in the hands of others, that is, some distributor(s) must be causally responsible for at least part of a recipient's circumstances.

Most of these six criteria – life, existence, self-consciousness, agency and autonomy, membership and responsibility on the side of a distributor – are easy to apply. If all of them obtain, one is a first-class recipient of social justice; if they do not, not. Complications arise, first, when two potential recipients are not members of the same 'society', that is, if different distributors carry responsibility for their welfare – in particular, different local, regional, national or international governments. Secondly, animals are a problem: they lack self-consciousness, or at least the same degree of self-consciousness as humans, yet they are subjects of the distributors' responsibility. As to the degree of self-consciousness, let us assume that there are only two possibilities: a recipient either does or does not have the potential to make plans of life – he, she or it is either a human or an animal. This overlooks the differences among animals in terms of sensitivity to pleasure and pain, but it serves well to bring out the basic issue: do we owe less justice to lesser recipients or should we give them full justice but a lower priority?

Answering that the needs and wants of humans and animals are not the same will get us nowhere. Animals do have basic needs, of sorts. They share some of our needs, or they would not be like enough to be morally relevant. They even share with us a sense of further wants: cats and dogs can be quite choosy in their food preferences. In so far as they have basic needs and further wants, their interests are relevant with regard to justice – they merely have fewer wants and therefore less need of justice. The real difference is in their interests themselves. Animals apparently lack responsibility and reasons, and they lack full or extended plans of life. Their basic 'reasons' hardly go beyond instinctive urges to eat, drink, avoid pain, save their skins and procreate – as far as we know. This makes them also less sensitive to justice: denying basic needs to a human harms his interests now *and* in the future, whereas denying the needs of self-conscious animals harms them only for the limited time that it experiences (an equivalent of) harm. In a situation in which one of the two has to die, killing the animal is clearly less unjust – though still not ideal. A similar argument can be made with regard to the further wants of humans and animals: animals, one may suppose, suffer less when deprived of 'luxury' than humans. We cannot say the same for a comparison between human wants and animal needs. Our conception of minimal justice cannot assign a priority here, as needs and wants are judged by different measures; the question must remain unresolved. Hence:

(9) *Needs and wants of recipients are to be given priority in proportion to their potential for making plans of life: the basic needs of humans have priority over the needs of self-conscious animals; the further wants of humans have priority over those of self-conscious animals.*

Responsibility for the quality of exploitable social relations poses a comparable problem: does distance diminish duty? A recipient is likely to be embedded in a whole series of social relations, local, regional, national and international. If one basic institution dodges its responsibility by neglecting the just distribution of what it is supposed to distribute, or if it cannot fulfil its tasks, the question arises whether another, unlike the first not directly responsible for that particular right, should interfere. It is an issue that emerges in the most diverse circumstances: in cases of civil war or massive famine, when a national government is no longer able to keep its citizens alive and international organizations are asked to rise to the occasion, as well as in cases of inequality on a local scale, when, due to differences in local taxes, the national rules for unemployment benefits make the jobless in some communities worse off than in others, and local governments are asked to compensate those affected. Fortunately, the problem is more of a polit-ical and administrative than of an ethical nature, and in so far as it is an ethical problem, it is one of just dispositions rather than just procedures. What matters to the victim of injustice is that *someone* takes responsibility. If one distributor neglects the duties to which it is bound, say, if it refuses to pay the welfare benefits it promised, other basic institutions would in turn duck their respons-ibilities if they had the means to intervene but did not. It is first and foremost people who matter, not people*s*, let alone the sacrosancticity of contingent, artificial or even accidental spheres of sovereignty (*pace* Rawls 1993b).

Still, there is a procedural aspect to the issue: a basic structure must be trust-worthy, a sound basis of expectations. An anarchy of mutually unrelated institu-tions covering separate needs and wants – say, a collection of distribution agencies without a co-ordinating government – does not offer the kind of certainty demanded. Distributive justice would then depend on the incidental good will of agencies to take up duties neglected by others, instead of on a reliable procedure agreed to and announced in advance.

(10) In a just basic structure, institutions should together guarantee that each takes its responsibility for the just distribution of rights to their recipients.

Principles of minimal social justice

The principles of minimal justice which we discussed above can be rearranged according to levels of decreasing generality and increasing precision as follows:

I   (Was: 10) In a just basic structure, institutions should together guarantee that each takes its responsibility for the just distribution of rights to their recipients.

II   (9) Needs and wants of recipients are to be given priority in proportion to their potential for making plans of life: the basic needs of humans have priority over the needs of self-conscious animals; the further wants of humans have priority over those of self-conscious animals.

III   (4) Each person's full reasons are inviolable; no social institution is allowed to distribute or redistribute (rights to) this vital aspect of the self.

IV   (5) Each person has an unconditional right to his or her natural endow-ments, in so far as these are essential to that person's full life, and an inalienable right to his or her other natural endowments; no social institu-tion is allowed to redistribute or limit rights to either category.

V   (8) The basic needs and further wants of recipients should be covered by a just social structure of distributive institutions, at least to the extent necessary for the protection of their options and the containment of envy.

VI   (6) Conditional rights are to be distributed as rights that are limited by a restraint principle: the object of a conditional right should not be destroyed

214

      unless that is unavoidable; if it cannot be used without destroying it, it should be replaced by an identical object; if that is impossible, an equivalent object should be made available; if that is also impossible, a proper compensation should be provided.

VII   (7) Distribution rules should not give rise to unreasonable expectations.

VIII   (1) Rights to basic necessities are to be distributed so as to give recipients equal options for a full life. Unavoidable inequalities should be as small as possible and should be randomly distributed, with an equal chance for all to win or lose.

IX   (3) Rules for the distribution of rights to further wants must be compatible with the respect archpointers owe to recipients of justice. This principle excludes: distribution rules chosen without consideration of arguments pro or con; rules based on logically fallacious arguments, on arguments inconsistent with the facts they refer to, and on arguments that are inconsistent with or not supported by the moral theories in terms of which they are defended; rules presupposing responsibility for more or less than what one is actually responsible for; rules based on judgements on full reasons; and rules that are incompatible with the principles of natural justice.

X   (2) Rights to further wants are to be distributed according to rules that minimize envy, first down to a level preventing the distributing institution from breaking down, after that down to a level at which no-one prefers leaving this institution above staying, and beyond that down to a level at which the pursuit of plans for a complete life is minimally hindered.

Throughout this part of the book, I have been engaged in designing principles that correspond to the conception of impartiality at the archpoint. However, the beginning of Chapter 6 also contained another test for principles of justice: criteria for the output of the archpoint (R11–16). I shall now consider whether our ten principles satisfy these criteria.

Generality and *universality* pose no problems and hardly need further discussion. *Publicity* is satisfied in one respect (the principles do not require secret application, and with Rawls we may assume that they are public knowledge), but underdeveloped in another: Rawls claims that publicity should have 'desirable effects', that is to say, it should incite individuals to behave in accordance with the principles for the basic institutions of society. I shall return to the question of justice as an individual virtue in the epilogue. *Finality* was already ensured at the beginning of Part II, where we distinguished minimal justice from communitarian justice as (by definition) the set of minimal requirements for the latter. The demand for an *ordering of alternatives* is nearly completely satisfied: we have given equal and inalienable rights to natural endowments, adequate decision rules for the distribution of basic needs and further wants and priority rules for most of the claims of the various kinds of recipients. One obvious difficulty remained unresolved: that of deciding between the needs of animals and the further wants of humans. Perhaps we should let convention decide on this.

Simplicity may be another matter. I should of course leave this to the judgement of the reader, but being a reader myself, I think I may point to, and if possible explain, some of the major obstacles to simplicity. The set of principles outlined above contains at least four elements that allow neither simple application nor simple comprehension. First, they assume the relevance of several differences between recipients. Things would be a lot easier if either only 'normal' human beings with the same nationality were recipients and certain allowances had been made for animals and for international justice, or if the interests of every creature able to experience were equally relevant. However, that is not the way the world looks from the archpoint. Second, things would have been simpler if there had not been so many kinds of rights and valid claims, and if those rights were not so ambiguously defined. Unfortunately, the logic of impartiality does not allow us to treat every right as being equally important, equally necessary, or interchangeable.

Third, the reader's life would have been made even more simple if I had not defined, as in fact I did, society and the basic social structure from the point of view of an individual in a modern world with its plentitude of governments and other distributive institutions. One state with one government and one level of government would indeed have allowed us to describe more clearly how a just basic structure should function and what virtues its preservation would demand of the average (that is, or would have been, every) citizen. But again, that is not how the world works.

Fourth, all this makes it quite difficult to imagine what a just society should look like and how a distributor should implement the principles of minimal justice. This last complication asks for a more detailed answer. The principles together obviously form a matrix. Following Nozick, we would therefore expect it to be of a morally substantive type, allowing statements on the just society or the 'just state of affairs' (cf. Miller 1972: 17–20), statements like 'a just society is one in which every person has a guaranteed bundle of fundamental rights and (subjectively) enough wealth and every other means to live as he or she likes'. Such statements are indeed possible, but they can never be so precise as to really represent a substantive ideal; beyond posing some limits to substantive ideals of society, the scale remains formal or, in Nozickean terms, procedural. It imposes side-constraints on the political freedom of society, allowing a broad range of private substantive ideals and ideal worlds, among which perhaps the one on which we all could or should, but as yet do not, agree. However, we do not need meticulously detailed models of just individuals in a just state of affairs. Comparisons of things with their ideal shape (the perfectly oval world, the young Wittgenstein, Mozart on his death-bed) are of little use for the evaluation of the ways and methods chosen to reach a realistic goal – nor are they the kinds of comparisons we would want to make if we desired to remain impartial. From an impartial point of view it is more sincere to compare, instead, procedural principles with actual conditions and developments, while at the same time respecting the individuals' freedom to form and practice their own view of the good.

If it is difficult to evaluate justice, it will also be difficult to implement it. The greater the number of individuals, claims and distributing institutions, the less we can be certain of the justice of a policy. All this is probably contrary to the desires of many policy-makers, who would welcome universally applicable principles covering all aspects of life and generating distributions that are exactly just down to the fifth decimal. But precision is not necessarily a virtue in justice, nor in politics; justice is rather a craft or an art. Precision has its disadvantages. It requires access to all sorts of information, and information implies severe restrictions on privacy. The principles advanced here are based on the information recipients are *willing* to give. Precision, furthermore, denies the discursive and uncertain character of justice. If justice is a mean between too much and too little, the art of doing justice seems to be one of keeping the mean between arbitrarily throwing things at people and meticulously calculating their rations, an art of sailing between chance and fate.

Epilogue: the good, the bad and the aesthetically challenged

At the end of this book, I want to stand some distance from its themes and discuss the theoretical and practical implications of justice as impartiality. I shall focus on three issues. First, I want to address the Good: the contribution of this theory to the liberal debate on social justice, to politics and the analysis of politics. Secondly, I shall turn its Bad aspects, the premises and suppositions that ought to be, but were not, defended or sustained. Thirdly, I shall discuss an Ugly aspect of the theory: the almost total absence of accounts of retributive justice, of communitarian justice, of justice as an individual virtue, and of the relation between social justice and other virtues of societies.

The good

There are two types of liberalism in political philosophy. One is modest in its political ambitions and firm in its modesty. It – let us call it moral liberalism – claims no knowledge of an ultimate truth, it recognizes and affirms moral pluralism, and it pays allegiance to one principle only: that we should each, as well as possible, find salvation in our own way and after our own taste. The other type, political liberalism, is slightly schizoid: it professes the same formal political principle as moral liberalism, yet it is at the same time deeply committed to substantive ideals like liberty, equality and occasionally fraternity. Unlike moral liberalism, it has a view of the good life, albeit one that accepts and mostly affirms moral pluralism. Moral liberalism is liberalism in its original form; political liberalism is its modern offspring, the dominant way of thinking in the debate on liberal social justice.

Moral liberalism is perfectly compatible with the idea of justice. If justice demands that we give each person his or her due, a moral liberal will point out that the (physically) same reward or penalty may mean different things to different people, as their views of use, value, worth and, in general, the good life diverge. A true stoic will not be impressed by medals and honours, a true utilitarian will probably be less affected by them in a capitalist than in a feudal society, and the same person who feels deeply honoured by her first medal may care less about every next decoration. Thus, and still according to moral liberalism, if a society is to be just and practise justice, it should take account of these differences and be impartial – or as impartial as possible – with regard to all theories of the good. It should be guided first of all by a minimal rather than a communitarian theory of justice.

Political liberalism, on the other hand, has problems with impartiality. In its incarnations as theories of justice it often – and often unconsciously – contains substantive ethical ideals and ideas in the form of 'thin' theories of the good, of assumptions about rational behaviour, or of postulates regarding the overall importance of equality and political liberty. As I argued in Chapter 2, one cannot serve two masters: either impartiality has to give way to substantive notions of the good, or impartiality has to take precedence at the expense of 'higher' – but in moral liberal eyes ultimately unsustainable – values.

In the preceding chapters, I have offered a view of social justice that stays closer to moral liberalism than modern theories of liberal social justice tend to. The attempt to take impartiality seriously led us to two important results: a new conception of impartiality and, as a result, a relatively unpretentious theory of distributive justice. With the conceptions of impartiality and of an impartial point of view developed in Part II, I intended to avoid (at least most of) the foundational problems of political liberalism sketched above. The notion of full reasons is central to this conception of impartiality. It allowed us to fruitfully combine uncompromising impartiality regarding the fundamental aims and ends of an individual's life (the plan for a full life) with flexibility towards ways and means (the plan for a complete life). Hence, our conception of impartiality does not sacrifice respect for other people and their views to scepticism and – ultimately – indifference. At the same time it does not make theories of the good sacrosanct. It does not prohibit critique, nor a public examination of the legitimacy of rights, claims to rights and the use of rights. All it does is scrap one imaginable topic from the agenda of the public debate, full reasons, a topic for which no standards of truth or worth are available. Incidentally, this means that we have given some substance to a notion that remains purely abstract in Brian Barry's version of justice as impartiality: the notion of that-which-is-crucial in a theory of the good or plan of life (Barry 1995: 84).

As to the resulting theory of distributive justice, one cannot say that it is generally characterized by stringent criteria for just and unjust distribution, by sweeping statements condemning existing unjust practices, or by ambitious schemes for society-wide and worldwide (re)distributions of wealth, opportunity and happiness. It was not my intention to describe the ultimately just society or the liberal utopia (*pace* Rawls 1971: 288). Indeed, we found that adherence to impartiality made it nearly impossible to formulate criteria for the good, better or best society. I argued instead that apart from certain basic rights required for the full life, everything flows. Nearly all rights are conditional, nearly all actual allocations of rights are temporary, nearly all distribution procedures are provisional, and nearly all the institutions of a just society are contingent. I did, nevertheless, try to provide some clue for correctly affixing the adjective 'just' to change and development: the ten principles listed in this chapter. In communitarian societies – in so far as our societies are communitarian societies – convention may rule. Every change, every distribution of conditional rights in a community is just as long as it is compatible with these ten principles. In pluralistic societies – in so far as our societies are pluralistic – compromise or a local attempt at impartiality (cf. Barry 1995: 11, 76) rules, again within the borders set by the principles of minimal justice. In the latter case our theory obliges us to use phrases like justice and injustice more sparingly. Claims regarding further wants in pluralistic societies are not by definition inspired by a shared, even if partial, ideal of the just society. Where they are not, where they are inspired by *private* convictions, morally and politically controversial convictions, they cannot be defended as 'just' or as answers to 'injustice', except rhetorically. A decision on their legitimacy cannot be based on a recognition of the intrinsic value of the claim; it is merely the result of pure politics.

The bad

The theory of justice sketched in this book leaves many fundamental questions unresolved or unasked. Some are simply too complex and too remotely related to the theme of justice to be dealt with here. I cannot but admit this, albeit only for a selection of the shortcomings I myself find in the text. In the last chapter, for instance, I assumed that the basic needs of humans can be compared to the needs of animals. This was one of several occasions on which the issue of intersubjective (inter-human, inter-cultural, inter-species) understanding surfaced, an issue which, to be properly addressed, would require a long journey into epistemology.

Another issue that deserves more attention than I can give it here is the conception of the self that would be required to sustain my theses on the moral relevance of full reasons, on the designation of recipients, and on the existence of inviolable rights to natural endowments. Perhaps alternative theories of the self could fit our framework equally well, but I chose to rely on the Parfitian conception of the self (implicitly in Chapter 4 and explicitly in Chapters 7 and 8). According to Parfit (1984), the (morally relevant aspect of the) self is 'relation-R', conscious connectedness to prior memories, whatever the cause of the connection may be. If the chain of remembrances is cut (for instance if I become senile and start to appreciate soccer), a new self, a new personality has come into existence and an old one has ceased to exist. Parfit's conception is plausible partly because competing conceptions are not: physical continuity, psychological continuity, and the supposition of a 'deep further fact', an essence of self below the surface of attributes, can all be refuted. To be completely plausible, relation-R should be defensible in its own right, which I believe it is – mostly. Yet I still believe, because of the way that I may be remembered by others, that I would rather *really* die than start to like soccer.

Further, we could have spent more time considering *in which way* rather than how and for what reasons (un)equals should be treated (un)equally: what political institutions are required and where do market forces come in? After all, how convincing a theory of social justice is does not depend on its consistency and rationality only, but also on its practicability. The question may be politically relevant, and as such philosophically relevant, but I nevertheless had to decide that it was not directly relevant to a purely theoretical discussion of justice. The principles developed here, and the environment from which they originated, should be what justice is: 'free of change, forever and entirely pure'. Their strength lies first of all in their critical potential, in their capacity to judge existing practices and compare them – not with an ideal, which would require a True View of the good life, but with the opinions of disinterested, impartial beings with human faculties and a human consciousness. Justice as impartiality offers ways to interpret and change the world, and its application may in turn prompt us to calibrate the theory, but it cannot point the way *to* anywhere.

The aesthetically challenged

A genuinely complete theory of justice would give principles for retributive as well as distributive justice, it would account for communitarian justice as well as for minimal justice, and it would discuss justice as a virtue of individuals as well as social justice. This treatise of justice between imperfection and impartiality begot a theory about minimal distributive social justice only. The theory is adequate to its purpose – that of laying down principles of justice for pluralistic societies – but it remains ugly without the rest. Again, I can only admit the shortcomings and indicate the direction in which answers might be found.

Basic structures have no life or mind of their own. They cannot be just unless they practise justice, and they cannot practise justice unless the individuals running the institutions or claiming shares from them act justly. Hence, a conception of a just structure of society needs to be accompanied by one of individual justice, of citizenship and, as the feminist critique of social justice has shown (e.g. Kearns 1983: 36; Baker 1995: 96), one of justice in the family. We do not perhaps have to demand more of our claiming and distributing citizens than accommodation to the principles of minimal justice – with Rawls, we may trust or even assume that a just basic structure will mobilize its own support, and that a good education and socialization will temper whatever contrary inclinations people may have. It is an optimistic view of human perfectibility, but even if it turns out to be untrue the blame should not necessarily be put on the theory. There are necessarily limits to the kinds of behaviour any *moral* theory can tolerate.

Justice cannot be practised solely on the basis of the principles of minimal justice. They offer only the outlines of a just society; society itself has to fill in the empty spaces. Sometimes a society does so unanimously or apparently unanimously. Here communitarian justice, a sincere consensus on the good, and minimal justice, demanding envy-containment, coincide. Often, however, a society deviates from minimal justice, *apparently* with full consent of all its members. The age-old and worldwide discrimination against women or the apartheid system in South Africa were (often) defended that way: it was argued that women and blacks themselves assented to the 'natural' distribution of rights, and of course that dissenters were blind to these facts. In the Soviet Union, similar 'weakness of the brain' where the truths of Marxism–Leninism were concerned made dissenters end up in similar places: in 'internal exile' or in psychiatric hospitals, prisons and graves. Obviously – it is not worth more words – full consent was lacking in these cases. Yet even if there had been consent, a deviation from minimal justice in the name of community values cannot be fundamentally just. If you cannot justify your society's acts to an archpointer, they cannot be justified in all possible societies; if they are, from an impartial point of view, unjust in some societies, they cannot be totally just. Whatever precise shape we give to justice in concrete societies, even in communities, must be compatible with minimal justice. Still, not all deviations are necessarily *unjust*. A society of happy anarchists without any permanent basic structure or a communitarian caste society without a just basic structure are not unjust – provided that they are prepared to *become* minimally just societies covering the basic needs of their members, should the communitarian consensus break down one day.

A complete set of principles of justice is also expected to include principles for fair prices and fair punishments. In this case, the subject is so far removed from that of social justice that I need to say little more than the obvious, namely that principles of retributive and minimal justice ought to be compatible. Whether a society is basically just is not a matter of retributive justice. It does not depend on whether, how and how well it punishes individual criminals, nor on what happens between consenting and responsible adults, but on how well it protects the innocent and powerless.

Finally, as justice is not the only virtue that we may desire from a society, minimal justice should be related to other virtues like stability, compassion, perfection, liberty, equality, privacy, solidarity and tolerance. Justice is, in theory, one side-constraint among others; in practice, it is a goal worth striving for, one among others. Justice is an advancement over a state of perpetual predation, but for a society to prosper we need more than justice and at least more than minimal justice. A society that limits itself to the tasks of providing basic needs and keeping the peace offers little more than a relatively permanent cease-fire. Its impartiality makes it imperfect.

Notes

1   *L'homme est né libre et partout il est dans les fers*: Jean-Jacques Rousseau, *The Social Contract* (1973: 165).

2   A remark *in margine*: in view of the reactions it evoked (e.g. special issues of *Political Studies* and *Utilitas* in 1996, Kelly's (1998) collection of essays), Barry's *Justice as Impartiality* (1995) seems to have done what Barry himself expected to be impossible (cf. Barry 1991): it revived the debate on grand theories of justice, which for the preceding five years had been overshadowed by discussions of a far more limited and technical nature. The evidence supports David Miller's recent observation that 'the social justice industry' (Miller 1998) is still going strong. See e.g. Cupit (1996), Powers (1996), Roemer (1996), Shapiro (1996) and Paden (1997a, 1997b).

3   Shields (1941: 26) says that '(t)he first appearance of the phrase social justice known to this writer was in A. Tapparelli's *Saggio teoretico di dritto naturale*, published in 1845'. But Shields did not explicitly look for a primal source; nevertheless, he may well have discovered its first appearance in Thomistic literature (Tapparelli being a Jesuit), the history of which he did investigate rather thoroughly.

4   Note that any transfer of goods or rights in a society can be assessed from a distributive and a commercial point of view. The worker's wage can be judged, commercially, as a just or unjust reward for his or her services; it can also, distributively, be judged as a just or unjust share in the product of co-operation. It all depends on whom one considers to be the 'true' owner of a good: a collective body, or a (set of) individuals. The more a liberal theorist believes that personal talents or qualities are undeserved, the less likely he or she is to take the point of view of commercial justice, and let the distribution of rights and goods be a result of market forces.

5   From Justinian's *Institutions*, quoted in Freund (1962: 94).

6   On the centrality of (personal) virtue in Thomistic ethics see also Bourke 1986: 64 ff.

7   Cf. Marx' critique of one-sided solutions (either distributive or general justice) to the class struggle in the *Communist Manifesto* (Marx and Engels 1967: 105 ff.; 1965: 15 ff.).

8   This point has also been made by Klaus Scherer (1992: ix), David Miller (1972) and most recently John Rawls himself (1995: 138). A rare exception is Ewald (1986).

NOTES

9 One can even interpret the later Wittgenstein as an agnostic on this point (cf. Lock 1991: 42). For a systematic examination of interdisciplinary research on social justice, leading to a conclusion similar to the one I draw here, see Bell and Schokkaert (1992).

10 If Erasmus is right, this argument should even be accepted by religious non-liberals: intolerance leads to war and other sins; it is therefore inconsistent with the Christian faith (or most others). For more arguments in defence of liberal tolerance, see Barry (1990).

11 The original position is a *kind of* state of nature in the contractarian sense: it places human beings (more or less reduced to the features essential to a theory of justice) in a state where there are either no principles of justice, or where those principles are open to debate, revision and replacement. The original position, however, is not a state of nature in the classical sense of leading to a contract by which a polity or a sovereign is instated; cf. Rawls (1958: 176) and Gough (1957: 3).

12 I therefore do not think that there is a contradiction between my analysis of Rawls's theory as using prior principles, and Rawls's statement about his original position being built without an appeal to 'self-evidence in the traditional sense of general conceptions or particular convictions' (Rawls 1971: 21). Rawls's 'considered judgements in reflective equilibrium' may even be a classic example of a method to test self-evidence in accordance with Sidgwick's conditions (cf. Rawls 1971: 51).

13 The distinction is originally Hart's (cf. Rawls 1971: 5n; Gray 1980: 510).

14 See for example several of the contributions to Copp's and Zimmerman's *Morality, reason and truth* (1985): Copp (1985: 5 ff.), Harman (1985: 27), Sturgeon (1985: 50), and Zimmerman (1985: 79); see also Jackson (1988: 312) and Galston (1980: 5).

15 An exception would be Spinoza, one of the earliest 'impartialists' – but that is a matter of metaphysics and epistemology rather than one of ethics.

16 Cf. Bell and Schokkaert (1992: 249). For a contrary opinion, based on a definition of absolutism that includes transcultural, human-made criteria see Jackson (1988: 312–14). For another, accusing Rawls of relativism, see Galston (1980: 5).

17 For communitarian critique of these ideas and some replies see Bovens (1990b), Galston (1980, 1991: 43 ff.), Gutmann (1985), Jackson (1988), Mulhall and Swift (1992), Rawls (1985: 245, 1988: 4, 1993a: 42), Sandel (1984), M. G. Singer (1976, 1987), Walzer (1981, 1983, 1984, 1988), and Williams (1985).

18 Cf. for instance Goodwin (1978, esp. 7–9), Goodwin and Taylor (1982: 15 ff.), Kateb (1972: 4–9), Olson (1982: 143 ff.), Popper (1960: 67 ff.) and Wissenburg (1989: 393–5).

19 For a similar description of community, leading to similar conclusions, see B. Singer (1998).

20 One can find more than one formulation of the categorical imperative in Kant's work; for an inventory see e.g. Wissenburg (1991).

21 Of course, one theory of action (e.g. self-interest) may prescribe that we (act as if we) believe in another (e.g. altruism) (cf. Parfit 1984: 23 ff.). But considering this possibility will only complicate, not solve, our problem: if the Enlightened View prescribed action in accordance with, or belief in, one's private Current View, and the Current Views prescribed the same with regard to the Enlightened View – the legitimation problem would remain the same.

22 That is, the contingent features of human life: capacities, (dis)abilities, race, sex, figure, intelligence, etc., as well as exterior circumstances like the structure of society, the economic climate, and laws and constitutions.

23 Imagine, for instance, a society where privately owned material goods are considered less important or even dangerous – say, among the Kalahari bushmen in Jamie Uys's movie *The Gods must be crazy* (1980).

24 'Republican' in political philosophy refers to a semi-communitarian school of thought inspired by Aristotle and Machiavelli, emphasizing notions like civic virtue, civic responsibility and citizenship. Not to be confused with the Grand Old Party.

25 Cf. Scanlon (1982) and Barry (1995: 67). Note once more the difference with their notion of impartiality, which is based on *current* sets of individuals, plans of life and conceptions of the good.

26 Cf. the essence of Rawls's understanding of the reasonable (Rawls 1993a, 1995: 150).

27 Note that where full reasons *actually* stem from is assumed not to matter *ethically*.

28 In the words of Martha Nussbaum: grounding experiences (Nussbaum 1988: 38).

29 The two are often used interchangeably, together defining for instance (see Griffin 1984: 72–3) personhood.

30 Note that Berlin did not criticize the idea of positive freedom as such, but the consequences of political attempts to further individual positive freedom.

31 A few pages later, Walzer makes the more modest claim that this conception catches the 'deepest meaning' of the social contract (Walzer 1983: 91), that of reconciling social consciousness and social practice. However, in this respect even brain surgery will catch this deepest meaning.

32 For a similar interpretation of the social contract as rational reconstruction, see Hampton (1986: 269 ff.). For Hampton's interpretation of Rawls's contract as a device to (re)construct freedom and autonomy (self-rule and self-determination), see Hampton (1980: 337). For Rawls's hardly implicit confirmation of Hampton's analysis, see Rawls (1995: 140).

33 Cf. Wissenburg (1998); for a well-argued contrary opinion see DeGrazia (1996).

34 I presume for a moment that a third option, fighting, only enters the agenda when negotiations are unsuccessful, and I presume that capitulation (or voluntary enslavement) is a special case of exit.

35 Again, I am assuming something: that there may not be enough pleasure in having children or caring for them to explain the fact that someone has them or cares for them. Though she refuses to draw this conclusion herself, Susan Moller Okin's quite modest summary of the disadvantages of marriage and motherhood unavoidably encourages a certain hesitation about the rationality of procreation (Okin 1989: 139 ff.).

36 Abundance as a burden is not uncommon. In December 1993, for instance, the European Union had 649 grams of butter in stock on a daily basis for every European citizen, 1404 grams of beef, half a litre of olive oil, 342 grams of cheese, and so forth. Source: *NRC/Handelsblad*, 22 January 1994.

37 As Grahame Lock pointed out to me, the people in Rawls's original position have access only to relevant *social* scientific information. It may be argued that the results of 'hard' science – like the invention of the wheel or the discovery of electricity – are at least as relevant to the understanding of differences between human societies. For that reason I assume that archpointers should rather have access to *general* scientific knowledge.

38 The fact that in Gauthier's model the contracting parties *are* particular persons imagining themselves in the shoes of all others is irrelevant: we can clearly distinguish both roles.

39 For comparable conclusions see Okin (1989) and Baker (1995: 94).

40 For a contrary opinion see Barry (1995: 67 ff.), and in that context also Barry (1995: 46, 166 ff.).

41 Or in absence of an ordering in terms of strict preferences, as the alternative that is ranked highest may be the most just alternative but need not be politically feasible.

42 For further literature and discussion of this and similar Last Person Arguments, see Lee (1993).

43 For an alternative and less distateful way of posing this type of question, see Wissenburg (1998).

44 We cannot be held responsible for not understanding that which is incomprehensible. Hence, if Evelyn can be harmed or benefited without our being able to recognize this and without our attributing Evelyn with recipiency, we are not at fault – to Evelyn's misfortune.

45 I leave 'life' undefined; until Dr McCoy aboard the Enterprise finds something that 'is life, Jim, but not as we know it', our everyday conception of life with all its borderline cases is quite sufficient for our present purposes.

46 For further discussion of shared and unattributable responsibility see e.g. Bovens (1990a) or Benton (1993: 128 ff.).

47 A noteworthy exception to this rule is offered by libertarian anti-distribution theorists like Robert Nozick, in whose theory redistribution is nearly always an illegitimate violation of individual natural rights. Even though Nozickian libertarians will agree that good or bad luck are in a sense undeserved, they find that to be insufficient reason to justify the violation of other people's rights.

48 See Barber (1975: 292 ff.), Koller (1987: 93) and Rawls himself (1974: 37–8) for Rawls's non-neutral reasons for choosing maximin; see also Lehning's discussion (Lehning 1980: 124 ff., 205 ff.) of this theme.

49 My formulation of the criteria of exploitability and changeability makes it difficult to see how the human concept of 'society' could be applied to the 'social' life of animals – pace e.g. Ted Benton (1993: 53 ff.).

50 There is a second limit to the equal representation of each person's interests in justice: the assumption of a self-sufficient society principally excludes the interests of foreigners – whoever foreigners may be.

51 Throughout this chapter, I shall use originally legal terms like ownership and rights as if they were purely moral concepts without any legal meaning. Thus, when I say that someone X does not (legitimately) own Y or should not have ownership rights to Y, I merely say that X's having (possessing) Y is not morally defensible.

52 That is, there is no longer a need to make a claim, to thereby effectuate one's natural freedom and create an entitlement; the pure and objective existence of a natural right is enough to create an entitlement.

53 This section is an extended version of section 1.3 in Wissenburg (1998: 18–23).

54 For further reading, on the other hand, see Steiner (1994) and Schmidtz (1996).

55 R-molecules can be seen as elements of what is known in deontic logic as atomic rights (Lindahl 1977: 38 ff.). Although it is odd to see molecules as the basic stuff of atoms, I decided it was safer to deviate from the conventional terminology: I would not want to pretend that my r-molecules are a-tomos, indivisible.

56 Condition ℭ is perhaps controversial. Its implication appears to be that rights cannot exist when they cannot be exercised – Cissy's right to vote, for instance, would supposedly not exist as long as there were no elections, or if there were but she

happened to be held hostage. However, these two cases must be distinguished. In the latter, someone *violates* Cissy's right, which is not the same as denying its legitimacy or creating a law of nature that makes it utterly impossible for her to vote. In the first case, during the absence of elections, Cissy does still have a right to vote: a right to vote *as soon as* there are elections.

57　See also our discussion of the standard rights concept in deontic logic at the end of this section.

58　For further interpretations of these operators see Lindahl (1977: 52 ff.).

59　Remark that, as said before, conditional rights of this kind are in practice inviolable.

60　For a more detailed – and more destructive – critique of mixing–owning see Onora O'Neill's excellent article on Nozick's theory of entitlement (O'Neill 1981).

61　For a classic example see Robert Nozick's story of Wilt Chamberlain (Nozick 1974: 161 ff.).

62　The formal freedom to live the full life of one's choosing should not to be confused with a complex right to the same. A formal freedom is limited by the rights and freedom of others; a complex right satisfies condition $\mathfrak{C}$ and therefore precisely and completely defines what is and what is not allowed.

63　Note that this implies a right, not a duty, to political participation. As Rawls remarked, probably as a comment on the republican *ceterum senseo* of the need for citizens to actively participate in politics, constantly participating in politics may be a rewarding way of life for some, but it need not be part of everyone's plan of life (Rawls 1995: 170).

64　I discuss the complexities off the concept of (in)equality only in so far as this is directly relevant to the issue of equalisanda. For a more fundamental discussion of equality, see Larry Temkin's seminal *Inequality* (1993).

65　See e.g. Vlastor (1962: 31 ff.) and Bell and Schokkaert (1992: 245). David Miller (1972: 27) distinguishes need, desert and rights.

66　For some modern and stronger versions of utilitariansm cf. several contributions to Sen and Williams (1982). For an overview of the alternative uses of utility in modern economics, see Schokkaert (1992).

67　I presume for a moment that the woman in question acts irresponsibly and that there are objective criteria for irresponsibility.

68　Brian Barry, personal communication.

69　Call P the set of rights to basic needs, instruments of option equality, and EC the set of rights to further wants, the instruments of envy-containment. Then either (1) $P = EC$ (identity), (2) $P \subset EC$ & $P \not\supset EC$, (3) $P \not\subset EC$ & $P \supset EC$ (total inclusion), (4) $P \not\subset EC$, $P \not\supset EC$ & $P \cap EC \neq \varnothing$ (partial inclusion), or (5) $P \not\subset EC$, $P \not\supset EC$ & $P \cap EC = \varnothing$ (mutual exclusion). I argue that either (4) or (5) must be the case.

70　Provided that they do not entail judgements on full reasons, random distribution of unavoidable inequality is compatible with *reasoned* choices for one rather than another life, for instance because of the existence of ties and obligations towards family or friends (reasons that are probably irrelevant for *social* justice, as we may expect state institutions not to have families or friends). In fact, any rule satisfying the conditions of the third principle that will be discussed shortly can be compatible with the idea of a random choice. For further reading on chances and random distribution, see Wasserman (1996).

71　Having a voice is not necessarily the same as having the vote. Compare in this connection Ronald Dworkin's helpful distinction between political influence and political impact (Dworkin 1988: 4); the latter equals voting influence, the first consists of impact *and* influence on other people's impact. Having a voice in politics is having influence rather than impact only.

72 For those interested in the debate on criteria for admission to citizenship, see Barry and Goodin (1992).

73 Assuming the rationality of such a move – which may be questionable.

74 Other examples could be segregation, clothing prescriptions (yellow stars, school uniforms), limitations on civil rights, and so forth.

75 The implication is that bargaining, both for equality and for relative advantages, in itself violates a principle of justice, unless further good reasons for the distribution rule are brought forward in the bargaining process.

References

Ackerman, B. A. 1980. *Social justice in the liberal state*. New Haven: Yale University Press.

Ackerman, B. A. 1983. What is neutral about neutrality. *Ethics* **93**, 372–90.

Aquinas, Thomas 1975. *Summa theologiae*. London: Blackfriars.

Aristotle 1959. *Ethica Nicomachea*. Oxford: Clarendon Press.

Aristotle 1981. *The politics*. Harmondsworth: Penguin.

Baier, A. 1987. The need for more than justice. *Canadian Journal of Philosophy*, suppl. vol. **13**, 41–56.

Baker, J. 1995. A reply in defense of impartiality. *Political Theory* **23**, 92–100.

Barber, B. R. 1975. Justifying justice: problems of philosophy, politics and measurement in Rawls. See Daniels (1975), 292–318.

Barber, B. R. 1983. Unconstrained conversations: a play on words, neutral and otherwise. *Ethics* **93**, 330–47.

Barry, B. M. 1965. *Political argument*. London, Routledge & Kegan Paul.

Barry, B. M. 1989. *A treatise on social justice. Volume I: theories of justice*. London: Harvester Wheatsheaf.

Barry, B. M. 1990. How not to defend liberal institutions. *British Journal of Political Science* **20**, 1–14.

Barry, B. M. 1991. Untitled. Paper presented at The concept of the state in policy analysis conference, Wassenaar, the Netherlands.

Barry, B. M. 1993. Intergenerational justice in energy policy. In *Justice: key concepts in critical theory*, M. Fisk (ed.), 223–37. Atlantic Highlands, NJ: Humanities Press.

Barry, B. M. 1995. *A treatise on social justice. Volume II: justice as impartiality*. Oxford: Clarendon Press.

Barry, B. M. & R. E. Goodin (eds) 1992. *Free movement: ethical issues in the transnational migration of people and of money*. New York: Harvester Wheatsheaf.

Bedau, H. A. 1982. Social justice: what it is and why it matters. See Bradie & Braybrooke (1982), 85–98.

Beitz, C. R. 1979. *Political theory and international relations*. Princeton: Princeton University Press.

Beitz, C. R., M. Cohen, T. Scanlon & A. J. Simmons (eds) 1985. *International ethics: a Philosophy and Public Affairs reader*. Princeton: Princeton University Press.

Bell, J. & E. Schokkaert 1992. Interdisciplinary theory and research on justice. See Scherer (1992), 237–53.

Benton, T. 1993. *Natural relations: ecology, animal rights and social justice*. London: Verso.

Berlin, I. 1969. *Four essays on liberty*. Oxford: Oxford University Press.

Binmore, K. 1993. *Game theory and the social contract. Volume I: playing fair*. Cambridge, Mass.: MIT Press.

Boudon, R. 1976. Review of John Rawls 'A Theory of Justice'. *Contemporary Sociology* **5**, 102–9.

Bourke, V. J. 1986. Recent Thomistic ethics. See De Marco & Fox (1986), 58–72.

Bovens, M. A. P. 1988. Tussen Kant en conventie: de rechtvaardiging van beginselen van rechtvaardigheid. *Acta Politica* **3**, 333–57.

Bovens, M. A. P. 1990a. *Verantwoordelijkheid en organisatie: beschouwingen over aansprakelijkheid, institutioneel burgerschap en ambtelijke ongehoorzaamheid*. Zwolle: Tjeenk Willink.

Bovens, M. A. P. 1990b. Liberalisme als gemeenschap. See De Beus & Lehning (1990), 109–29.

Bradie, M. & D. Braybrooke (eds) 1982. *Social justice*. Bowling Green Studies in Applied Philosophy vol. IV. Bowling Green, Ohio: Bowling Green State University.

Brandt, R. B. (ed.) 1962. *Social justice*. Englewood Cliffs, NJ: Prentice-Hall.

Brandt, R. B. 1979. *A theory of the good and the right*. Oxford: Clarendon Press.

Brandt, R. B. 1988. The structure of virtue. See French & Uehling (1988), 64–82.

Braybrooke, D. 1982. Making justice practical. See Bradie & Braybrooke (1982), 1–14.

Brehmer, K. 1980. *Rawls' 'Original Position' oder Kants 'Ursprünglicher Kontrakt': Die Bedingungen der Möglichkeit eines wohlgeordneten Zusammenlebens*. Koenigstein: Forum Academicum.

Broad, C. D. 1930. *Five types of ethical theory*. London: Routledge & Kegan Paul.

Brown, C. 1992. Marxism and the transnational migration of people: ethical issues. See Barry & Goodin (1992), 127–44.

Buchanan, J. M. 1975. *The limits of liberty: between anarchy and Leviathan*. Chicago: Chicago University Press.

Cohen, G. A. 1986. Self-ownership, world-ownership, and equality. See Lucash (1986), 108–35.

Cohen, G. A. 1991. *Incentives, inequality and community*. Lecture, University of Nijmegen, the Netherlands.

Cohen, G. A. 1993. Equality of what? On welfare, goods, and capabilities. See Nussbaum & Sen (1993), 9–29.

Copp, D. 1985. Introduction. See Copp & Zimmerman (1985), 1–24.

Copp, D. & D. Zimmerman (eds) 1985. *Morality, reason and truth: new essays on the foundations of ethics*. Totowa, NJ: Rowman & Allanheld.

Cullen, B. 1992. Philosophical theories of justice. See Scherer (1992), 15–64.

Cupit, G. 1996. *Justice as fittingness*. Oxford: Clarendon Press.

Daniels, N. (ed.) 1975. *Reading Rawls: critical studies on Rawls' A theory of justice*. Oxford: Blackwell.

Daniels, N. 1985. Two approachs to theory acceptance in ethics. See Copp & Zimmerman (1985), 120–40.

Davies, B. & M. Walsh (eds) 1991. *Proclaiming justice and peace: one hundred years of Catholic social teaching*. London: Flame.

De Beus, J. W. & P. B. Lehning (eds) 1990. *Beleid voor de vrije samenleving: politiek-theoretische opstellen*, Jaarboek Beleid en Maatschappij 1989. Amsterdam: Boom.

De Crespigny, A. & K. R. Minogue (eds) 1975. *Contemporary political philosophers*. London: Methuen.

DeGrazia, D. 1996. *Taking animals seriously: mental life and moral status*. Cambridge: Cambridge University Press.

De Marco, J. P. & R. M. Fox (eds) 1986. *New directions in ethics*. London: Routledge & Kegan Paul.

Diehl, K. & P. Mombert (eds) 1984. *Sozialpolitik: ausgewählte Lesestücke zum Studium der politischen Ökonomie*. Frankfurt am Main: Ullstein.

Dobson, A. N. H. & P. Lucardie (eds) 1993. *The politics of nature: explorations in green political theory*. London: Routledge.

Dooyeweerd, H. 1957. *A new critique of theoretical thought*. Amsterdam: Presbyterian & Reformed Publishing Company.

Dryzek, J. & R. E. Goodin 1984. *Risk sharing and social justice: the motivational forces of the post-war welfare state*, Essex Papers in Politics and Government 11. University of Essex.

Dworkin, R. M. 1975. The original position. See Daniels (1975), 16–53. Quoted as Justice and rights, from Dworkin (1978), 150–83.

Dworkin, R. M. 1978. *Taking rights seriously*, 2nd edn. London: Duckworth.

Dworkin, R. M. 1981. What is equality? Part 2: equality of resources. *Philosophy and Public Affairs* **4**, 283–345.

Dworkin, R. M. 1985a. *A matter of principle*. Cambridge, Mass.: Harvard University Press.

Dworkin, R. M. 1985b. Liberalism. See Dworkin (1985a), 181–204.

Dworkin, R. M. 1985c. Why liberals should care about equality. See Dworkin (1985a), 205–13.

Dworkin, R. M. 1988. What is equality? Part 4: political equality. Unpublished paper, University of Oxford.

Elster, J. 1987. The possibility of rational politics. *Archives Européennes de Sociologie* **1**, 67–103.

Epictetus 1966. *Moral discourses, Encheiridion and fragments*. London: Everyman.

Erh-soon Tay, A. & E. Kamenka (eds) 1979. *Justice*. London: Edward Arnold.

Ewald, F. 1986. *L'état providence*. Paris: Grasset & Fasquelle.

Fishkin, J. S. 1983. Can there be a neutral theory of justice? *Ethics* **93**, 348–56.

Fisk, M. 1975. History and reason in Rawls' moral theory. See Daniels (1975), 53–80.

Fisk, M. (ed.) 1993. *Justice: key concepts in critical theory*. Atlantic Highlands, NJ: Humanities Press.

Flathman, R. E. 1983. Egalitarian blood and skeptical turnips. *Ethics* **93**, 357–66.

Frankena, W. K. 1962. The concept of social justice. See Brandt (1962), 1–29.

Frankena, W. K. 1963. *Ethics*. Englewood Cliffs, NJ: Prentice-Hall.

Freeden, M. 1978. *The new liberalism*. Oxford: Clarendon Press.

French, P. A., T. E. Uehling Jr. & H. K. Wettstein (eds) 1988. *Ethical theory: character and virtue*, Midwest Studies in Philosophy, vol. XIII. Notre Dame, Ind.: University of Notre Dame Press.

Freund, P. A. 1962. Social justice and the law. See Brandt (1962), 92–117.

Frey, R. G. (ed.) 1984. *Utility and rights*. Minneapolis: University of Minnesota Press.

Galston, W. A. 1980. *Justice and the human good*. Chicago: Chicago University Press.

Galston, W. A. 1982. Moral personality and liberal theory. *Political Theory* **4**, 492–519.

Galston, W. A. 1991. *Liberal purposes: goods, virtues, and diversity in the liberal state*. Cambridge: Cambridge University Press.

REFERENCES

Gauthier, D. 1985. Justice as social choice. See Copp & Zimmerman (1985), 251–69.

Gauthier, D. 1986. *Morals by agreement*. Oxford: Clarendon Press.

Goodin, R. E. 1984. *Supply side politics: circumventing the claims of justice*, Essex Papers in Politics and Government 18. University of Essex. Also in Goodin (1988), Chapter 9.

Goodin, R. E. 1988. *Reasons for welfare*. Princeton: Princeton University Press.

Goodin, R. E. 1992. If people were money ... See Barry & Goodin (1992), 6–22.

Goodwin, B. 1978. *Social science and Utopia: nineteenth-century models of social harmony*. Hassocks: Harvester Press.

Goodwin, B. 1992. *Justice by lottery*. New York: Harvester Wheatsheaf.

Goodwin, B. & K. Taylor 1982. *The politics of Utopia: a study in theory and practice*. London: Hutchinson.

Gough, J. W. 1957. *The social contract*, 2nd edn. Oxford: Clarendon Press.

Gray, J. 1980. On negative and positive liberty. *Political Studies* **28**, 507–26.

Gray, J. 1993. Can we agree to disagree? *New York Times Book Reviews*, 16 May, 35.

Griffin, J. 1984. Towards a substantive theory of rights. See Frey (1984), 137–60.

Gutmann, A. 1985. Communitarian critics of liberalism. *Philosophy and Public Affairs* **14**, 308–22.

Hampton, J. 1980. Contracts and choices: does Rawls have a social contract theory? *Journal of Philosophy* **77**, 315–38.

Hampton, J. 1986. *Hobbes and the social contract tradition*. Cambridge: Cambridge University Press.

Hardin, R. 1990. Incentives and beneficence. *Social Justice Research* **2**, 87–104.

Hare, R. M. 1982. Ethical theory and utilitarianism. See Sen & Williams (1982), 23–38.

Harman, G. 1985. Is there a single true morality? See Copp & Zimmerman (1985), 27–48.

Harrison, J. (ed.) 1990. *Time-travel for beginners and other stories*. Nottingham: Nottingham University Press.

Harsanyi, J. C. 1982. Morality and the theory of rational behaviour. See Sen & Williams (1982), 39–62.

Hayek, F. A. 1976a. *The road to serfdom*. London: Routledge & Kegan Paul.

Hayek, F. A. 1976b. *Law, legislation, and liberty. Part II: the mirage of social justice*. London: Routledge & Kegan Paul.

Hickel, R. 1984. Sozialpolitik in Geschichte, Theorie, und Praxis. See Diehl & Mombert (1984), v–liv.

Hodges, W. 1977. *Logic*. Harmondsworth: Penguin.

Hook, S. 1976. *Revolution, reform, and social justice*. Oxford: Blackwell.

Horton, J. 1996. The good, the bad, and the impartial. *Utilitas* **8**, 307–28.

Hübner, K. 1992. Transnational migration of money and capital: a Marxist perspective. See Barry & Goodin (1992), 145–54.

Inwood, B. 1985. *Ethics and human action in early stoicism*. Oxford: Oxford University Press.

Jackson, M. W. 1988. Rationality, reality, and morality. *Man and World* **21**, 307–26.

Jeffrey, P. (ed.) 1981. *Reading Nozick: essays on Anarchy, State, and Utopia*. Oxford: Blackwell.

John of Salisbury 1990. *Policraticus*. Cambridge: Cambridge University Press.

Kanger, H. & S. Kanger 1966. Rights and parliamentarism. *Theoria* **2**, 85–115.

Kant, I. 1928. *Kritik der praktischen Vernunft*. Wiesbaden: VMA-Verlag.

Kant, I. 1974. *Kritik der praktischen Vernunft & Grundlegung zur Metaphysik der Sitten*. Frankfurt am Main: Suhrkamp.

Kateb, G. 1972. *Utopia and its enemies*, 2nd edn. New York: Schocken.

Kearns, D. 1983. A theory of justice – and love: Rawls on the family. *Politics* **2**, 36–42.

Kelly, J. S. 1988. *Social choice theory: an introduction*. Berlin: Springer-Verlag.

Kelly, P. 1998. *Impartiality, neutrality and justice: re-reading Brian Barry's justice as impartiality*. Edinburgh: Edinburgh University Press.

Kitschelt, H. 1980. Moralisches argumentieren und Sozialtheorie: prozedurale Ethik bei John Rawls und Jürgen Habermas. *Archiv für Rechts- und Sozialphilosophie 1980*, 391–429.

Kley, R. 1989. *Vertragstheorien der Gerechtigkeit: eine philosophische Kritik der Theorien von John Rawls, Robert Nozick und James Buchanan*. Bern: Paul Haupt.

Koller, P. 1987. *Neue Theorien des Sozialkontrakts*. Berlin: Dunckler und Humblot.

Kukathas, C. & P. Pettit 1990. *Rawls: a theory of justice and its critics*. Cambridge: Polity Press.

Kymlicka, W. 1995. *Multicultural citizenship*. Oxford: Clarendon Press.

Laslett, P. & W. G. Runciman (eds.) 1967. *Politics, philosophy, and society*, 3rd series. Oxford: Blackwell.

Lee, K. 1993. Instrumentalism and the last person argument. *Environmental Ethics* **4**, 333–44.

Lehning, P. B. 1980. *Politieke orde en rawlsiaanse rechtvaardigheid*. Delft: Eburon.

Leo XIII 1991. Rerum Novarum. See Davies & Walsh (1991).

Lindahl, L. 1977. *Position and change: a study in law and logic*. Dordrecht: Reidel.

Lock, G. E. 1989. Marx, Rawls, l'égalité et la justice. Unpublished paper.

Lock, G. E. 1991. Jeu politique et jeu de langage: Althusser et le statut de la philosophie. *M* **1**, 41–6.

Locke, J. 1924. *Two treatises of government*. London: Everyman.

Lucash, F. F. (ed.) 1986. *Justice and equality here and now*. Ithaca: Cornell University Press.

Lukes, S. 1985. *Marxism and morality*. Oxford: Oxford University Press.

Macintyre, A. 1985. *After virtue: a study in moral theory*, 2nd edn. London: Duckworth.

Maritain, J. 1947. *La personne et le bien commun*. Paris: Desclée De Brouwer.

Marx, K. H. & F. H. Engels 1965. *Manifest der kommunistischen Partei*, Reproduktion der Erstausgabe (London 1848). Berlin: Dietz.

Marx K. H. & F. H. Engels 1967. *The communist manifesto*. Harmondsworth: Penguin.

Matson, W. 1983. Justice: a funeral oration. *Social Philosophy and Policy* **1**, 94–113.

Ma-tsu 1981. *De gesprekken*. Baarn: Wereldvenster.

Mcbride, L. W. 1975. The concept of justice in Marx, Engels, and others. *Ethics* **85**, 204–18.

McMurrin, S. M. (ed.) 1980. *The Tanner lectures on human values 1980*. Salt Lake City: University of Utah Press.

McMurrin, S. M. (ed.) 1988. *The Tanner lectures on human values 1985*. Salt Lake City: University of Utah Press.

Mill, J. S. 1969. *Autobiography*. Boston: Houghton Mifflin.

Miller, D. 1972. *Social justice*. Oxford: Clarendon Press.

Miller, D. 1998. Prospects for social justice. Paper presented at Political Thought Conference, Oxford.

Min, K. 1984. *Ordnungspolitische Untersuchung der Gesellschaftsvertragstheorie von John Rawls: Grenzen seiner Gesellschaftsvertragstheorie*. PhD thesis, Freiburg im Breisgau.

Minogue, K. R. 1975. Michael Oakeshott. See De Crespigny & Minogue (1975), 120–46.

Mulhall, S. & A. Swift 1992. *Liberals and communitarians*. Oxford: Blackwell.

Nagel, T. 1974. What is it like to be a bat? *Philosophical Review* **83**, 435–50.

Nagel, T. 1986. *The view from nowhere*. Oxford: Oxford University Press.

Nagel, T. 1991. *Equality and partiality*. Oxford: Oxford University Press.

Narveson, J. 1973. Moral problems of population. *Monist* **57**, 62–86.

Nielsen, K. 1986. Marxism, morality and moral philosophy. See De Marco & Fox (1986), 92–112.

Nozick, R. 1974. *Anarchy, state, and Utopia*. New York: Basic Books.

Nozick, R. 1989. *The examined life: philosophical meditations*. New York: Touchstone.

Nussbaum, M. 1988. Non-relative virtues: an Aristotelian perspective. See French, Uehling & Wettstein (1988), 32–53.

Nussbaum, M. & A. K. Sen (eds) 1993. *The quality of life*. Oxford: Clarendon Press.

Okin, S. M. 1989. *Justice, gender and the family*. New York: Basic Books.

Olson, T. 1982. *Millennialism, Utopianism, and progress*. Toronto: University of Toronto Press.

O'Neill, O. 1981. Nozick's entitlements. See Jeffrey (1981), 305–22.

Paden, R. 1997a. Rawls's just savings principle and the sense of justice. *Social Theory and Practice* **23**, 27–51.

Paden, R. 1997b. Reconstructing Rawls's law of peoples. *Ethics and International Affairs* **11**, 215–32.

Parfit, D. 1984. *Reasons and persons*. Oxford: Clarendon Press.

Passmore, J. A. 1979. Civil justice and its rivals. See Erh-Soon Tay & Kamenka (1979), 25–49.

Plato 1974. *The republic*. Harmondsworth: Penguin.

Popper, K. R. 1960. *The poverty of historicism*, 2nd edn. London: Routledge & Kegan Paul.

Popper, K. R. 1986a. *The open society and its enemies. Volume I: the spell of Plato*, 5th edn. London: Routledge & Kegan Paul.

Popper, K. R. 1986b. *The open society and its enemies. Volume II: Hegel and Marx*, 5th edn. London: Routledge & Kegan Paul.

Powers, M. 1996. Forget about equality. *Kennedy Institute of Ethics Journal* **6**, 129–44.

Pufendorf, S. 1991. *On the duty of man and citizen according to natural law*. Cambridge: Cambridge University Press.

Raphael, D. D. 1981. *Moral philosophy*. Oxford: Oxford University Press.

Rawls, J. B. 1958. Justice as fairness. *Philosophical Review* **67**, 164–94.

Rawls, J. B. 1967. Distributive justice. See Laslett & Runciman (1967), 57–82.

Rawls, J. B. 1971. *A theory of justice*. Oxford: Oxford University Press.

Rawls, J. B. 1974. Concepts of distributional equity: some reasons for the maximin criterion. *American Economic Review* **64**, 34–9.

Rawls, J. B. 1982. Social unity and primary goods. See Sen & Williams (1982), 159–85.

Rawls, J. B. 1985. Justice as fairness: political not metaphysical. *Philosophy and Public Affairs* **3**, 223–51.

Rawls, J. B. 1988. A conception of democratic equality. Unpublished paper.

Rawls, J. B. 1993a. *Political liberalism*. New York: Columbia University Press.

Rawls, J. B. 1993b. The law of the peoples. *Critical Inquiry* **20**, 36–68.

Rawls, J. B. 1995. Reply to Habermas. *Journal of Philosophy* **92**, 132–80.

Raz, J. 1986. *The morality of freedom*. Oxford: Clarendon Press.

Roemer, J. E. (1996). *Theories of distributive justice*. Cambridge, Mass.: Harvard University Press.

Rousseau, J.-J. 1973. *The social contract & discourses*. London: Everyman.

Sandel, M. 1982. *Liberalism and the limits of justice*. Cambridge: Cambridge University Press.

Sandel, M. 1984. The procedural republic and the unencumbered self. *Political Theory* **12**, 81–96.

Scanlon, T. M. 1982. Contractarianism and utilitarianism. See Sen & Williams (1982), 103–28.

Scherer, K. R. 1992. *Justice: interdisciplinary perspectives*. Cambridge: Press Syndicate of the University of Cambridge.

Schmidtz, D. 1996. Critical notice of Hillel Steiner: an essay on rights. *Canadian Journal of Philosophy* **26**, 283–302.

Schmitt, C. 1987. *Der Begriff des Politischen*. Berlin: Duncker & Humblot.

Schokkaert, E. 1992. The economics of distributive justice, welfare and freedom. See Scherer (1992), 65–113.

Sen, A. K. 1970. *Collective choice and social welfare*. San Francisco: Holden-Day.

Sen, A. K. 1975. Rawls versus Bentham: an axiomatic examination of the pure distribution problem. See Daniels (1975), 283–92.

Sen, A. K. 1980. Equality of what? See McMurrin (1980), 196–220.

Sen, A. K. 1993. Capability and well-being. See Nussbaum & Sen (1993), 30–53.

Sen, A. K. & B. Williams (eds) 1982. *Utilitarianism and beyond*. Cambridge: Cambridge University Press.

Shapiro, I. 1996. Elements of democratic justice. *Political Theory* **24**, 579–619.

Sharples, R. W. 1986. Soft determinism and freedom in early stoicism. *Phronesis* **3**, 266–79.

Shields, L. W. 1941. *The history and meaning of the term social justice*. PhD thesis, University of Notre Dame, Indiana.

Shklar, J. (ed.) 1986. *Justice and equality*. Ithaca: Cornell University Press.

Sidgwick, H. 1962. *Methods of ethics*, 7th edn. London: Macmillan.

Singer, B. 1988. An extention of Rawls' theory of justice to environmental ethics. *Environmental Ethics* **3**, 217–31.

Singer, B. 1998. Reconciling liberalism and communitarianism. In *Memory, history and critique: European identity at the millenium*. Proceedings of the fifth conference of the International Society for the Study of European Ideas, F. Brinkhuis, S. Talmor (eds). Utrecht: University for Humanist Studies.

Singer, M. G. 1976. The methods of justice: reflections on Rawls. *Journal of Value Inquiry* **10**, 286–316.

Singer, M. G. 1987. Moral theory and justification. *Philosophy* **62**, 517–22.

Singer, P. 1979. *Practical ethics*. Cambridge: Cambridge University Press.

Singer, P. 1985. Famine, affluence and morality. See Beitz, Cohen, Scanlon, & Simmons (1985), 247–61.

Smart, J. J. C. 1986. Utilitarianism and its applications. See De Marco & Fox (1986), 24–41.

Spinoza, B. 1951. *Tractatus theologico-politicus & tractatus politicus*. New York: Dover.

Spinoza, B. 1972. *Ethica ordine geometrico demonstrata*, 2nd edn. Heidelberg: Carl Winters Universitätsbuchhandlung.

Steiner, H. 1994. *An essay on rights*. Oxford: Blackwell.

Sturgeon, N. L. 1985. Moral explanations. See Copp & Zimmerman (1985), 49–78.

Swift, J. 1959. *Selected prose and poetry*. New York: Rinehart & Winston.

Talmon, J. L. 1970. *The origins of totalitarian democracy*. London: Sphere Books.

Taylor, C. 1986. The nature and scope of distributive justice. See Shklar (1986), 34–67.

Temkin, L. S. 1986. Inequality. *Philosophy and Public Administration* **2**, 99–121.

Temkin, L. S. 1993. *Inequality.* Oxford: Oxford University Press.

Terpstra, M. J. 1990. *De wending naar de politiek: een studie over de begrippen 'potentia' en 'potestas' bij Spinoza.* PhD thesis, University of Nijmegen, the Netherlands.

Tester, K. 1991. *Animals and society: the humanity of animal rights.* London: Routledge.

Timmons, M. 1987. Ethical foundationalism. *Ethics* **97**, 595–609.

Van Den Enden, F. 1992. *Vrije politijke stellingen en consideratien van staat.* Amsterdam: Wereldbibliotheek.

VanDerVeer, D. 1977. Of beasts, persons and the original position. *Monist* **3**, 368–77.

Van Parijs, P. 1992. Citizenship exploitation, unequal exchange and the breakdown of popular sovereignty. See Barry & Goodin (1992), 155–65.

Vlastor, G. 1962. Justice and equality. See Brandt (1962), 31–72.

Waddell, H. (ed.) 1968. *Mediaeval Latin lyrics.* Harmondsworth: Penguin.

Walzer, M. 1981. Philosophy and democracy. *Political Theory* **9**, 379–99.

Walzer, M. 1983. *Spheres of justice.* New York: Basic Books.

Walzer, M. 1984. Liberalism and the art of separation. *Political Theory* **12**, 315–30.

Walzer, M. 1988. Interpretation and social criticism. See McMurrin (1985), 1–80.

Wasserman, D. 1996. Let them eat chances: probability and distributive justice. *Economics and Philosophy* **12**, 29–49.

Wegener, B. 1990. Equity, relative deprivation, and the value consensus paradox. *Social Justice Research* **1**, 65–86.

Weithman, P. J. 1992. Natural law, solidarity and international justice. See Barry & Goodin (1992), 181–202.

Wempe, B. E. 1986. *Beyond equality: a study of T. H. Green's theory of positive freedom.* Delft: Eburon.

Wenz, P. S. 1988. *Environmental justice.* Albany: State University of New York Press.

Williams, B. 1983. Space talk: the conversation continued. *Ethics* **93**, 367–71.

Williams, B. 1985. *Ethics and the limits of philosophy.* Cambridge: Harvard University Press.

Wissenburg, M. L. J. 1989. Karl Popper over de betere wereld. *Acta Politica* **24**, 385–408.

Wissenburg, M. L. J. 1991. Holle frasen, lege woorden: drie onmogelijke versies van de categorische imperatief. *Parodos* **29**, 4–16.

Wissenburg, M. L. J. 1993. The idea of nature and the nature of distributive justice. See Dobson & Lucardie (1993), 3–20.

Wissenburg, M. L. J. 1994. *Justice from a distance: an outline of a liberal theory of social justice.* PhD thesis, University of Nijmegen, the Netherlands.

Wissenburg, M. L. J. 1998. *Green liberalism: the free and the green society.* London: UCL Press.

Wolff, R. P. (ed.) 1977. *Understanding Rawls.* Princeton: Princeton University Press.

Woodward, J. 1992. Commentary: liberalism and migration. See Barry & Goodin (1992), 59–84.

Zimmerman, D. 1985. Moral realism and explanatory necessity. See Copp & Zimmerman (1985), 79–103.

Index

For Product Safety Concerns and Information please contact our EU
representative GPSR@taylorandfrancis.com
Taylor & Francis Verlag GmbH, Kaufingerstraße 24, 80331 München, Germany

www.ingramcontent.com/pod-product-compliance
Ingram Content Group UK Ltd.
Pitfield, Milton Keynes, MK11 3LW, UK
UKHW010813080625
459435UK00006B/63